Tips for
Quilting

by the Staff of
THE OLD COUNTRY STORE

Intercourse, PA 17534
800/762-7171
www.GoodBooks.com

Thank you, quilters for contributing your tips and hints about so many parts of quilting. We are grateful that you've shared your know-how. We're touched by your generous spirits.

Cover design by Koechel Peterson & Associates, Inc.,
Minneapolis, Minnesota

Design by Cliff Snyder

TIPS FOR QUILTING
Copyright © 2013 by Good Books, Intercourse, PA 17534
International Standard Book Number: 978-1-56148-804-9
Library of Congress Control Number: 2013950308

Publisher's Cataloging-in-Publication Data
Tips for Quilting / by the staff of the Old Country Store.
    p. cm.
    ISBN 978-1-56148-804-9
    Includes index.

1. Quilting. 2. Patchwork. I. Old Country Store (Intercourse, Pa.). II. Title.

TT835 .O43 2013
746.46 --dc23   2013950308

Contents

CHAPTER 12

Machine Quilting   221

CHAPTER 13

Embellishments   242

CHAPTER 14

Technology   256

Introduction

We love hearing what our customers plan to do with the fabric they buy at The Old Country Store, but even more, we love when they lean in close and tell us a quilting secret. So we asked the whole group of them for their quilting secrets and tricks and collected the best ones in this book for you. After all, not all of us come from a quilting family or hang out in a local quilt store. Sure, you can read a quilting book, surf the internet tutorials, and take a quilting class, but who will give you the lowdown on all the batting choices (see Chapter 9) or help you figure out how to store your templates (see Chapter 4, Section D)?

Here is a collection of behind-the-scenes, not-mentioned-in-tutorials tips from many thousands of our experienced quilting customers, as well as from us, the staff of The Old Country Store.

Here is a collection of behind-the-scenes, not-mentioned-in-tutorials tips from many thousands of our experienced quilting customers, as well as from us, the staff of The Old Country Store.

If you're a beginner, you will be glad for the basic tips that help you get started and steer you in the direction of a finished quilt you will love. If you're an experienced quilter, you will benefit from the different advice on every topic, allowing you to pick and choose what seems best to you.

The sheer breadth of methods and opinions in this tips book is wonderfully freeing for a quilter. One of our staff thought you could only hand quilt with a floor frame and she didn't have room for that! Then, a friend introduced her to a lap hoop, and now she happily drags her quilt in process with her wherever she goes. And there are still more ways to hand quilt without a frame in the section on Quilting Frames (see Chapter 11, Section A).

Wondering if you should try quilt-as-you-go? See Chapter 12, Section F.

Want to know the best way to store a quilt for a long time? See Chapter 18, Section A.

Thinking of dyeing your own fabric? See Chapter 3, Section E.

This handbook is a cheering section for incorporating more quilting in your life, in whatever way works for you. No quilt police here!

Want to know the best way to store a quilt for a long time?

You'll notice there are sometimes opposite viewpoints on the same topic (Wash your fabric before you sew! Don't wash out the factory finish before you sew! See Chapter 3, Sections A and B). You can decide for yourself which pros and cons you agree with and read the reasons that our quilters give for what they do. This is the beauty of many quilters talking shop with each other, generously sharing their wisdom and experience with anyone lucky enough to listen in.

This handbook is not a collection of tutorials and how-tos. It's just a friendly boost from many quilters who quilt like they breathe.

When our quilters named names for products and authors, we included them. We figured you'd want to know what to search for at the store or online as you experiment with new methods and products. We'll include any updates to these at our website, **www.oldcountrystorefabrics.com**.

May this handbook prove to be as fun and useful to read as it was for us. We have fresh ideas and tools to bring to our next quilts, thanks to our generous quilters.

— The Staff of The Old Country Store

CHAPTER 1

Getting Started

A. Choosing What to Make

❶ First, I think about the person for whom I am making the quilt. Second, I look at pictures or patterns for inspiration. Third, I go to my "stash" and look at fabrics to see what I already have that can be incorporated into the quilt. If all of these things come together, I am on my way. If not, I go back to #1 and start again.

Mary Jane Hollcraft, Indianapolis, IN

❷ My quilts are always started with someone in mind, so that's the first decisive factor. If it's for a baby or young child, I choose a simple design, solid seams and intersections, machine appliquéd (not hand needle turn), and often minky or flannel backing. For a teenager, I go with their favorite colors or themed fabric. For adults, they often want a color for a specific room. My mother-in-law loves aqua and purple batiks, my son wanted it to match his bright red couch, and my daughter wanted blue, greens and yellow with imprecise blocks, so I chose a Jan Mullen pattern.

Anne Zinni, Hertford, NC

❸ I usually have a new technique or ruler I'd like to try, or I fall in love with a fabric line or quilt I see in a magazine.

DeAnna Dodson, Aubrey, TX

❹ Sometimes I just want something that is simple, that I can finish quickly. I usually have several quilts going at the same time, so it's nice to finish an easy one in the midst of larger projects that take a long time.

Carol Lattimore, Ozark, AL

❺ I go to a local quilt shop, and if I like the project they are doing, then I will take that class and make the quilt.

Rosemary Bowlby, De Soto, IL

❻ If color scares you, pick one fabric you love, then look on the selvage (side) where there will be little circles of color. These are the dyes used to make the fabric and if you match those colors to other fabric, everything will work just fine. And if you like the colors, that is what matters.

Carol Nussbaumer, Estes Park, CO

❼ I love trying new patterns and find that making small charity quilts with an unfamiliar pattern offers a great opportunity to decide if I am interested in making a full-size quilt using that pattern. Inspiration often comes from a quilt magazine or from a picture in social media.

Signa Ferguson, Pelham, AL

❽ I get bored easily, so I don't like to make anything that is very repetitive.

Charlotte Kewish, Gibsonia, PA

❾ I am constantly on the lookout for quilts that are beautiful *and* that are at my ability level. I save patterns and pictures of these quilts for a later date. When I'm ready to start a new quilt, I go through those pictures and patterns. Then I go through my stash to decide what will work, and lastly, I shop for more fabric that will be needed.

Allison Evrard, Coopersburg, PA

10 I really lean toward small projects such as runners, table toppers, and baby or throw quilts. These are so much more manageable
to me. *Martha Bean, Hanover, PA*

11 I usually make quilts as gifts, so whatever inspires me about
that person, I try to match to a pattern. It's not always easy, but it is
interesting to see what I come up with. *Brenda Seth, Waterford, PA*

12 I have a list I call my "HSY list" (pronounced "hissy"). HSY
stands for "haven't started yet." Sometimes I will choose a quilt
from that list that I know will go perfectly with some fabric I have,
and other times I choose one that works for the time I have right
then to devote to making a new quilt. *Janet Espeleta, Boonville, MO*

13 Attend quilt shows to be exposed to all the different kinds of
quilting so that you can start to focus on what really appeals to you.
Anne Jackson, Prior Lake, MN

14 I love quilts with unusual angles, especially 60°
angles and a fair amount of piecing. Quilts combin-
ing two blocks to create a secondary design appeal
to me, and quilts that throw together a lot of large
squares and rectangles are boring to me.
KC Howell, Medina, OH

> *I love quilts with unusual angles.*

15 I start with a color combination or focal fabric that inspires
me. I collect the fabrics and *then* find a pattern that works with the
fabrics. It seems backwards to some, but I make a lot of scrap quilts
and have a lot of fabric already on hand. I would prefer to be totally
inspired by color or a single fabric, rather than finding fabrics to fit
a recipe. *Nancy Henry, Rochester, NH*

16 I have recreated two of my grandmother's quilts that had
become worn from years of loving use in new fabric.
Signa Ferguson, Pelham, AL

17 I'm mostly inspired by nature when I'm thinking of what quilt
to make next: flower shapes, butterfly patterns, trees, lakes or

rivers, too. For example, when I created my first granddaughter's quilt, I remembered her mother liked the moon, so I incorporated that into it.   *Caroline O'Connor, Ypsilanti, MI*

18 After a few projects, you will find that you stick to pretty much the same color palette or fabric lines. Don't be afraid to "get out of

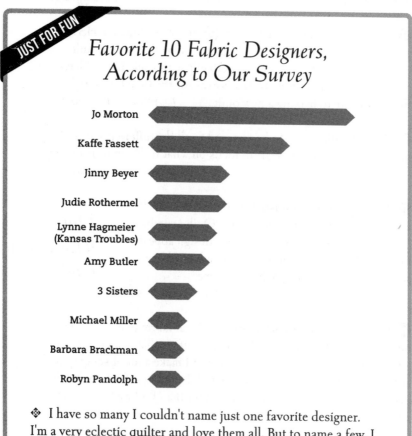

JUST FOR FUN

Favorite 10 Fabric Designers, According to Our Survey

- Jo Morton
- Kaffe Fassett
- Jinny Beyer
- Judie Rothermel
- Lynne Hagmeier (Kansas Troubles)
- Amy Butler
- 3 Sisters
- Michael Miller
- Barbara Brackman
- Robyn Pandolph

❖ I have so many I couldn't name just one favorite designer. I'm a very eclectic quilter and love them all. But to name a few, I would say Kaffe Fassett because of his astounding sense of color theory. The combinations of colors he comes up with are always blowing me away. Amy Butler and Pat Bravo never cease to amaze me with each new collection they come out with. And Tula Pink always fascinates me with her sense of design and themes in her collections. I love the way she thinks.   *Francis Stanley, Slidell, LA*

the box." When I was asked to sew samples for a local quilt store, I had to work with fabrics I never would have worked with on my own. It opened up a whole new world for me. Now I see scraps from those quilts in other projects I've made and think how proud I am of myself for taking a chance.   *Susan Chandler, Solon Springs, WI*

⓳ I figure out the who (is it for), the why (celebration or just a cozy), what (color the who likes), when (how much time do I have to complete it), and where (to buy the fabric). What fun it is to choose a quilt!   *Annette Jordan, Portville, NY*

⓴ Don't try too hard to match the decor of a room. When I started I was stuck on the thought that I had to make a quilt that would go in a certain room. It just would not come together.

When I let go of the idea that I had to match the room, I made an awesome quilt that went with nothing in my house. So I painted a guest room to match the quilt! The best thing I learned by doing this is that every quilt can stand alone. If you are inspired by and love what you create, you will want to make more quilts!

Nancy Henry, Rochester, NH

㉑ Time is always the great decider for me. How quickly do I want my quilt? If the answer is "yesterday," then a simple, no-nonsense pattern is just the thing. If time is no problem, then I have the luxury to explore more intricate designs and techniques.

Penny D'Aloia, Coburg, Australia

㉒ I begin with the people the quilt is going to be made for: what are their likes or dislikes, do they have a favorite color, will the quilt be used or just displayed? Are they organized people or artistic, have they planted their garden with the tulips all in a row or randomly? This tells me what kind of design they are looking for, as they often don't know.

After I can answer these questions, I then begin to look at old magazines and old quilt books. These hold such great beauty in design and color and often lead me in my thinking regarding color or design. This allows me to begin to develop in my mind the quilt I am looking to design.   *Kellie Hewitt, Marion, VA*

㉓ If the quilt is for myself, I often like to try new techniques, so I can expand my quilting experience. If the quilt is a gift, I try to base my choice on the recipients' likes and how they will be using it.

Karen Vecchioli, Staunton, VA

㉔ There have been times I make up my own pattern because I want to use my current stash or scraps.

Peggy Quinlan-Gee, Salt Lake City, UT

㉕ I look on the web and places such as Flickr to see pictures of quilts. I find that before I even finish the quilt top that I'm currently sewing, I'm already thinking and deciding my next project. I write a list of quilts I like to make and cross them off as they're completed, but for every quilt I cross off the list, I seem to add two or more.

Kerilee Corrie, Ross, Australia

㉖ My favorite place for quilt design lately is my EQ 7 program (quilt design software by Electric Quilt company). I can move blocks in and out, color them, and really play with the quilt before I ever commit anything.

Victoria Page, Amarillo, TX

㉗ For my first quilt, I chose my favorite color, blue, and my favorite object, snowflakes, and the quilt just evolved from there.

Bethany Beiler, Smoketown, PA

Some of my best ideas come while performing routine household tasks.

㉘ My creative process does not respond well to requests from friends or family members for a quilt of a particular color. In general, I do not dream well in other people's colors. The combination of pattern and color vibrates when I know I have it right. A great deal of my inspiration comes from looking at 19th century quilts, but I can also be inspired by modern designs. Color combinations often come to me based on scenes I see through my car window while driving, and some of my best ideas come while performing routine household tasks such as washing dishes or ironing.

Betsy Scott, Richmond, VA

29 The recipient gets input on the colors, but the pattern decision is mine. Then I spend time going through the patterns and books I've collected over the last 20-plus years.   *Mary Coudray, Belleville, WI*

30 I browse in a good quilt store with lots of samples, patterns, and books. I also subscribe to a number of quilt magazines, and I go to local quilt shows whenever possible. I have more quilts in mind than I'll ever have time to do.   *Deborah Gross, Willow Grove, PA*

31 I love the vintage quilts. I want to learn as much as possible so the traditions won't die. I have a list of "someday" quilts, from a Wedding Ring to a Dahlia, Log Cabin, I want to make them all!
    Barb Mikielski, Dallas, PA

32 Several things prompt me to make quilts: classes to learn a new technique or improve skills, seeing a pattern I like, or a group of fabrics I want to put together. This year I wanted to enter a themed contest. I didn't get the quilt done in time to enter it, but I had a wonderful time designing the quilt.   *Kirsten Franz, Denver, CO*

B. Specific Quilt Patterns

1 I've just discovered the Disappearing Nine-Patch blocks. These are so simple to do, but are so effective with the opportunity to move them around to make different designs.
    Barbara Falkner, Wellard, WA

2 The Nine-Patch is my favorite pattern. It is so versatile. I appreciate the economy of the design: small pieces can be easily used in this block, and yet the overall design can look very pulled together if you have a good color sense. With today's rotary cutters, it doesn't take long to put together a whole group of blocks.
    Celeste Collier, Guntersville, AL

❸ Currently my favorite pattern is Grandmother's Flower Garden. This is a project that I am currently hand piecing, and I always carry my hexagons with me because I can work on it anywhere since it is so portable. *Geralyn McClarren, Harrisburg, PA*

❹ I love Grandma's Flower Garden quilts done in '30s fabric, especially if they have a Nile green diamond path. I went to a bed turning a few years ago. When the narrator took off the quilt and showed one just like my favorite, I got a huge lump in my throat and tears in my eyes. My husband thought I was nuts, but most of the women seated near me gasped when they showed this quilt. It was pristine, perfect and well documented. I will never forget that quilt as long as I live. What a legacy some grandma left for her family! *Donna Clements, Hoquiam, WA*

❺ I like Pickle Dish quilts because I can do so many interesting things with them. *Sue Sacchero, Safety Bay, Australia*

❻ The Missouri Star is my favorite quilt block. I have made my four granddaughters quilts using a variation of this block called The Wonderland Block. It's just amazing how, even though it's the same block, when using different colors, the effect of each one is unique. *Anne Ryves, Thornlands, Australia*

❼ Baltimore Album style quilts can tell a story. You can instantly connect with the quilt maker and understand the story. It becomes more personal. *Betsy Pyle, Lancaster, PA*

❽ I find the Mariner's Star beautiful and versatile and rather exotic. I also love all star patterns because they make me think of heaven. *Carol Baruschke, Dunedin, FL*

❾ I love pinwheels and star blocks of all sorts. I like a lot of motion in my quilts. *Victoria Page, Amarillo, TX*

❿ I like Churn Dash because it is a quick and easy pattern. *Chris Tamsett, Red Hill, Australia*

11 Most patchwork is squares and angles, but I am drawn to circles. I like the softer curved lines of Orange Peel (my very favorite), Dresden Plate and Yo-Yo's.   *Diane Bachman, Leola, PA*

12 I love half-square triangles because they are so versatile and you can make so many different patterns for a block by the way you arrange them.   *Billye Wilda, Eagar, AZ*

13 My favorite pattern is 54 Forty or Fight. This became my favorite block after I was introduced to the Tri-Recs rulers by Darlene Zimmerman. I highly recommend quilters use these to make the "peaky" and "spike" triangle units for this and many other blocks.   *Janet Espeleta, Boonville, MO*

14 I love Puzzle Box for big prints; it's perfect for that traditional poinsettia Christmas fabric and those gorgeous big hydrangea prints.   *Wendy Akin, Terrell, TX*

15 The traditional block pattern that I use most often is the Double Irish Chain. I like it because it is quick and easy to put together, and it looks like it has taken a lot more work than it actually has. Non-quilters think that you sew each tiny piece of fabric together, one at a time!   *Barbara Johnson, Dallas, OR*

16 You know you married the right man when he likes the Ohio Star as much as you do. The ceramic tile in our kitchen has an Ohio Star in the middle. It was his idea!   *Debbie Henry, Lucinda, PA*

You know you married the right man when he likes the Ohio Star as much as you do.

17 The Tennessee Waltz by Eleanor Burns is my favorite pattern. I had been quilting for only a year when I made this, and it was, at times, like putting a puzzle together, but this was the most rewarding quilt I have ever made. It can look totally different with the choice of fabrics, and I'm preparing to make another one soon.   *Nancy Chase, Columbus, MT*

18 The New York Beauty is my favorite block. I love all of the spikes and curves in this block.   *Audrey Clark, Red Lodge, MT*

19 I love stars. Stars can be any color or size and go with traditional or contemporary designs. I am particularly into oversized blocks right now. I have a large star that is essentially the quilt top (about 50" or so). It's a beautiful quilt and pretty quick and easy, and can be used with brights for a baby or reproduction prints for a wall hanging or table topper.   *Vicki DiFrancesco, Conowingo, MD*

20 I like simple patterns that show off the fabric such as Nine-Patch, Variable Star and Square-in-Square.   *Jill Bowman, Jamestown, NC*

21 My favorite quilt block design is the Blooming 9-Patch, where the colors blend into each other until the center of the quilt can be quite different from the edges. I enjoyed figuring out how to put the quilt together after seeing it in a book. I used a neutral palette, with black at the edges, blending to brown, then tan, and finally, white in the center.   *Eileen D. Wenger, Lancaster, PA*

22 I like blocks that create secondary patterns, like Jacob's Ladder. Mary Ellen Hopkins would call it a two bell block.
          Jann Dodds, Kenthurst, Australia

I enjoy designs that stack the same repeat of the fabric.

23 I enjoy designs that stack the same repeat of the fabric, such as Stack n Whack and Four Patch Posie. I then work those into traditional settings such as pinwheels or simple squares set on point.
          Marian Gowan, Hendersonville, NC

24 My all-time favorite quilt block is the Log Cabin. It's a very simple block, but the layout options are endless.   *Cincy Bailey, Valrico, FL*

25 Pinwheels are always fun because one can make them spin in different directions and look different with all kinds of color combinations. These blocks can be made in so many different ways and they add so much to so many different types of quilts, from baby quilts to elegant flower garden quilts, to novelty kids' quilts. They also make a wonderful scrappy look with your stash or a new line of fabrics you can't wait to try.   *Shannon Nay, Austin, TX*

26 I like the Carpenter's Block. It can be easily redesigned to any size you want, and it looks great in three tones of fabric.
Kim Clark, Lakewood, CO

27 I like the Lemoyne Star. It makes an elegant quilt.
Marti Blankenship, Pleasant Valley, MO

28 I will never get tired of making Dresden Plates. I love the old fashioned look using '30s reproduction fabrics as well as modern fabrics. Anything works with them and you have to love that for stash busting.   *Francis Stanley, Slidell, LA*

c. Sources of Inspiration

1 Nature inspires me. I take a daily walk and soak up the colors and textures I see. I am still working on my plan for a quilt with a series of panels showing the four seasons looking out over the lake.
Deborah Vivrette, Hidden Valley Lake, CA

2 I look for designs everywhere. I once did a quilt using the design in the ceiling tiles in a doctor's office.   *Marie Sugar, Lancaster, PA*

3 I am so happy that my first quilt came from Sunbonnet Sue blocks that my grandmother had completed and never put together as a quilt. After she died, I found the blocks and it provided a real connection between us when I made them into a quilt. She made it so easy for me: all the hard work was done.
Carol M. Johnson, Greenville, SC

4 One time I designed a small appliqué quilt based on an October ale carton.
Annie Morgan, Johnson, VT

5 The old quilts in museums are masterpieces made by our fore-mothers. There are mistakes, fabrics that don't match, and many have been mended and repaired. But, there they are speaking to us from across the generations saying "Just make it! It doesn't have to be perfect, you don't have to have a degree in sewing, you just have to have a love for it and it will be a masterpiece!"
Diane Bachman, Leola, PA

6 Recently, I attended a shop hop with 11 stores; each one had multiple quilts on display which also inspired me.
Amy Kentera, Highland Mills, NY

7 I visit Pinterest, quilting blogs, or check out books at the library.
Karen Woodhull, Lumberton, NJ

A single color can pull at me to work with it and devise a colorway that revolves around that one hue.

8 I am in awe of nature, particularly wild nature, so I am drawn to scenery that includes mountains, the sea, wildlife and flora.

I am a keen gardener and can be totally inspired by a single bloom or the colors of autumn in my garden.

Color is pivotal to my quilting ideas—a single color can pull at me to work with it and devise a colorway that revolves around that one hue.
Anne Clutterbuck, Ocean Grove, Australia

9 Lately I've been recreating the graphics on boats. I take a picture of a section of an image painted on a boat, and make a quilt that matches the image.
Noelle Clesceri, Oakwood Hills, IL

10 My favorite is appliqué because I love hand work. My next favorite is trying to reproduce an antique quilt, so I prefer Civil War fabrics.
Wilma Scholl, Kaufman, TX

⑪ My business is doing long-arm quilting for customers. I get inspired when I see some of my customers' quilts.

Susie Young, Anthony, KS

⑫ In my church sewing group, we receive a lot of donated fabrics, so it can be challenging putting together a quilt with fabrics that you may not have picked at the store. I love that challenge.

Nina Banagay, McMinnville, OR

⑬ One quilt I need to make is a depiction of Pachelbel's Canon in D. It's my favorite piece of music, and I *must* translate it into fabric.

Cathie Shelton, Montgomery Village, MD

⑭ Much inspiration comes from members of my quilt guild. We participate in a number of Blocks of the Month which make us go outside of our comfort zone at times and try something we have never tried before.

Sharon Purves, Cannifton, Ontario

⑮ I take photos of architecture, natural lines and shadows in winter landscapes, and keep my eyes open for daily structures, fences, shapes, and discarded broken items. These may provide ideas that I can apply to the spaces in my quilt that require quilting.

Dagmar Yaddow, Rhinebeck, NY

⑯ I enjoy checking out books from libraries and browsing through until a special quilt just jumps out—and that is all I can think about!

Marcia Dionne, Laconia, NH

⑰ I have recently started looking a lot more at quilting blogs instead of magazines or books. I think blogs are a great reference for quilters because usually you can ask the quilters a question directly without trying to guess the methodology behind their patterns and it makes it easier to learn how they come up with their designs and how to execute them successfully. A lot of the patterns are also free which is great.

Nina Banagay, McMinnville, OR

18 I look at pictures for inspiration. Magazines! Catalogs! Then if I need a real shot in the arm, I go to the quilt fabric store. It gets the juices flowing.   *Virginia Olcerst, Marriottsville, MD*

19 I make family reunion quilts every two years. I will pick one color or several colors and ask my family members to send me fabrics, then make a final decision on the quilt based upon the fabric I receive. If I keep running across a particular quilt pattern again and again, I make that quilt—like the Sister's Choice/Farmer's Daughter block when we made a memorial quilt for my sister after she passed away. I find it a great challenge to use some fabrics that I would never have chosen, but the final quilt for that particular family reunion is always quite beautiful.

Margaret Dabrowski, Lowell, MA

20 Some event needs to inspire me. For example, I tried to grow weeping cherry trees and they all died, so I was inspired to quilt a small weeping cherry tree.   *Mary Andra Holmes, Prescott, AZ*

21 I have 20 years of quilting magazines that I look through all of the time. Something I didn't really like 15 years ago may be the perfect design now. I take tons of pictures at shows and museums: I may use the layout from one and the border from another, the colors from this one and the blocks from a history book.

Diane Meddley, Parrish, FL

22 I read quilt magazines and when a quilt design inspires me, I tear it out and slip the pages in a plastic sleeve for safekeeping until I'm ready to start a new project. I gravitate toward piecing projects that employ timesaving techniques like strip piecing, half-square triangles, etc. I'm also easily attracted to scrappy quilts, not necessarily as a way to use up my stash, but because I find them more visually interesting than quilts with limited fabric selections.

Jan Mast, Lancaster, PA

23 When I go into a building, I look at the floors and the walls to see how the tiles are laid out. Sometimes that gives me the inspiration for different projects.   *Patricia Baptista, Dartmouth, MA*

24 I look at online quilt shows to see exhibits too far away for me to attend. My favorite is the Tokyo show. I also attend 3 or 4 shows a year, including the international show in Houston.

Eileen Ellis, Tabernacle, NJ

25 A favorite memory is taking the train from Minneapolis, Minnesota, to Portland, Oregon in July. I had a queen-size quilt that I hand quilted as I looked out to see the amazing yellow canola fields and the periwinkle flax fields, then the river water gurgling along right next to the train, then to wake up Sunday morning to see Mt. Hood across the Columbia River. . . .   *Marlys Wiens, Edina, MN*

26 My quilting friends never let me down. Often I pair up with one or more gals and we all make the same quilt using different fabrics.

The public library is also a great source of inspiration. I check out quilting books. If I find I am checking it out more than once, then it is a book I must buy to put in my own collection. I have bookcases of books, patterns, quilt magazines and newspaper clippings. A couple hours browsing in my patterns usually inspires me to focus in on a couple quilts.

Marti Blankenship, Pleasant Valley, MO

27 I'm interested in the creative process, so I challenge myself to create little quilts to express feelings. I read the story of the 12 × 12 quilting challenge and I decided to try my hand at it, so I wrote down a series of topics such as centrality, joy, Venice, embellishment, and so on and created a doll-sized quilt for each topic.

Silvia Triches, Udine, Italy

> *I challenge myself to create little quilts to express feelings.*

28 Nature inspires me most. The colors in nature and gardens fit so well together that it is hard to improve on! I do a lot of landscape appliqué.   *Nancy Henry, Rochester, NH*

29 I get inspiration from books with pictures of old quilts, such as museum catalogs and state documentation books.

Beth Fisher, San Antonio, TX

Look at your window: it's an outline of a quilt. Now, use your imagination to divide it into three vertical panels.

30 My eyes see pattern, design, shape and color in the things and places that surround me. Sounds a bit "arty," but it's not. Look at your window: it's an outline of a quilt. Now, use your imagination to divide it into three vertical panels. In each panel what are the three or four main colors? For me, first panel, it's blue/grey sky, terracotta roofs, green cyprus tree. Second panel: blue/grey sky, terracotta roof, cream weather board, greens of pot plants and two spots of intense red, the last of my autumn flowers. Third panel: blue/grey sky, charcoal metal roof, cream weather boards. Now imagine all those things are just squares and rectangles of color. Go on, tweak the colors and shapes in your head a little bit, but keep it simple. You have a quilt! *Penny D'Aloia, Coburg, Australia*

31 I am inspired by chat groups on Yahoo. I belong to several appliqué groups: Appliqué-Addicts, Sue Garman, and Ladies of the Sea. *Karen Nick, Lutz, FL*

32 For reproduction fabrics—Jo Morton or Barbara Brackman. For contemporary fabrics—Martha Negley or Amy Butler. For batiks—McKenna Ryan. For traditional—French General.

Jan Mast, Lancaster, PA

33 Going on a quilt retreat is a huge inspiration for me—I sew with an awesome group of quilters that take my breath away with their workmanship and creativity. *Karen Martin, Breezy Point, MN*

34 I visit Pinterest for inspiration. I could get a lot more sewing done if I had never discovered Pinterest. *Gale Priesmeyer, Bellville, TX*

35 I subscribe to several magazines and buy patterns. In order to keep all these quilts in mind, when I get a new magazine, I mark the page of the quilt project that interests me and then add that information to a notebook, organized by magazine.

Lisa Sachs, Hackettstown, NJ

36 I am inspired by all kinds of sources for quilts. Some have been:
  • pictures in magazines
  • the carpet design at an airport
  • quilts others have made
  • a sound barrier wall design on the side of a busy road
  • the challenge of what to do with pre-cut fabric
  • a design on a napkin
  • a fence

Anna Osborn, Omaha, NE

D. Finding Time To Quilt

1 First of all, I think it is important not to get hung up on how much time it takes to make or finish a quilt. Make a decision to sew every day and never leave your sewing machine without setting up what you will sew next. That way, if you only have 10 or 15 minutes, those will be productive minutes. It is amazing how much you can get done in small increments of time.   *Betsy Scott, Richmond, VA*

2 I try to prepare hand sewing or quilting projects over the weekend that I can work on during the evening hours while I spend time with my family.   *Blair Mahan, Medford, NJ*

3 I make time: quilting is my stress reliever. I am self employed, work long hours, and sometimes it feels out of my control. I go to the "dungeon," my basement sewing room that has my comforts: the sewing machine, lots of fabric and books for perusing, a TV, tablet and phone. I kick off my shoes, turn on some mindless TV and sew. If I'm particularly stressed, I organize the room, straighten up the fabric, refold and put away new purchases and get out the next project. Sometimes 20 minutes may be all I can give, but I am relaxed after and the calmness is profound. The family knows where I am, there's a chair for them when they come visit, but don't touch! Everything has a place and I like it organized my way.

Barb Mikielski, Dallas, PA

❹ When I was in 6th grade, I greatly admired Olivia Martinez's saddle shoes which were always spic-and-span brown and white. I asked her how she found time to polish them and she told me, "I *make* time." This has stuck with me for many years and when I have a little block of time, I do at least one thing on my quilt.

Elizabeth Beardsley, Boulder, CO

❺ As I'm doing chores, quilting is the carrot at the finish, even if it's only 5 minutes looking at a pattern or auditioning fabrics.

Barbara Augustine, Woodbridge, VA

❻ I never watch TV without a piece of handwork in my lap.

Eileen Ellis, Tabernacle, NJ

❼ I do not watch a lot of TV, so every day after dinner, I set this time aside for my quilting.   *Jean McCrea, Thornhurst, PA*

❽ I separate my quilting into three categories: hand work that can be done while chatting, watching TV, etc.; cutting and machine piecing which I do in the sewing room whenever I have 10 minutes free; and design work I incorporate into my daily life by always looking for inspiration in my surroundings. I have a sewing room right off my kitchen. In there, at the ready is always a project in the works.   *Kathleen Keough, Berwyn, PA*

❾ There is always something else I need to be doing. There are always errands to run, groceries to buy, food to cook, children to care for, appointments that must be kept. Quilting is on my To Do List just like all those things. I pencil in time at least a few times a week just for me.   *Diane Meddley, Parrish, FL*

❿ I really enjoy it when my husband goes hunting with a male buddy and I stay home. I have everything ready: fabric, thread, patterns, batting, audio books, coffee, and microwave food. Day one: clean house and do laundry. Days 2–6: sew, sew, sew! Day 7: vacuum, dust, change sheets and hand wash the coffee cups in the dishwasher because that's all that's in it!   *Nancy Chase, Columbus, MT*

⓫ As a rule I have a hand-piecing "kit" in my purse for found moments while I wait. This tip came from Jinny Beyers' book on quilting. I have always hand quilted at least fifteen minutes per day before or after work. It is surprising how much you can accomplish within small blocks of time over a month.

Shelia Smith, Goldthwaite, TX

⓬ I have a 20-minute rule. Every day, I find 20 minutes to do a quilt-related thing. No exceptions! Many days, I get a lot more time to quilt, but that is my minimum and some days that's it.

Mary Kastner, Oakland, CA

⓭ About 20 years ago I read *10-20-30 Minutes to Sew* by Nancy Zieman. I literally couldn't put it down. I have lived by that book ever since. She taught me what to do in 10 minutes, then put the item away, then 20 minutes, etc. I am able to quilt every single day and I still work a full-time job. I also do this with my housework. i.e., I spend 30 to 45 minutes every night cleaning something, maybe an hour. When I break every task down into segments, it goes very fast and I'm not overwhelmed.   *Jenean McGuigan, Chicago, IL*

> *I am able to quilt every single day and I still work a full-time job.*

⓮ Sometimes you just have to skip cleaning the house! Quilts are permanent and bring joy; the floors just get dirty again.

Wendy Akin, Terrell, TX

⓯ Being retired, I consider my quilting time what I want it to be. I don't have so many deadlines I have to meet or obligations I have to keep. Kids are grown and it's now my turn. So what if the house isn't spotless, it's still clean. Meals don't have to be on the table a certain time anymore, so I can quilt a few more minutes. This is one

of the few advantages of getting older: being a little selfish with my
time.   *Francis Stanley, Slidell, LA*

16 Quilting is my therapy. I am a teacher, and we are experiencing
stressful times in education. I find time to play in my sewing room
every day after work. I try to have simple, repetitive blocks cut and
waiting by the machine (I love scrap quilts) so I can just send things
through the machine and work with all the pretty fabrics after a
long day. People often say "How do you find the patience to sew all
those small pieces together?" My answer is that the sewing gives me
patience for everything else in my life.   *Lorraine Vignoli, Commack, NY*

17 Even though I am retired, there never seems to be enough
time to quilt! I try to look at the week ahead and plan to quilt on
days that have a large chunk of free time. I also look at the weather
forecast ahead of time, knowing which days I won't be working in
my garden.   *Allison Evrard, Coopersburg, PA*

18 My local quilt store has a sit-and-sew every Monday, which I
regularly attend as it provides me regular sewing time. I tend to be
so energized that when I get home, I sew the rest of the day.
                                                       KC Howell, Medina, OH

*Quilting serves
to recharge my
emotional battery,
and that is why
I never reach the
end of my rope.*

19 It is vital for me to set aside quilting
time because of the hectic daily activities of
going to work, running a household, being
a grandmother, a volunteer, and actively
engaging in a number of choruses and
other cultural activities... Quilting serves to
recharge my emotional battery, and that is
why I never reach the end of my rope.
                                       Dagmar Yaddow, Rhinebeck, NY

20 I rush through cleaning the house. I sew in between loads
of laundry and always try to cook enough for two days' worth of
meals.   *Pat Zimmerman, Kissimmee, FL*

㉑ I make time! Thursdays are "my" day. I don't do laundry, clean the house, or run errands.... I sew all day with no guilt or interruptions. We have a sushi date for dinner and I hang on until the next Thursday.   *Christy Proost, Mechanicsville, VA*

㉒ I set aside 5 hours every Monday to work on UFOs (unfinished objects). I try to fit in other time during the week as I can, which isn't always easy, but at least I have my Mondays.

Amy Braunagel, Columbia, MO

㉓ I give up a few hours of sleep a week and totally ignore housework and sometimes cooking.   *Joyce Carey, Waterford, MI*

㉔ I make the time. I worked a full time job and learned to sew in 20–30 minute increments. I never put my projects away, so they are always ready when I have the few minutes to sew. I also get up early and reward myself with a half hour of sewing before I leave for work. I make time every day to cut, sew, iron and play with designs. Both my children grew up with me quilting and they both have a strong sense of color and design. They also learned the importance of their mother having time for herself to do the things that gave her pleasure (and they also had a father who is a great cook).

Anne Gallo, Chelmsford, MA

㉕ Everyone has 24 hours in a day. An older woman once told me if you don't organize your time, someone else will. Make an appointment with yourself.   *Barbara Porter, Arroyo Grande, CA*

㉖ I make time. Quilting is an important part of my life, and I would become very stressed if I were not able to sew. I work full time, so weekends are my main quilting opportunities. I like to get up early, prepare my dinner (usually in a slow cooker), do a load or two of laundry, then have the rest of the day free to sew.

Pat Deck, Oreland, PA

㉗ I hand sew every day during my lunch hour at work. I call it "me time."   *Patricia Henseler, Maple Grove, MN*

28 I just try to do 15 minutes a day. I also keep track of what I have done on a small calendar and I can see when I haven't done anything for a while. That usually gets me going again. It also allows me to know when I started and finished a project.

Barbara Hughes, Elkins Park, PA

29 I have recently learned that if I can't sleep, sitting at the sewing machine and just doing a little is when I quilt the best.

Susan Lesko, Bloomingburg, NY

30 I do a lot of hand appliqué and used to do hand piecing. A project like that was essential to be able to take with me when I attended the kids' baseball practices, doctors' waiting rooms, etc. I actually started *and* finished hand piecing a quilt on a 6-week family car trip when my kids were really little! *Nancy Henry, Rochester, NH*

31 I quilt best in the mornings, so I put off housework or errands until afternoons. *Nancy Jolley, Tucson, AZ*

32 I work full-time, so it is difficult, but for my own sanity, I need to spend at least 30 minutes a day in my quilting room. Either Saturday or Sunday of every weekend, my husband takes charge of the house, and I have the entire day to quilt. *Ann Hay, Carlisle, PA*

33 I had more time to quilt before I retired. I would get up an hour earlier than I had to to go to work. I would race through getting ready then set the timer and sit and sew. When the timer went off, no matter where I was, I had to stop and leave for work. Since I retired, there are weeks that go by and I don't have time to sew.

Terry Green, Attica, NY

We take off every Wednesday to sew.

34 I am my husband's caregiver, and when he naps during the day, I quilt. *Doris Carbone, Dracut, MA*

35 I have two girlfriends and we take off every Wednesday to sew. It is an appointment every week, and it takes a *lot* for one of us to cancel our appointment! It is a time of sisterhood in fabric. We help each other, share ideas and fabric and have fun! We are very different in age and sewing ability and experience, but each has something to offer. It is a mental health day in the middle of the week that gets us through the rest of the week.   *Diane Bachman, Leola, PA*

36 I schedule quilting time into each day like it is a meeting I need to keep. This is my therapy, so it is like an appointment with the doctor.   *Kim Clark, Lakewood, CO*

37 I am fortunate in that my husband of 54 years is interested in my quilting. He pins quilts on the longarm while I do piecing at the domestic machine. How neat is that? He is also experienced at frogging (ripping out stitches in quilting). Our daughter bought him an ergonomic seam ripper for his Christmas stocking gift.

I do stay organized. Doing laundry while piecing a quilt is a snap. Slow cookers were surely invented by quilters. There may be a little dust on the furniture or crumbs on the kitchen floor but with the love and support of my family, I (almost) never feel guilty about making quilting one of my life goals.

Marti Blankenship, Pleasant Valley, MO

E. A Sewing Space

1 Have a sewing room. I had to use my kitchen table for years, but finally got a room that I can just shut the door on and make dinner without having to clean up first.   *Nancy Chase, Columbus, MT*

2 You really need the ability to display your fabric stash—you can't create with it if you can't see it.   *Peggy Quinlan-Gee, Salt Lake City, UT*

3 It's nice to have cork boards to pin up anything that you don't want to go missing after you put it in a "safe" place—for example,

JUST FOR FUN

Favorite 5 Fabric Companies, According to Our Survey

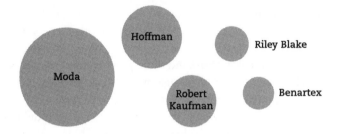

Hoffman

Riley Blake

Moda

Robert Kaufman

Benartex

❖ This is the best time ever in the history of the world to be a quilter. There is such a fabulous array of designers. Judie Rothermel does such lovely reproduction fabrics. For bold colors, there is Kaffe Fassett, and then Moda has some designers who do traditional styles. And all the modern, contemporary looks featuring citron and gray! And the anonymous folks who do batiks. Wow! *Valerie Turere, Brooklyn, NY*

directions you most often use, inspiring pictures, small appliqué pieces, etc. *Dolores Smith, Westford, MA*

❹ Get a card from Superior Threads to hang on a bulletin board (a must) in your sewing room that identifies the types of thread and how to use them. *Nancy Chase, Columbus, MT*

❺ I have a sewing machine in my kitchen. When I put potatoes on to boil, I can sew two seams. When I wait for the coffee to perk, I can square up a block or paper piece some seams. It's amazing how much I can accomplish minute by minute. Slow and steady wins the race! *MaryJean Bower, Bloomsburg, PA*

❻ A plastic case that a certain brand of chewing gum comes in makes a wonderful disposal for bent pins, dull needles and dead rotary blades. Just tape the little door shut when it's full and throw in the garbage.   *Debbie Daugherty-Ball, Salisbury, MD*

❼ Make sure you have adequate electrical outlets for machine, iron, lighting, and radio/TV.   *Rachel Applegate, Slingerlands, NY*

❽ Clock! I'd be up all night if I didn't have one in my sewing space!   *Kris Newlin, West Chester, PA*

❾ Outstanding lighting is important for sewing. Try the new LEDs—lots of clean light and no heat!   *Jana Pratt, Barnegat, NJ*

❿ A sewing space needs lots of storage, good light, and a design wall if you can swing it.   *Teresa Caldwell, Long Valley, NJ*

⓫ Since I don't have a lot of wall space for a design wall, I rigged up a flannel-backed vinyl tablecloth that hangs from the ceiling that I can let down or roll up. I also like a floor that is easily cleaned, not carpet.   *Cathy Jolley, Fillmore, UT*

⓬ I don't have room for a design wall, so I use my king-size bed top.   *Vicki Kasten, Rosemount, MN*

⓭ I have designed (in my head) storage to hang on the front of my cupboard doors. Using a quilt I don't love anymore, I will attach pockets to it made of see-through plastic like a hanging shoe holder, and have all my templates and rulers on display. That way I'll be able to get my hands on them easily when I want to use them.   *Louise Lott, Healesville, Australia*

⓮ I seem to flip between projects, so I need lots of room in my sewing space. It's helpful if this room is close to the kitchen so I can run in and check on the Crockpot now and then, and close to the utility room with washer and dryer so I can throw in a load.   *Nancy Fairchild, Crossville, TN*

⓯ An ashtray, with its raised sides, is perfect for holding little bits of thread or fabric.   *Verna Fitzgerald, West New York, NJ*

⓰ I keep objects in my sewing room that I enjoy seeing. I have a couple of bulletin boards—one with quilt pins and other pins I have collected and one with pictures of quilts I have made or would like to make. I also have other items on my sewing room wall that just speak to me: handmade art from my children and friends and old irons and sewing related items.   *Pamela Olson, South Windsor, CT*

⓱ I keep a tweezers in my sewing space; they help grab so many things.   *Nancy Koyanik, Troy, VA*

⓲ When I'm seated too low at my machine, I use door stops to prop the back side of the machine up. It really makes the throat plate more visible.   *Karen Asman, Martin, OH*

A magnetic pincushion is great for getting pins off floors.

⓳ Keep a dust mop or vacuum nearby to keep the floors neat. A magnetic pincushion is also great for getting pins off floors.   *Robbin Golden, Summerville, SC*

⓴ I have a cork floor which is good for standing on for a period of time as I cut fabric.   *Norma Whaley, Salt Lake City, UT*

㉑ I use a pretty flowerpot near my machine to store all of my scissors. I have a clear vinyl shoe pocket rack that I hang on the wall with my notions clearly visible: one for marking pens, one for tape measures, one for rotary cutters, one for glues, etc.   *Carolyn Vidal, Newport, WA*

㉒ I use a pencil box to place my sewing notions in (cutter, markers, small scissors, etc.) so that I can easily see what I want and store them efficiently.   *Emily Schanck, Taftsville, VT*

㉓ I have four pairs of scissors in my sewing room: two on the cutting table, one at the machine and the other just floats around where I need it.   *Mary Helen Ames, Perkiomenville, PA*

㉔ Clean up every surface of your workspace at least once every week and put things where they belong instead of where it is convenient.   *Michelle Harrison, Morganton, GA*

㉕ When you finish a project, press and fold extra fabric and stow it away, sweep the floor, clean the machine and change the needle, put supplies and notions where they belong and start the next project with a clean room and machine.   *Nancy Chase, Columbus, MT*

F. Advice for People Who Want to Learn to Quilt

❶ I've heard that you should never give away your first quilt. Keep it so you can see how your skills improve over the years.
                                            Susie Curry, Chesterbrook, PA

❷ Out of my first 20 quilts, some were lovely, some were dreadful and the rest just average. I get better with every quilt—and more adventurous. You just have to start somewhere, but make sure you pick fabrics that you really love. Then the finished quilt will please you no matter what pattern it is and how many mistakes you can find.   *Deb Spencer, Greenwith, Australia*

❸ Join a guild in your area. One advantage of belonging to a guild is that you have opportunity to take classes from very good quilting teachers at reduced costs.   *Charlotte Kewish, Gibsonia, PA*

❹ Don't take one instructor's methods as the only way to do things—every instructor I've taken a class from has been convinced that her way is the ONLY way to do things, but you have to experiment with other methods to find what works for you.
                                            Carol Moll, Schnecksville, PA

5 Eleanor Burns is the best. I tell beginners to buy an Eleanor Burns book and do what she tells you to do, page by page. It's almost no fail.   *Cincy Bailey, Valrico, FL*

6 If you want to learn machine quilting, it is important to already be familiar with your sewing machine. It is very difficult to learn sewing and quilting simultaneously.   *Sandra Leigh, Birmingham, AL*

7 Remember that all those beautiful quilts you look at have mistakes that each quilter is aware of but no one else is.
                                            Kellie Hewitt, Marion, VA

8 Find a quilting buddy. My friend and I started quilting together in 1989, she in New York, me in Florida. We started by doing a wall quilt each month as we both sewed, but had no quilting experience. We would comb through magazines to decide on the pattern for that month, buy and cut the fabric together, and then "race" each other to finish the quilt by the first of the month so that we could display them. We still check with each other to see if we remembered to change the quilt each month.   *Amy Israel, Port St Lucie, FL*

9 Take your time and just enjoy your work. It does not have to be perfect—nothing is ever perfect. Some of my biggest mistakes have become the unique feature I like the best in the finished quilt. I try to blend the mistake in and make it look like it was a planned feature.   *Mary Marlowe, Hedgesville, WV*

I'm teaching myself with YouTube.

10 I took a class long ago before I was even married and it didn't go well for me. So this time around, I'm teaching myself with YouTube. It's free and nice and quiet just the way I like it.
                                        Kimberly Dutcher, Brighton, MI

11 Watch YouTube videos for any areas of quilting that you may have doubts or questions on. Don't get discouraged.
                                        Barbara Merritt, Brackney, PA

⑫ Find a mentor. My grandmother was my mentor, and my memories of learning to sew with her are the best from my childhood. I am currently mentoring my best friend who comes from a non-sewing family and my 8 year old daughter. I get to share in their joy when they master a new technique or finish a project. Your love and joy of quilting are doubled when you share what you know with someone else! *Diane Bachman, Leola, PA*

⑬ Don't worry about finishing everything. Sometimes learning you don't like a technique or a fabric is valuable enough. UFO's are not necessarily bad. Sometimes you just lose interest for a while and will come back to a project. Sometimes it's better to do a big project in manageable chunks instead of telling yourself you can't start anything else until it's finished. Nothing will kill your enthusiasm for quilting faster than plowing through a project you have lost interest in. *Sally Eshelman, York, PA*

⑭ You have to love to iron! And you have to be willing to take things apart when they aren't right. If you're the type that says "close enough," then quilting probably isn't for you because being just a little bit off on your blocks will throw off the whole quilt. *Cheryl Desmond, Bristol, CT*

⑮ I think if you want to learn, you need to have that spark of curiosity about the craft, backed up by a willingness to commit time to mastering techniques. It is important to begin with a project you can achieve in a realistic time frame—something simple but appealing. That first project is what will get you hooked, so it has to be something that you can see yourself finishing and enjoying. *Anne Clutterbuck, Ocean Grove, Australia*

⑯ Checking quilting books out of your local library lets you learn without spending a lot of money. *Karen Vecchioli, Staunton, VA*

⑰ Quilt making is not like sewing clothes with a pattern. It is like putting together a puzzle, one piece at a time. Much of it is repetitive and slow and can be very relaxing if you are chain piecing. *Donna Royson, Blythewood, SC*

18 A great book to begin with is Jinny Beyers' *Quiltmaking By Hand* with DVD.   *Shelia Smith, Goldthwaite, TX*

19 Don't let anyone tell you you can't do something in quilting. There are no rules in quilting except close your rotary cutter each time you use it. If it feels good to you, it will look good to you ... it's in your heart, not a book or anywhere else.   *Mardi Niles, Scotia, NY*

20 Read! I was laid up from two back-to-back surgeries, so I bought *Quilting For Dummies* and Eleanor Burns' *It's Elementary* among other beginner quilting books and just read for all of my 12 weeks of bed rest and recovery. I also watched Eleanor Burns and Fons & Porter on PBS, and by the time I could get back into the sewing room, I had so many ideas!   *Lisa Hughes, Richland, NY*

21 Focus on the process and enjoy that. The finished product is not as important as the process. If you don't enjoy the process, you probably shouldn't keep quilting.   *BJ Chadwick, Marmora, NJ*

22 For people who are afraid that they will buy the wrong fabrics or use the wrong stitches and not make quilts as nice as they would want them to be, take lessons from your local quilt shop.

For people who love the creative process more than the finished product and who see a mistake as a branch into something just not thought of, pick yourself some fibers, get a good techniques book, and go for it.   *Louise Bem, Indiana, PA*

23 I made my first quilt reading one of the *Quilt in a Day* books by Eleanor Burns. I had only been a garment sewer until then.

Joyce Ciembronowicz, Lake Zurich, IL

24 I suggest taking a beginner class for quilting, not just a class that beginners can do. The difference is, a beginner class teaches things you will always need to quilt: measuring, pressing, piecing, layout, etc.

A class that beginners can do will teach you a pretty simple project, but once you finish it, you will only know how to make that

one thing. You want to learn things you can expand on and use in
your next project.   *Diane Meddley, Parrish, FL*

㉕ Lots of churches have sewing groups that do charity sewing.
Many of those ladies are also quilters and are great sources of
information.   *Karen Martin, Breezy Point, MN*

㉖ Start with a small project so you don't become overwhelmed.
Take a class with a teacher who is relaxed and not looking for
perfection, or you will become discouraged.   *Ann Hay, Carlisle, PA*

㉗ This is the best advice I have after 20 years of quilting: join a
quilt guild and purchase your fabric at a local store. Both of these
will give you a source of free advice and a chance to make new
lifelong friends.   *Mardelle Tanner, Sodus, NY*

㉘ Take a beginning quilting
course at a local quilt shop.
Both shops where I currently
do business have 8-session
classes that cover the whole
realm of getting started in
quilting, plus taking classes
puts you in contact with other
quilters of varying experience.
After that, subscribe to online
resources such as The Quilt
Show. There's a lot of free
material out there to get you
familiar with the whole field

I learned to quilt from my grandmother in the '60s, and worked with that knowledge until I retired, at which time I really got my eyes opened from online resources to new and better ways of cutting, piecing, and quilting.

and what is new. I learned to quilt from my grandmother in the
'60s, and worked with that knowledge until I retired a few years ago,
at which time I really got my eyes opened from online resources to
new and better ways of cutting, piecing, and quilting.
                                  Carol Moll, Schnecksville, PA

29 Buy the Hargrave's series *Quilter's Academy*. They are the best books to learn how to quilt I've seen so far (and I have a lot of books!).

Silvia Triches, Udine, Italy

30 Don't try to do every technique in your first quilt.

Debbie Daugherty-Ball, Salisbury, MD

31 You don't need every gadget ever made and you don't need an expensive sewing machine. Just the basics will do fine.

Ann Hay, Carlisle, PA

32 Try out as many rulers, marking tools, thimbles, needles, scissors as you can. There are differences and tools are expensive. Try asking friends to borrow their favorite ruler for a few days just to see if it works for you. Ask why they like it and what they use it for. Just because it is their favorite does not mean it will be your favorite.

Mary Andra Holmes, Prescott, AZ

33 Purchase good materials and tools—or use a friends' until you know you want to do this. Don't try to do it with old crummy fabric that stretches, or a ruler that slides around, or a rotary cutter or scissors that are too dull to cut, or a sewing machine that continually has tension problems or comes unthreaded every time you use it. Any of those will make you throw up your hands and say "I don't like quilting" when what you really are doing is trying to quilt with bad materials or tools!

Ruthie Hoover, Westerville, OH

34 Always look at your projects from 15 feet, not 5 inches, so you're looking at the whole picture.

Amy Rochelle, South Lyon, MI

CHAPTER 2

Selecting Fabric

A. Planning Colors and Fabrics

1 It is always best to make a sample block and live with it for a day or so to be sure it's what you want. A good way to see what the finished quilt will look like is to place 2 mirrors at right angles on a table, then place the block on the table against the 2 edges of the mirrors. The reflections will let you see how the blocks will look when connected.   *Diane Bachman, Leola, PA*

2 Piece a block (or a few) and see how you like it on the design wall for a few days. Once, I removed a single piece from a completed Double Wedding Ring top because it was the one piece that drew everyone's eye. I replaced it with a more blending color, not too much of a hassle for a major improvement!

Libbie Ellis, Tarpon Springs, FL

❸ I understand the color wheel and know about complementary and contrasting colors. I also know that too much matchy matchy is boring.   *Jann Dodds, Kenthurst, Australia*

❹ If you have trouble with picking colors or discerning whether fabrics are light, medium or dark, try making a black and white photocopy of the quilt you have in mind. It'll help you get past the "color" and you'll be better able to distinguish the tones of the fabrics instead.   *Barbara Gentner, West Seneca, NY*

❺ Think outside the box at least a little and try something new. You might be pleasantly surprised. This is not brain surgery. If you goof it up, no one will die.   *Annemarie (Nancy) Poorbaugh, Montgomery, AL*

❻ If you have a lot of small prints, your quilt is not dramatic when viewed from farther away. Scale is important.
          Danette Lockler, Denver, CO

❼ I focus on the contrast between a pattern's pieces. There are always certain parts of a block that I want to bring forward and others that I want to recede. A general rule is warm colors (red, yellow and orange) will come forward; cool colors (blue, green and purple) will recede.   *Kathleen Keough, Berwyn, PA*

❽ I allow the pattern to dictate the colors. If I'm making a modern quilt, I'll use bold, bright, primary colors. If I'm making a traditional quilt, I'll use more subdued, grayed colors, and if I'm making an Americana quilt, I'll mostly use various tones of red, white, and blue. My personal favorites are scrap quilts with medium dark, and dark fabrics (all colors) with some tans thrown in for contrast.
          Jan Fusco, Collegeville, PA

❾ Advertising companies spend *a lot* of money picking color combinations for the packaged food items we buy. Pick one or two from your pantry and pull your colors from that.
          Maria Goodwin, Washington, DC

10 I almost never use solid fabrics. I prefer fabrics that, when you squint your eyes, *look* solid. They add more interest in a quilt.

Nancy Henry, Rochester, NH

11 A good beginner's tip is to take a piece of typing paper and cut a 2–3" square out of the middle, then lay this down on your bolt to see the perspective you'd have if you cut it into a square. A color may appear too bright when you are looking at an entire bolt, but if you are just using 3" squares, it just may be the punch you need.   *Susan Bonilla, Clinton, UT*

> *Take a piece of typing paper and cut a 2–3" square out of the middle, then lay this down on your bolt to see the perspective you'd have if you cut it into a square.*

12 I like my quilts to have a "feel" to them—like bright and bold, soft and romantic, earth tones, or masculine. Once I have a feel for how I'd like the end result to look, it's easier to audition possible fabrics for the quilt.

Barbara Gentner, West Seneca, NY

13 Since I am usually making quilts for other people, I go on what color they are using for the baby's room or their bedroom. Or it may be just a grouping of fabrics that seem to be that person. I made a quilt for my son, and my husband looked at it and said, "It looks like him." Exactly what I was going for!   *Karen Kunte, Rome, PA*

14 For soothing quilts, colors should have low contrast, and for lively ones, most contrast. I'm very picky and only choose what's pleasing to me, for quilting is a hobby and I want to feel joy in working with the colors I choose.   *Karla Santoro, Stanley, NY*

15 Usually there is one fabric that I build off of. Sometimes it's the fabric itself that caught my attention, or it could be that when thinking of the person for whom the quilt is intended, I find one fabric that he/she will love. Then I use the quilter's color wheel and the pattern to build the rest of it.   *Beth Artman, Red Lion, PA*

⑯ I use a digital camera to help me finalize my picks. I lay out the potential fabrics side by side, take some photos and download them to my computer. It gives me a better perspective.

Suzanne Beringer, Greenacres, WA

Don't go all matchy-matchy. Quilting is about contrast, not matching.

⑰ Don't go all matchy-matchy. Unlike getting dressed in the morning, quilting is about contrast, not matching.   *Janice Simmons, Fresno, CA*

⑱ When I am planning a quilt, I leave the fabrics fanned out on the sewing table and look at them over several days. I will lay out more fabrics than I need and take things away until I have just the look I want. When a fabric is just not quite right, I keep looking for one that is, or I may go another color way with a different fabric. I recently worked on a quilt that started from a beautiful Hoffman cabbage rose print. I started working with the greens and gold in it, but in the end went more toward the burgundies based on the fabrics I liked layered on the table.

Stephanie Wagner, Bear, DE

⑲ I use Electric Quilt 7 to see how the colors will play and, many times, I end up moving my colors around for a more pleasing effect. Before purchasing EQ7, I used to sketch out the design on graph paper and color it with coloring pencils.

Donna Royson, Blythewood, SC

⑳ Make sure to incorporate fabrics that allow the eye to rest—too much pattern can be exhausting in a larger quilt.

Anne Jackson, Prior Lake, MN

㉑ Sometimes I like to go with a quilt just as I've seen it made. If I can't find the exact fabric, I study the quilt. I learn what role each fabric is playing. I then try to find new fabric that can play a similar role to achieve the same effect. I can change color schemes. There is much to be learned. What recedes. What comes forward. What are the hues? Values? How do they relate to the overall quilt? Those fabrics adjacent to them?   *Amy Rochelle, South Lyon, MI*

22 Be careful of designs with checks and lines; they don't always print straight on the fabric, and it is hard to match them up.

Shirley Valk, Ellerbe, NC

23 Don't forget to use solid colors. The beautiful patterns will really pop out at you with a little plain color used here and there. It helps make the quilt more restful and relaxing to look at, too, instead of just too busy. My early quilts were more busy and the prettiest fabrics were lost in the mix.   *Paula Clark, Ethridge, TN*

24 I'm big on making sure the colors flow without a dominant color that takes over the quilt. I love white to tone and balance.

Barb Mikielski, Dallas, PA

25 The more happy colors the better! I like a lot of contrast and movement, and I almost always use red somewhere in every quilt.

Christy Proost, Mechanicsville, VA

26 You should always line your fabrics up in the quilt store, take a few steps away from them, and look at how they blend before you decide to buy them. Sometimes I'll even walk out of sight of the fabrics so that when I look again I can be surprised by the stack of fabric. In this way, I can decide if I like how the fabrics look together from far away.   *Kat Gatrell, Tucson, AZ*

27 If the quilt will stay in my home, I consider the colors in the room where the quilt will be located. If it is for donation, I often select a color grouping I like but that will not work in my home.

Nancy Koyanik, Troy, VA

28 I like vibrant colors and use a lot of black in my projects as it makes the pattern stand out.   *Lee Waltenberry, Wales, WI*

29 I make bed-size scrappy quilts and use only 1800s reproduction fabrics in them. If I'm using any and all colors, then I try to use a common background color to tie everything together and give the eye a place to rest in viewing the quilt. Or, sometimes I select two colors, i.e. pink/brown, and use varying shades of those colors. I'm currently working on a quilt using 5 different fabrics and scrappy background colors—it all works together because it is reproduction fabrics.

Nora Manley, Athens, AL

30 I prefer limiting myself to 3–5 colors, but then I like to have many, many selections from those color families.

Jan Mast, Lancaster, PA

31 Start with a "focus" fabric and arrange the other fabrics in matching colors, then add one fabric in a deviate color so there will be something exciting to look at.

One of my color scheme books taught me to be happy with 95% of my fabrics/colors and take a risk with the last 5%.

Ellen Boes-Smit, The Hague, Netherlands

32 I usually audition fabrics, starting with a fabric that excites me and working out fabrics that work with it. I look for contrast as well as harmony in the colors. I sometimes include a color that would normally be considered discordant to add some zing to the color scheme.

BJ Chadwick, Marmora, NJ

> *I usually buy a collection of fabrics so that the colors are already coordinated.*

33 I usually buy a collection of fabrics so that the colors are already coordinated. The artists that design fabric lines have much more artistic skill than I do.

Stephanie Leuthesser, San Ysidro, CA

34 I particularly enjoy sewing with multi-colored fabrics—those you'd have trouble defining as one color because they have equal amount of several colors in them. I make a lot of controlled scrappy quilts—that is, I choose pastels or brights and I don't mix them in the same quilt. Scrappy quilts are bordered and bound in a single fabric used in the quilt body to draw it all together.

Nancee McCann, Wilmington, DE

35 I usually use colors that I like or have in my home.

Susie Young, Anthony, KS

36 I start with one fabric that I really like and then find complementary fabric to go with it. Then I look for one color that pops and use a limited amount of it so my eyes will move across the quilt.

Robbin Golden, Summerville, SC

37 I've done quilts in combinations I never thought were possible, whatever pleases my eye. I recently completed a magnificent quilt in purples, blues and rusts. I love to go outside the box with colors!

Sue Levin, Blue Bell, PA

38 I slip into my comfort zone of the 1800–1900 colors. I love turkey red and ick (olive) green, browns, cheddars, federal blues and pinks. I am not fond of bright jewel tones or of dyed fabrics.

Joanne Picicci, Spokane, WA

39 When I'm shopping for quilt fabric, I love to take my daughter along with me even though I've been quilting for quite some time, and she is not a quilter. She definitely has an eye for putting fabrics together that I may not have considered.

Geralyn McClarren, Harrisburg, PA

B. Color Inspiration

1 Nature gives us beautiful color combinations. Have you ever looked at a flower garden? Just the blends of the zinnia patch can present ideas. Or how about the variations of blue and white skies adjacent to a hundred shades of green of a wooded scene?

Color is my favorite part of quilting.   *Sharel Etheridge, Lennon, MI*

2 Paint chips are my favorite color play. I own color wheels from all the major paint manufactures, and I mix and match all the time.

Susan Ache, Jacksonville, FL

❸ When I was teaching, I was often amazed at some of the garish cloth people would bring in. But I was the one surprised, because when we were finished cutting and sewing, none of the quilt tops were ever ugly. I tell my students that handmade quilts seem to mystically take on some special attribute, and the quilts become infused with love for the intended recipient, and all become beautiful, regardless of color or design.   *Violet Thetford, Forest Grove, OR*

❹ I love the website Design Seeds. It takes any photograph and breaks it down into the color story. Many of the pictures I use are of nature, or other forms of art such as a painting.
Kathleen Keough, Berwyn, PA

❺ When we travel, I often come home with fabrics that remind me of where we went. Yellow and turquoise from San Diego, navy and camel from Charleston, red and black from Disney World...
Mary Jo Millonzi, Mt. Prospect, IL

❻ I love to peruse books on vintage quilts and find lots of inspiration there.   *Karen Martin, Breezy Point, MN*

❼ Nature is inspiring. I love to try to reproduce a summer sky, a sunset, or a winter landscape. I use a lot of batiks for those. For reproduction quilts, I try to visualize what my predecessors would have used to make a quilt, relying on books, websites, or designers for guidance.   *Deborah Gross, Willow Grove, PA*

❽ I find clues in nature. For instance, one of my favorite roses has petals with deep pink, pale yellow, and peach. What a pretty quilt that would make for a baby girl.   *Carole Sibley, Mt. Laurel, NJ*

❾ I look at oriental rugs, paisleys, and tapestries for color inspiration. For tonal quilts, I find flowers are great inspiration.
Beth Miller, Arena, WI

❿ I love following the Pantone Color of the Year and then a fun seasonal fabric each season.   *Anne Jackson, Prior Lake, MN*

⑪ A *major* source of fabrics for me is the scrap/share table at my guild meetings. Even scraps as small as 3″ square can inspire very large wall quilts. There are also a variety of old or vintage fabrics and also fibers other than cotton. Scrap tables are incredibly

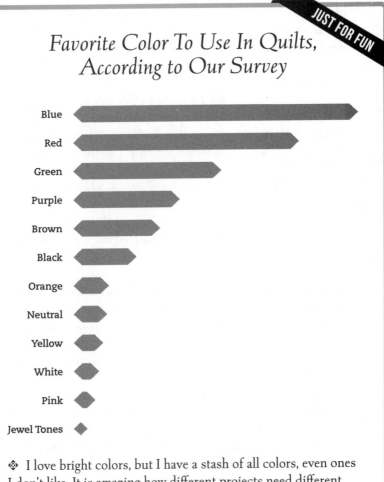

Favorite Color To Use In Quilts, According to Our Survey

JUST FOR FUN

Blue
Red
Green
Purple
Brown
Black
Orange
Neutral
Yellow
White
Pink
Jewel Tones

❖ I love bright colors, but I have a stash of all colors, even ones I don't like. It is amazing how different projects need different colors to create the effect I want.

Bev Day, Grand Bay–Westfield, New Brunswick

popular at my guild meetings—the tables are rushed and the fabric goes flying. Every piece is taken. This is a guild fundraiser.

Valerie Turer, Brooklyn, NY

12 I love the internet! I have a folder on my computer labeled "quilt inspiration" and save pictures of random items there. The last photo I saved there was of an advertisement for a Mother's Day flower arrangement. I just loved the colors, and it immediately made me think how pretty the colors would be in a quilt.

Terri Overton, San Tan Valley, AZ

Look at nature. There are many greens that don't match, but they look beautiful together.

13 I went to a color lecture by Jane Blair, and she said look at nature. There are many greens that don't match, but they look beautiful together. I do that with my quilts. It really adds a special punch to the quilt.

Kris Newlin, West Chester, PA

14 Once, I challenged myself to create a quilt which reflected the feeling of a painting I liked.   *E. Anne Hendrickson, Toledo, OR*

15 Don't be afraid to try your hand at choosing your own fabrics. Yes, there are beautiful kits to be had, but it is okay to try that for yourself. Every one of us manages to dress ourselves in a present-able way each day. Trust your instincts and what you love in the colors you wear.   *Colleen Coffman, Mulino, OR*

16 I received a beautiful bouquet of flowers from my son on my birthday. I took a picture of it because I just loved the colors and said that would be awesome colors in a quilt. I downloaded the picture on to my computer and saved it there until I found the right fabrics. Four months later, I made the quilt.

Ann Ouellette, Meriden, CT

17 Sometimes I see museum displays—such as Egyptian art—with interesting color combinations.   *Valerie Turer, Brooklyn, NY*

18 My husband and I spent almost 4 years cruising on a small sailboat throughout the Bahamas and the Caribbean. I love the colors seen in the waters there, the deep blues to soft turquoises to pale greens. The bright fruits and flowers and the brilliance of the sunrises and sunsets are so cheerful and vibrant and show up in many of my projects. But I also favor the deep greens and browns of the temperate rain forests I grew to love during my high school years on the Olympic Peninsula in the state of Washington.

Libbie Ellis, Tarpon Springs, FL

19 My husband is a hobby photographer, so he has lots of interesting photos to analyze for color.   *Laroletta Petty, Breckenridge, CO*

20 I am most often inspired by a photograph, so I always carry a camera with me. I also clip photos out of magazines and save these in a scrapbook for future reference.   *Barbara Merritt, Brackney, PA*

21 One day, when I was making a pot of minestrone soup, I took a photo of the bacon, onions, carrot and celery. The colors all mixed together as they were frying off were amazing.

Louise Lott, Healesville, Australia

22 I live in Southwest Virginia, tucked in a "holler" in the Appalachian mountains. I can see greens, purple, white, pink, browns, and yellow right from my window. Whenever I wonder if this shade will match with that shade, I think of the mountains.

Kellie Hewitt, Marion, VA

23 I get a lot of quilting inspiration from Monet, the French Impressionist painter.   *Susan Lesko, Bloomingburg, NY*

24 I find color inspiration in unusual displays in stores, accidental placing of towels in my linen cupboard, magazines, paint chips and other quilters' work.   *Adrienne Wilson, Ada, MI*

25 I find inspiration taking a walk through the woods; there must be 45 different shades of green.   *Denise Mincek, White Lake, MI*

㉖ I sometimes sew bright cheery colors in the winter and colder colors in the summer to help balance the seasonal temperature.

Paula Clark, Ethridge, TN

c. *Fabric Quality*

---

❶ I recommend 100% cotton or organic cotton for all quilting. I do not use any poly-cotton blends. Cotton is easy to work with, will not stretch out of shape, and always looks crisp and clean.

Sharon Sutton, Lindsey, OH

❷ There's no need to waste your time sewing something if you're going to use inferior fabric. The fabric will fight you along the way, and the finished piece will not withstand the test of time. Buy the best quality fabric you can afford from a reputable quilt fabric store. Yardage should come off the bolt (not flat goods that are strike-offs or remnants) and should come from a respected manufacturer whose name should appear on the selvage.

Jan Mast, Lancaster, PA

❸ Established manufacturers such as Windham, Marcus, Moda, and RJR, to name a few, are known to carry excellent fabric.

Shelia Smith, Goldthwaite, TX

❹ Keep in mind that flannel will stretch more, so it is not as good for intricate piecing; it will usually shrink more in washing, too. Flannel is good for backing because it is soft and cuddly.

Sherry Waite, Albuquerque, NM

❺ The higher the thread count, the happier I am, therefore I'm especially partial to batiks. The tighter the weave, the easier is needle-turn appliqué and, it seems, the stronger and more long-lasting the quilt will be. I'm often found holding a single thickness of fabric up to a light to see how much light comes through the spaces between threads. Yes, it's subjective, but it works for me.

Libbie Ellis, Tarpon Springs, FL

6 Hold your hand under one layer of the fabric. If you see your hand, the thread count in the fabric is not high enough.

Faye Sykes, Rocky Mount, NC

7 Cheaper fabrics do not cut well or hold their shape. Simply tug a little at the cut edge of the fabric and you will know it's cheap if a bunch of threads pop out.   *Kevin Kern, Paradise Valley, NV*

Tug a little at the cut edge of the fabric and you will know it's cheap if a bunch of threads pop out.

8 If I like a fabric and I'm not sure it is 100% cotton, I use my lighter to burn a small piece of it. If it burns without making a sticky ball, only leaving a kind of powder, I am sure it is cotton.

Maria da Conceição Amado de Sousa Martins, Alges, Portugal

9 I look at the cut edge for fraying—it shouldn't fray much. I also look at the selvage edge for the fabric maker.

Mary Andra Holmes, Prescott, AZ

10 I find quality fabrics have better color intensity, and the fabrics fade very little or not at all when washed. Quality fabrics have a tight weave and feel silky.   *Beverly Baxter, Troy, PA*

11 A good quality fabric will make the project easier to cut out and sew together. There will be no stretching and the pattern will stay on grain.   *Tammy DeLeebeeck, Vittoria, Ontario*

12 Fabric of lesser quality is stiffer, and some hardly drapes at all. I only use it now for small pieces that aren't meant to last a long time: table runners, placemats, etc.   *Barbara Kunkel, West Bloomfield, MI*

⑬ Many fabrics of lower quality add *a lot* of sizing to try to hide the fact that their fabric is of lower quality. I have learned that excessive sizing makes fabric stiff and hard to work with.

Claudia McGriff, Piqua, OH

⑭ Fabric quality is very important to me. I want to make quilts that will be here long after I am gone. Good quality fabric stands up to washings and use, it's nice to work with, it lays better in the piecing, and looks better than less expensive fabric. While I always check to be sure that the bolt says 100% cotton, I also feel the fabric with my hands to be sure it is soft rather than hard, not thin/flimsy and has a nice density. If it doesn't "feel" nice, I won't buy it.

Kim Loar, Lancaster, PA

⑮ I look at the strength of the material. If I pull on the diagonal, will it return to its shape or look stretched out? If it returns to its shape, that's quality fabric.   *Arlene Greenwald, West Chester, PA*

⑯ The fabric can make or break a quilt…good quality is essential. Fabric with a lower thread count can be stiff, thin and shrink a lot. The batting can also beard in lower thread count fabric. Check to make sure the colors are printed correctly and in the right places.

Linnette Dowdell, Apopka, FL

⑰ I check the weave by using my nail to see if I can move the threads. If the weave is loose, the fabric probably has a low thread count and will likely deteriorate with use. If I put my hand behind it, and see the outline of my hand, this is a lower quality fabric.

Rosemarie Garone, West Islip, NY

⑱ Good quality fabric means higher thread count, less shrinkage, less color fading, durability, stability and consistency. Quality fabric gives much less frustration for someone new to quilting; there is enough to deal with without worrying about if the fabric is going to fade or bleed.   *Teresa Caldwell, Long Valley, NJ*

19 If I plan to hand quilt the project, I look at the fabric to make sure it is not too dense as that makes it difficult to get tiny stitches in the quilting. *Dagmar Yaddow, Rhinebeck, NY*

20 I always look at the back of the fabric where you can more easily see the quality of the dye and the weave of the fabric. *Barbara Merritt, Brackney, PA*

I always look at the back of the fabric where you can more easily see the quality of the dye and the weave of the fabric.

21 I want my fabric to be of good quality, for I think anything that I make will be around for grandchildren and beyond. It is my legacy.
Nancy Olsen, Scotia, NY

22 You won't save money buying cheap fabrics. You will make a temporary quilt. *Diane Bachman, Leola, PA*

23 I always buy good quality fabric which I can tell by look, feel, and price. I am fortunate I can afford this. I dislike when people look down on other people with cheaper fabric, because if the cheaper price enables them to sew, then that's terrific.
Jude Simmonds, Hobart, Australia

24 I have been disappointed sometimes to find that a higher price does not always mean a quality fabric. I check quality by feeling the fabric and looking to see how tight the weave is.
Charlotte Kewish, Gibsonia, PA

25 Checking for fabric quality, I look for color brightness and fastness. I will take a white cotton t-shirt and rub it together with the fabric to be sure color does not rub off, which means it will likely run in the wash. This is particularly important when using red fabric, as it has a tendency to run. *Ellen Volker, Lancaster, NY*

26 If it does not have a name on the bolt or selvage, I don't usually buy it. *Cathy Washburn, Tucson, AZ*

27 I would say fabric quality is about 80% important to me. Since I do a lot of fusible appliqué, the quality for the small appliqué pieces does not have to be of the highest caliber. My borders and pieced blocks, however should be of the best quality I can afford.
Barbara Theriault, Brooksville, FL

28 I scrunch it with my hands and feel it to see if it is wrinkled. If it is, it is too thin and of poor quality for my quilts.
Karen Richards, Cerritos, CA

29 A very sweet smell means too much stabilizing product in the fabric. Heavy dyes smell, too.   *Mardi Niles, Scotia, NY*

30 If you rip out a mistake in poor fabric, you can ruin it.
Brenda Radzinski, Albion, NY

31 I think you have to judge fabric quality on an individual basis and not just by where you bought the fabric. There is good and bad fabric in every store. Sometimes I make real scrap basket quilts and everything goes!   *Cincy Bailey, Valrico, FL*

32 I like a good, tight weave; I don't like to use fabric if I can hold it up to the light and see through it!   *Linda Hahn, Chelsea, MI*

D. Shopping Online

1 I do a lot of online shopping. Usually I will have a small first order to test the company's product quality, promptness, and customer service.   *Karon Chigbrow, Marysville, WA*

2 If shopping online, I read customer comments, policies, and "about us." I want to make sure I am dealing with a shop with a good reputation and good customer service. If I get something I don't like, or the order is not correct, are they going to fix it for me nicely and quickly?   *Colleen Froats, Alanson, MI*

❸ When you live two hours from the nearest quilt shop, you depend on the internet a little more. Our little shop can't afford to get all the latest fabrics in. That is also why Block of the Month quilts are so handy for me. I get to use all the latest fabrics and some wonderful patterns. I can always use more shops that do these Blocks of the Month!   *Carol Lewin, Hay Springs, NE*

❹ In an online fabric store, I appreciate handwritten notes from the women who cut and prepare my orders. I like to be on mailing lists about sales.   *Kathy Perry, Sugar Land, TX*

❺ I use True Up Sales Alerts (www.trueup.net) to find fabric sales online, but when I want a certain fabric, I buy it, regardless of whether it is on sale or not.   *Kathleen Keough, Berwyn, PA*

❻ The pros of shopping online: The prices are usually better. You can shop in the middle of the night.

The con: You can shop in the middle of the night so that makes impulse buying way too easy.   *Cincy Bailey, Valrico, FL*

❼ The best thing about shopping online is it's easy to see whole lines of fabric on one page. The down side is that there's no one to ask for an opinion, or help figure yardage, or maybe know where that perfect companion piece is hiding. When I buy online, it's usually for something very specific or more of something I already have. To me, shopping in a brick and mortar store is more casual, more social, more fun and, in the end, I usually spend more money.

Barbara Gentner, West Seneca, NY

> *The best thing about shopping online is it's easy to see whole lines of fabric on one page.*

❽ I work long hours, and many stores are closed when I have time to shop. Online shopping is more convenient and easier on my feet.   *Becky Garten, Overland Park, KS*

9 When searching for fabrics online, you have the advantage of shopping anytime, day or night with no waiting in line. You can also do your shopping on holidays when fabric stores are closed. You have the ability to search and compare prices without leaving the comforts of your home, without driving to different stores using up your gas.   *Debbie McAdam, Holbrook, NY*

10 It is very much easier to shop online but does nothing to support the wonderful people at my local quilt shop who are making a living in my community.   *Elizabeth Beardsley, Boulder, CO*

11 Shipping can be expensive if you don't buy a large quantity and the colors aren't always true. However, you can usually get some great deals, and often complete collections of materials if a "bricks" store is out of certain patterns.   *Linda Hahn, Chelsea, MI*

12 If you are just trying to add to your stash, online shopping may be okay, particularly if the fabric is on sale. Colors online do not always look the same in person, though.   *Faye Sykes, Rocky Mount, NC*

13 For me, the absolute best place to shop for fabric is eBay. There is always a great variety, you can ask as many questions as you like, and you can always find a sale.   *Kellie Hewitt, Marion, VA*

14 I have purchased fabric online but only after I've actually seen the same fabric in a shop. I like to be able to feel the fabric and see the colors. Usually, the online price is better.   *Ann Hay, Carlisle, PA*

I like sites that have design boards to view fabrics together.

15 Online shopping allows me to see more options. I like sites that have design boards to view fabrics together. As I age, I find online shopping takes less energy, and I like shopping in my jammies.   *Carolyn Simons, Apple Valley, CA*

16 I remember one time I was looking for something cute for a bathrobe, just a sweet little print. I found pretty red pairs of cherries on a buttery yellow background at this one online retailer. Well. When the fabric arrived,

I was *shocked*. My sweet little cherries were bigger than my fist! I made the bathrobe anyway and I get a chuckle every time I wear it.

Michelle Harrison, Morganton, GA

E. *Shopping in a Physical Store*

❶ Here is a valuable reason to buy from a local quilt store: if you don't, they may disappear and your *only* choice will be a chain store. The fabric may be more expensive than a chain store's for several reasons: chain stores buy in larger bulk and the quality is usually lesser. However, the quilt store is where many people learn to quilt, continue to get support and have their questions answered, and there is a much greater variety of fabrics. I can't stress how important it is to support your local quilt stores! *Nancy Henry, Rochester, NH*

❷ Buy what you love, and don't take the shop ladies' advice unless you have seen their quilts and you know that you like what they make. So many of us are brought up to please people, we find it hard to say, "Hmmmm. No, let me think about that one. I am not sure I want to put that fabric in this project."

Michelle Harrison, Morganton, GA

❸ I shop my local quilt shops first because they are dedicated to me, the quilter. The help, inspiration, classes, knowledge, and support from quilt shops are priceless to me. I sign up to receive quilt shop news so I am aware of new classes, fabric, events, and sales.

Darly Dulion, Laguna Beach, CA

❹ Look for salespeople who are passionate about quilting. They will be eager to help you find fabrics and not just make a buck.

Krista Schwabe, Lakeland, FL

5 There are two kinds of fabric shopping: browsing and focused. Browsing is wandering into a store or a web site in the expectation of a "wow" moment. If you love it, buy it right now, because fabric is so often unavailable a short time later. Focused shopping is going for the stuff you need to make or finish a quilt. If it is in process, I take swatches and always measurements.

Carol Nussbaumer, Estes Park, CO

6 Treat every trip to the fabric store as a design session. Take your pattern and swatches of fabric with you. I use a spiral notebook and double-stick tape to create a page for every project, so I have everything with me that I need.   *Barbara Merritt, Brackney, PA*

7 I take my notebook with the diagrams I drew, and the list of how much fabric I need for each part of the quilt, such as the main fabric, sashing, borders, backing, etc. I also take a small calculator to figure out if I need more or less depending on fabric width.

Karen Richards, Cerritos, CA

8 Every year I go to the Houston International Quilt Show. My best friend and I always make a "wish list." We decide what color fabric we are looking for, we select patterns for future quilts and then while we are at the show, we evaluate all the booths before we start buying. We write what booths we are going to re-visit and what we like at them. Yes, we spend about two days before we buy anything. Yes, there is a chance that the fabric or product might not be there when we re-visit, but that's the chance we take. If it was meant to be, it will be there!   *Carolyn Landers, Lincoln, CA*

9 Be sure the store has good lighting, or go to the window, or ask if you may take the fabric outside.   *Karen Crossland, Riverside, WA*

10 Wear comfortable shoes and carry a purse with a long enough strap for crossbody wear so both arms are available for toting bolts to the cutting counter. And I take my own bags to save the store money which I hope, in turn, saves me money!

Beth Fisher, San Antonio, TX

11 When exploring a new shop, I try to avoid weekends if possible. I take along a list, fabric to match and either the pattern or yardage requirements. My Smartphone is also a new tool in my bag—pictures, lists, names of gadgets are great to store and bring along. *Pamela Olson, South Windsor, CT*

12 Take a snack and some water. Shopping is tough work.
Pat Deck, Oreland, PA

13 I prefer to buy everything I need for the project at one time so I can match all fabrics, get assistance from a staff member if needed, and buy the necessary quantities with pattern in hand rather than guessing. If you need to refer to formerly bought goods, Swatch Buddies, the new plastic tags for adhering fabric swatches, are a helpful gadget. *Jan Mast, Lancaster, PA*

If you need to refer to formerly bought goods, Swatch Buddies, the new plastic tags for adhering fabric swatches, are a helpful gadget.

14 Get a business card or stamp from each shop you deal with. Keep all buys from each store in one bag. Snip off a little of your fabric each time you purchase and glue it and the business card into a book. Find any manufacturer's information on the selvage and write it in the book. Sounds like tons of trouble when all you want is to quilt, but it's so worth it when you're trying to track down another 25cm of the perfect fabric you have discovered in your stash. *Penny D'Aloia, Coburg, Australia*

15 When I need small amounts of fabrics, buying at a store will make my money go farther because I can buy as little as ⅛ yard, while the online minimum is usually ½ yard.
Kari Vojtechovsky, Centennial, CO

16 When I go fabric shopping with a group of friends, I try to have in mind a few particular items that I need. If I don't, I can get carried away and spend way beyond my budget on things that may end up not being used. *Susan Chandler, Solon Springs, WI*

17 Before leaving the house to go fabric shopping, I take a phone picture of my stash to remind myself how much blue (for me it's blue) fabric I already have. Always take someone with you—your mom or a friend—even if she doesn't sew or quilt. It's just more fun!   *Beth Artman, Red Lion, PA*

> *Before leaving the house to go fabric shopping, I take a phone picture of my stash to remind myself how much blue (for me it's blue) fabric I already have.*

18 I carry a swatch book of all my batiks so that I don't buy one I already have. My swatch book is the fabric cut in 3½ × 1" strips, laminated to the card stock.   *Barbara Hill, Huntsville, AL*

19 Always check out every quilt store when traveling because different shop owners purchase by their taste or their clientele, and you can discover fabrics that will amaze you.   *Susan Riley, Hingham, MA*

20 I love to visit quilt shops. I plan our vacation destination, and then I check out all the possible quilt shops I can visit. This summer, I have 11 quilt shops in one province and two states on the list to visit. I check out their websites. I check out new fabric lines from the different suppliers. Then I decide on next years' projects and make a list of what fabrics I am looking for. That way as I go from shop to shop, I can gather more of the various collections than by going to just one shop. When I'm shopping, I make notes, so when I get home and need additional fabric, I know where I shopped and can contact the store through the internet or by calling directly.
Bev Day, Grand Bay–Westfield, New Brunswick

21 Shop hops are the best for scouting new ideas or looking for a piece to complete a project. You usually visit many stores out of your area on a hop.   *Brenda Seth, Waterford, PA*

22 My quilting friends and I go on F.A.R.T.s (Fabric Acquisition Road Trips). It's fun!   *Suzanne Beringer, Greenacres, WA*

㉓ I take a small photo of my project and attach it to an index card with the yardage needed for each part of the quilt. Then as I shop I take a small swatch as I buy and attach it to the card so I can refer to the card when needed   *Arlene King, Baldwinsville, NY*

㉔ Always take along whatever fabrics you are trying to match. There are just way too many different shades of color to try to match by memory.   *Leanne Skoloda, New Holland, PA*

㉕ The Joen Wolfrom Color Tool is a good thing to take along when I go fabric shopping, as well as samples of fabric I want to use and pictures of quilts I like.   *Linda Arkens, Hatfield, PA*

㉖ I take the Ultimate 3-in-1 Color Tool with me, which is a spiral bound book with many various shades of colors. I write down the colors I'm trying to match before leaving home.
Michele Rutolo, Sinking Spring, PA

㉗ I shop for fabric all the time, not always with a project in mind. If I am looking for particular fabrics to match other fabrics I have, I snip a small piece of each fabric and use a safety pin to hold them together. I carry these with me when shopping for fabric until I find all the fabric I need.   *Barbara Isaak, Lakeville, MN*

㉘ I bring samples of fabric I need to match up, and often I have a quilt top that I leave in the car just in case I find the perfect backing or just one more border. Then if I see something that might suit, I go back to the car and retrieve the top to see how well suited it might be.   *Michelle Harrison, Morganton, GA*

㉙ I sometimes take a whole tub of fabric with me to the quilt shop if I am looking for something that needs to fit into a particular quilt—tiny swatches don't work for me! *Karen Martin, Breezy Point, MN*

㉚ A tape measure can also come in handy for measuring remnants.
Sharel Etheridge, Lennon, MI

31 If I am looking for fabric that will be cut into a certain shape, I cut that shape out of a heavy piece of paper or folder and take along the paper frame with the cut-out shape in the middle. That way I can hold it up to the fabric and see just the portion that would be in the quilt.   *Lorraine Reid, Pottstown, PA*

32 When I was working, I tried to shop for fabric one evening a month. I made dinner for the family and went for a hour or so to shop with my samples or patterns.   *Dianne Deaver, Yuba City, CA*

33 The best time to shop at a bricks-and-mortar store is in the morning on Tuesday, Wednesday, or Thursday.

Denise Rosbicki, South Prince George, VA

F. Fabric Bargains

1 One of the best times to shop is when there are stores near a big quilt show. There are many special sales that are going on then, and many stores will be stocking up on lots of fabrics, knowing that crowds will be coming. There are often great specials. Holiday weekends often are a great time for sales. Look in your local newspaper for ads from say, JoAnn Fabrics, or even various craft stores.

One of the best times to shop is when there are stores near a big quilt show.

Susan Louis, Briarwood, NY

2 Many times I will recycle or re-purpose some beautiful cotton fabric that started life as a dress, shirt, etc. I feel connected to my grandmothers when I take "nothing" and make it into "something."

Andrea Mitchell, Silver Spring, MD

❸ Don't buy pre-cuts unless it's the only way to find that fabric. You are paying a high price to have the fabric cut for you. If you're doing small blocks or appliqué, buy a quarter yard off the bolt rather than a fat quarter. It will be much cheaper in most cases.

Diane Linker, Scarsdale, NY

❹ I know people who will not quilt with anything other than the most expensive fabrics. But quilting as a craft started as a recycling project, and the quality of the fabric was not a consideration. The main consideration was if it had a worn out spot or not.

Nancy Quade, Newark, DE

❺ I am in a group of eight ladies who get together at each others' homes every other month to quilt for a weekend. We usually try to align it with a time when one of the local quilt stores is having a sale. Then we take a little break and a road trip to break up the day.

Susan Chandler, Solon Springs, WI

❻ Sometimes I'll use very old, worn fabric simply because I like how it looks in my quilt.   *Sandy Helin, Watsonville, CA*

❼ I don't remember the last time I bought a fabric that wasn't on sale. Being a scrap quilter makes that a lot easier to do. I usually buy ½ yd. That is plenty for anything I want to make, except sometimes borders. In that case, I will usually complete the quilt top, except for borders, and take it to the store with me.

Cincy Bailey, Valrico, FL

❽ I always look at thrift stores, consignment stores, yard sales, or even craigslist. Once I found the most awesome deal from a lady selling all her name-brand cotton fabric for dollars a yard. I spent about $200, but it was fabric I may never have bought at a store for full price.   *Bobbie Haynes, Shepherdsville, KY*

❾ I am on a very limited income, so price is very important to me. I don't feel I need to have the most expensive fabric to have a lovely quilt. I would prefer cheaper fabric and more opportunities to create. I expect my quilts to be used and not kept as heirlooms. When they wear out, I'll make another one.

Marion Eggers, Winter Park, FL

❿ I go to yard sales and see what people have. I get many old Key West Handprints fabric in my hometown of Key West, since they often gave the employees misprinted fabric. The factory is no longer operating, so these are collectible pieces that go back many years. I purchased my first piece in 1968 and recently used up the last of it.   *Margo Ellis, Key West, FL*

⓫ My husband reads the ads in the paper, and I have bought fabric at auctions.   *Vera Wolf, Union City, PA*

⓬ Try Goodwill, Value Village or Salvation Army thrift shops to find great cotton broadcloths in originally expensive men's shirts. I loved the multi-colored cotton plaid I found for the back of a cubicle quilt for my son.   *LynDee Lombardo, Olympia, WA*

⓭ Remember what our forebears did: recycle. I have started collecting cotton shirts and skirts from yard sales and second hand stores. Even at $3 for a man's shirt, it is a good buy when one considers that yardage from the store can be more than $12 a yard.

Sheri Ketarkus, Glidden, WI

⓮ We're on a tight budget here at home, so I've built part of my stash at yard sales by careful selection and also absolutely during quilt shop sales.   *Libbie Ellis, Tarpon Springs, FL*

⓯ I know a lot of people don't like excess emails, but I always sign up for quilt shop email lists because that's the best way to find out when their sales are and when new collections of fabric arrive.

Geralyn McClarren, Harrisburg, PA

I use Twitter to find out if my favorite shops are having a sale.

⓰ I use Twitter to find out if my favorite shops are having a sale, or to ask if they carry whatever I am looking for.

Mary Andra Holmes, Prescott, AZ

17 There seem to be sales for just about every holiday. Mother's Day, Valentine's Day, Veterans' Day, Super Bowl Widow day all seem to be good days to find sales at both your local quilt store and online stores.   *Janice Simmons, Fresno, CA*

18 Don't wait until November to buy Christmas fabrics. Look in the spring and summer for the best selection of those fabrics.
                                            Susan Vargo, Avondale, PA

19 I do shop sales at quilt shops, looking for suitable quilt backing fabrics. Neutrals are always good. I try to buy a 10-yard piece. That will back a king size quilt, with some fabrics left for pillow shams, etc. While I like to find fabrics on sale for the backs of my quilts, I won't use just any fabric. If I have gone to the expense of quality fabrics for the front, I definitely want equal quality fabric on the back of my quilt.   *Marti Blankenship, Pleasant Valley, MO*

20 If you find something you *love*, buy at least one yard. If it's on sale, consider it for a backing and buy five to seven yards!
                                      Lynne Fraas, Peachtree City, GA

21 Most clearance fabrics are located near the back of a shop, so I start there and work my way up to the front of the store.
                                      Robbin Golden, Summerville, SC

22 Be sure to buy enough yardage the first time as you can rarely track down the same goods as much as six months later, unless it's a "basic." The couple dollars spent for the extra ¼ yard will seem like a worthy investment, compared to running short by a ¼ yard and wasting hours searching for it.   *Jan Mast, Lancaster, PA*

23 I do not specifically shop sales, because I know what is going to be there: every fabric that has not sold previously. There are reasons fabric does not sell, and a lower price is usually not going to make a bad fabric look good.   *Barbara Hutton, Carolina Shores, NC*

CHAPTER 3

Preparing Fabric

A. How and Why to Prewash

❶ Wash fabric before putting it near your sewing room/area. That way you'll know that all fabric has been washed that is in your sewing area. No surprises! *Kris Newlin, West Chester, PA*

❷ Quilters sometimes intentionally use unwashed fabrics to assemble a quilt because the puckers left over after the first wash give the quilt a vintage appearance. If vintage isn't the look you're going for, it's best to prewash your fabrics.

Rosemarie Garone, West Islip, NY

❸ I have learned over the years that prewashed fabrics are better for hand quilting. *Nora Manley, Athens, AL*

4 My hands seem to become irritated and sore from a chemical or finish on the unwashed fabric, and I also sneeze more.

Ann Lineberger, Allentown, PA

5 I wash fabric first for three reasons: I do not like to sew with the bolt crease running down the middle of my yardage, some colored fabrics really do still run, even the expensive ones, and I like to "get to know" my fabric. Ironing the fabric while it is still damp is one of my very favorite things to do.   *Michelle Harrison, Morganton, GA*

6 Prewashing fabric cuts down on the dust in my sewing room. The sizing and fabric finish flake off when I handle the fabric, causing excess dust, but I wash that out with prewashing.

Barbara Johnson, Dallas, OR

7 I found that the quilts I've made with pre-washed fabric have a much nicer appearance after being washed and dried. They lay much better but still have the "old fashioned" look. The quilts I've made with unwashed fabric tend to pucker considerably more, too much, in my opinion.   *Susan McCurdy, Price, UT*

The quilts I've made with unwashed fabric tend to pucker considerably more, too much, in my opinion.

8 I buy a lot of used fabric from flea markets and such. Washing renders all the fabric "equal" and prevents surprises.

Sandy Helin, Watsonville, CA

9 I only prewash flannel fabrics as they shrink so much.

Judy McLeod, Alexandria, MN

10 I wash new fabric because most of it is not made in the United States, and I am concerned about the conditions surrounding its manufacturing.   *Barbara Gentner, West Seneca, NY*

11 Since I do a lot of fusible appliqué, I do wash most of the fat quarters I buy so I can remove the sizing. The fusible products work best with no sizing residue.   *Barbara Theriault, Brooksville, FL*

12 I have found that if I want to use freezer paper in the project, it adheres better to laundered fabrics. *Patricia Boyle, Bedford, TX*

13 As fabric is wound on the bolt in the factory, it can become distorted. Washing it returns it to its natural, relaxed state, so I don't end up fighting with it throughout the piecing process.
Colleen Coffman, Mulino, OR

14 I prewash fabrics because it eliminates the chemical odors that burst from a bin when I open it. This helps prevent allergy problems. *Charlotte Kewish, Gibsonia, PA*

15 For baby quilts, I think it is important to prewash fabric so that the sizing is washed out and does not affect the baby's delicate skin. *Amy Kentera, Highland Mills, NY*

16 Darks and reds I usually prewash to prevent bleeding. Most others I do not. However, I do like to press all the fabric to make sure there is no shrinkage in pressing. I find this happens more often than I would think. *Beth Miller, Arena, WI*

17 I prewash and dry my fabrics. Then, I iron them with Light Body Magic Sizing to make the fabric easier to work with and help it keep its shape. *Louise McFadyen, Auburn, NY*

18 I always wash my new fabric with no bleach or softener of any kind. I machine dry on hot. I want my fabrics to be ready to put in a quilt that will be washed and dried by machine.
Kris Newlin, West Chester, PA

19 I do prewash my fabric because even with the best cotton fabric on the market today, I find it still shrinks some. And if I'm mixing different manufacturer's fabric together, they shrink differently, some a lot more than others. Because I am a precision piecer, I don't like to find this out after I've cut all my pieces. Finding out that units I'm trying to sew together aren't matching, because they shrank from the steam or heat of the iron while I was pressing my seams, is frustrating to me. If I am in a class and need to add a fabric I cannot prewash, I spritz it good with water and iron it on the cotton setting with steam to eliminate shrinking possibilities.

Darly Dulion, Laguna Beach, CA

20 I don't always prewash fabric. I cut a 4" square of each of the fabrics, wash it with Woolite in a small bucket and rinse. Then I place the fabric squares in a garment bag and dry on low heat until almost dry. I measure each square to check for shrinkage. I then make my decision whether or not the fabric needs to be prewashed prior to cutting.

Sharon Sutton, Lindsey, OH

B. The Case Against Prewashing

1 I like working with the fabric as it comes from the store because it has a certain crispness. Besides, if I've purchased quality fabric, I find the colors don't run. If it shrinks a little the first time I wash the quilt, that's okay too, because I like the "old-fashioned" look of quilts.

Carolynn Thornton, Seguin, TX

2 When I first started quilting about 20 years ago, I prewashed everything because my quilt instructor said we had to. Over the years I have slowly done away with prewashing. I think manufacturers have come a long way in their dyes and stability. Reds and batiks make me a little nervous, so I will give them a quick wash.

Twila Sikkink, Clear Lake, WI

3 I do press all my fabrics with a hot iron after saturating them with spray-on sizing. I think I have better piecing results when I don't prewash, as the fabric seems to have more stability.

Karen Martin, Breezy Point, MN

I do press all my fabrics with a hot iron after saturating them with spray-on sizing. I think I have better piecing results when I don't prewash.

4 I use the method of testing a piece of fabric in water in a glass measuring cup in the microwave until it boils to see if it bleeds. I have found that the colors in good quality fabrics today seem to be more stable, so I no longer wash my fabrics before using them.

Janice Kraus, Durham, NH

5 I don't feel that most fabrics really bleed a lot anymore, and Shout Color Catchers are a wonderful tool. I always use a Color Catcher and wash my quilts in cold or warm water. I haven't had any issues.   *Debbie Westerman, The Colony, TX*

> *There has been some credible evidence that unwashed fabrics used in a wall hanging are better preserved.*

6 There has been some credible evidence that unwashed fabrics used in a wall hanging are better preserved.

Kathleen McLaughlin, Groton, CT

7 I don't prewash fabric if it is being used for making a wall hanging, because wall hangings are not likely to be washed, only dusted.   *Sally Petersheim, Gap, PA*

8 I do not prewash kits because if they shrink too much, I won't have enough fabric.   *Carol Nelson, Baxter, MN*

9 I do not prewash my quilting fabrics unless they are very old ones from my clothing-construction days (1950s thru 1990s). I feel the new fabrics are so colorfast, beautifully woven, and stable that they can be used without pre-laundering. I also *love* to feel new, unwashed fabric.   *Carol Keskimaki, Prescott Valley, AZ*

10 I do not prewash quilt fabric. Any time I've tried it, it frays badly, and the fraying on one piece of fabric tangles with the fraying of the others, and you get a big mess when it comes out of the washer. This means that the fabric is twisted around itself and needs significant ironing, followed by trimming of all raw edges in order to be usable. I haven't had a problem (yet!) with colors running after the quilt is made, but I don't use hand-dyes, and I always buy quality fabric.   *Carol Moll, Schnecksville, PA*

C. Raveled Edges in Prewashing

1 I always buy a couple of inches of extra fabric since raveling is always an unknown quantity.   *Susan Vargo, Avondale, PA*

2 I always buy enough extra fabric to not worry about the raveling issues in prewashing. I just cut the strings off before I put the fabric in the dryer and save them in a jar. When I have enough, I put the strings out for the birds to use for nesting. I love seeing wads of threads in my trees.   *Mary Andra Holmes, Prescott, AZ*

3 I've copied a clever way to fold the fabric, concertina-like with the cut edges to the outside. The cut edges are safety pinned together, and then the whole piece of fabric can be washed without too much damage.   *Barbara Falkner, Wellard, WA*

4 If I can be bothered, I will serge the fabric edges which stops the raveling. Otherwise, I will take a pair of scissors to the wash line when I am hanging out the fabric and clip off the threads.   *Marie White, Waiuku, New Zealand*

5 I usually zig-zag the raw edges before washing and throw a microfiber cloth in the dryer with the fabric to collect all the loose threads.   *Diane Bachman, Leola, PA*

6 I like to fold over the raw edges twice and pin with safety pins before washing and drying. No more tangled, frayed fabrics to have to undo!   *Francis Stanley, Slidell, LA*

7 I run a glue stick over the edges of the fabric and finger press it together before I wash it. The glue will wash off, but the fabric holds together better. I also spin in a delicate cycle.
          Debi Selin, Covington, GA

8 I clip the corners to help prevent raveling. I keep a scissors at the washing machine for that purpose. After washing, I clip the strings before the fabric goes in the dryer.   *Cathy Washburn, Tucson, AZ*

9 I notch the end of my fabric before it goes in the washer as it helps a little with the fraying. However, I find it fun to straighten the edges and get rid of the knotted up threads and tangles after the fabric is washed.   *Twila Sikkink, Clear Lake, WI*

10 I manage raveling by clipping all four corners of each fabric piece that I wash. It is just enough to eliminate the back-and-forth raveling issue that creates balls of string in the wash.
     Nancy Henry, Rochester, NH

11 I will normally put my fabric (if I don't have too much yardage) in lingerie bags in the washing machine, as that seems to keep it from raveling as much.   *Debbie Westerman, The Colony, TX*

I use my pinking shears to trim the fabric's cut sides to eliminate as much fraying as possible.

12 If I do prewash fabrics, I use my pinking shears to trim the fabric's cut sides to eliminate as much fraying as possible.
     Geralyn McClarren, Harrisburg, PA

13 If fabric unravels more than ¼" when it's washed, I don't use it in a quilt! That's a good sign it will pull apart easily if it's used in a quilt.   *Pat Smith, Sidney, NY*

D. Dealing With Bleeding Fabric

1 I test a particular fabric for bleeding by taking a small piece (2 × 2" square is enough) and getting it wet. Then I rub it against a white piece of paper. If there is no color deposited on the paper, it is likely the fabric is sufficiently colorfast and will be safe to use in my quilt.   *Celeste Collier, Guntersville, AL*

❷ Warm water will contribute to color migration, so use cold water when washing fabric/quilts.   *Celeste Collier, Guntersville, AL*

❸ If I am putting a very dark fabric next to a very light fabric in a quilt, I sew a strip of each together and wash it to make sure the colors are fast. If not, I want to know it before the quilt is finished.
Anne Hollenbach, Hudson, WI

❹ When I give a quilt as a gift, I pin a Shout Color Catcher to it with a note that says, "wash me with your quilt when you wash it the first time." I've had nothing but good results.
Susan Walters, Newark, DE

When I give a quilt as a gift, I pin a Shout Color Catcher to it.

❺ My grandmother taught me to pin clean white fabric to suspect fabric and wash it three times, adding a ½ cup of salt to the rinse cycle. It sounds tedious, but I think it's always better to do this instead of ruining a finished quilt.   *Bobbie Haynes, Shepherdsville, KY*

❻ While steam pressing will generally reveal shrinkage, washing is the only way to find out color bleeding.
Christine Baxter, Gordon, Australia

❼ I either add Retayne (to keep dye in) or Synthrapol (to get the dye out) when I wash fabric.   *Leslie Emma, Raleigh, NC*

❽ If I'm afraid a fabric might bleed, I soak the piece in a half vinegar, half water solution to set the colors.
Carolynn Thornton, Seguin, TX

❾ I wash every color separately and check for bleeding. If a fabric continues to bleed after two washings, it does not go in to my quilts.   *Ann Hay, Carlisle, PA*

10 My only exception to not washing is if I have a red fabric or really dark, rich color that I'm concerned will bleed. I will prewash that fabric in Retayne and prewash all other fabric going into that quilt.   *Cathy Warren, Perry, MI*

11 I run my fabric through a hot water wash with a cup of white vinegar, and one of my husband's old white socks or a white face cloth until the water runs clear.   *Doris Carbone, Dracut, MA*

12 Usually, I try to place bleeding fabrics aside. If I am putting my time and effort into a quilt, I do not want to have it shredding quickly or bleeding when it is first washed by the owner. If there are other projects like hotpads that are not going to be so intense as a quilt, I will use bleeding or weaker fabrics there.

Donna Dickinson, Harrington, DE

E. Dyeing

1 I dye a lot of my fabrics, because it's fun to be able to say not only did I make the quilt, but I created the fabrics that made the quilt. I love making 8–12 step, light-to-dark color runs, which are very hard to find in stores.   *Colleen Froats, Alanson, MI*

2 So many ways to dye fabric:
- color pencils
- block printing
- fabric paints
- fabric crayons
- food coloring
- silk screening
- heat transfer paper
- photosensitizing
- fiber reactive

- bleach
- dye powder
- spray/sponge design dyeing
- tie dye
- Rit
- oil paint sticks
- stamps/dip dying technique
- computer printer iron-on transfer

Quilters would want to dye their own fabrics for the purpose of making a custom look or color, or for making art quilts.

Bobbie Haynes, Shepherdsville, KY

3 If I make a quilt and do not like how my colors work together, I may overdye it to tone down the bright prints or give it an aged look.

Carole Wilder, Hastings, MN

> *If I make a quilt and do not like how my colors work together, I may overdye it.*

4 I love to age cotton fabric and lace with used tea bags, coffee grounds, onion skins and miscellaneous vegetation, and hardware such as nails and screws that will rust and stain. It's a surprise every time. *LynDee Lombardo, Olympia, WA*

5 I'm a great fan of Civil War fabrics. I have used both tea and purchased Rit dyes to dye a piece that is too light for a particular project. While it's really hard to find black Civil War fabrics with cream/tan/beige prints, there are lots of black and white prints that can be dyed to make them the right color.

Kathleen (Kathi) Miller, Vancouver, WA

6 When a white fabric with little flowers is just a bit too white, I will dye it in tea. I put 20 teabags in hot water, put the fabric in for a few hours, or shorter if I don't want it too dark. Then I rinse it out and put it in clean water with some vinegar to hold the color. I rinse it again, let it dry and iron it. *Ingrid Tuyl, Zwijndrecht, Netherlands*

7 I have only used tea dye or tan Rit dye on my fabric, mostly to make it look aged, but also to change the color slightly. Tan dye is good for toning down bright colors and whites.

Jill Bowman, Jamestown, NC

8 I have tea-stained a double-size quilt as a means to age it. I filled the bathtub with warm water and tons of tea bags. I let the tea bags steep for a while and then placed my quilt top in the water, submerging it as much as I could, trying to get out all the air bubbles. I then checked the quilt top every 30 minutes or so. When the color I was seeking was achieved, I took the quilt top out and rinsed it. This took about six hours from beginning to end, and the result was a beautifully antiqued quilt.   *Kellie Hewitt, Marion, VA*

9 I have painted Rit dye on with a brush, after masking with masking tape, if I need to tone down contrast on a finished top.

Valerie Turer, Brooklyn, NY

10 You may be able to purchase a large amount of a light fabric very economically, and then use it for different projects by dyeing it.

Linda Chadsey, Abbotsford, British Columbia

11 The sun-release dyes make awesome fabrics to use for appliqué or for base fabrics for creative thread work. I like to outline leaf shapes and veins with contrasting color threads. Then I quilt the pieces.   *Nancy Powell, Coatesville, PA*

12 The only technique I have tried is discharge with bleach. It is a fun experiment and you end up with what is basically a new fabric to work with.   *Kari Vojtechovsky, Centennial, CO*

13 Because I wanted to do my own creative color design and have something no one else has, I have dyed fabric eight different shades in an old-fashioned canner with eight quarts of water and dye.

Louise McFadyen, Auburn, NY

14 After you purchase your fabric, keep it in an area away from sunlight. I've gone to work on a project and at the fold—there is no color! The sun faded my fabric.   *Marlys Wiens, Edina, MN*

15 I have dyed some fabric with watered-down acrylic paint. While it was wet, I placed it on cookie sheets and laid it in the sun to dry. Fabric dyeing is great when I'm doing landscaping quilt projects and want to create an exact color.   *Gayle Saunders, Moneta, VA*

I have dyed some fabric with watered-down acrylic paint.

16 I like dyeing with natural, organic dyes made from plants. The bathtub or a washroom sink are nice places to dye in, but be careful to thoroughly wash the basin or tub after dyeing so as not to stain them.   *Amanda Kei Andrews, Vero Beach, FL*

17 One precaution for dyeing fabric is to avoid breathing in the dye powder by wearing a mask. Only use utensils for dyeing that aren't also used for food preparation.   *Susan Knudson, Janesville, WI*

18 I have dyed fabric in the microwave instead of the stovetop, following the directions on the dye package. It was my first try, and I found it an easy method.   *Joyce Shiels, Manteo, NC*

19 I have used fabric dyes from Dharma Trading to get a certain color or look in some quilts. I especially enjoy using the fabric paints/dyes to accent and shade appliqué patterns of flowers and foliage. It brings so much depth to the appliqués.   *Francis Stanley, Slidell, LA*

20 I do a lot of appliqué, so having hand dyed fabric to get shades of colors for flowers makes them look very realistic.   *Barbara Cascelli, Murrieta, CA*

21 I just recently did some fabric dyeing as a fun project with my granddaughters. They did some tie dyeing and I was doing other fabric manipulations to see what would turn out. It was a lot of fun

and I definitely plan on doing more. We used a good Procion MX
Dye, and I wore a mask to mix it up.   *Ann Ouellette, Meriden, CT*

㉒ When I absolutely need a color I cannot find, I contact a
professional fabric colorist, send a swatch of the color I am trying
to match, and get his/her help.   *Barbara Merritt, Brackney, PA*

㉓ I no longer can dye fabric now that I live in a house with no
outdoor space or a basement slop sink. I still use the Japanese inks
to color smaller areas, and I also sign up for dyeing workshops to
have a place to dye fabric.   *Stephanie Greenberg, Lawrenceville, NJ*

F. Pressing and Ironing

❶ Fabric should be pressed—not ironed. Ironing pushes the fabric back and forth and can cause it to be stretched, especially if you are using steam. The best way is to press the iron down flat on your fabric which flattens it.   *Susan McCurdy, Price, UT*

❷ After I've washed a fabric, I don't iron it if I'm not going to use it right away. I just smooth it and fold it. That way, it's easier to tell what has been washed and what hasn't. You always have to press it again anyway, if it's been folded in a closet, so why waste the extra step?   *Sally Eshelman, York, PA*

❸ I try to iron the fabric as it comes out of the washer, because it is damp and the wrinkles come out much better. I do not use starch, as I do a lot of appliqué and want my fabric soft to gently go around curves on the appliqué.   *Jennifer Padden, Austin, TX*

❹ Make a big ironing board. At the lumber store, buy a piece of plywood 2 × 4'. Cover this with two layers of cotton batting and ironing board fabric available at chain fabric stores. Wrap it around the edge and staple down on the back. This is small enough to lift on and off your regular ironing board and makes the big ironing jobs go fast.   *Wendy Akin, Terrell, TX*

❺ I have an ironing board extender that I could not live without when I'm ironing big pieces of fabric. It is made out of wood and covered with a pad. It fits on top of my ironing board.
          Carol Nelson, Baxter, MN

❻ A press cloth will keep any scorch marks off your fabric. If you do not have a press cloth, a bed sheet also works. Press the underside of the fabric and try not to stretch or pull at the fabric.
          Bobbie Haynes, Shepherdsville, KY

7 I steam iron a lot. I iron my fabrics on the straight of grain with a light hand on the raw edges so as not to warp or misshape the fabric. Some fabrics may be on the thin side, and with these, I use spray sizing to give more body to the fabric. It really does make a difference in the ease of cutting and sewing because the cuts are more accurate.   *Francis Stanley, Slidell, LA*

8 Because I prewash fabric, the sizing has been removed. Spray starch gives body and stability and can prevent stretching. Sometimes I spray starch and iron a fabric several times.
      Anne Hollenbach, Hudson, WI

9 I like to air-fluff fabric first in the dryer, iron all over quickly and then use starch to eliminate all wrinkles. If a fabric won't respond, I sprinkle it with water, roll it up into a ball and let it rest; I then iron it slightly damp.   *Susan Riley, Hingham, MA*

10 I make a concoction that when sprayed onto folded fabric takes out wrinkles and fold lines—replace one cup from a gallon of distilled water with one cup of vodka.   *Joanne Picicci, Spokane, WA*

11 I stay away from starch because I live in the South, and it will sometimes draw silverfish.   *Joan Oldham, Panama City, FL*

12 Starch the fabric heavily, then put it in a zip-lock plastic bag. I put this bag in the freezer overnight. That makes the fabric so easy to iron. My fabric is as stiff as paper, so cutting is a breeze.
      Frances Courson, Maryville, TN

13 If using spray starch or sizing, cover the floor around your ironing board. Use a protective waste fabric over your ironing board cover. Wash that protective cover often. Clean your iron often.
      Michelle Harrison, Morganton, GA

14 I try to remove fabric from the dryer slightly damp, and then I use Mary Ellen's Best Press when I iron it.
      Elizabeth Merkle, Levittown, PA

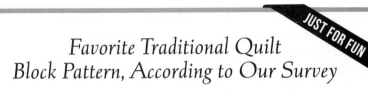

Favorite Traditional Quilt Block Pattern, According to Our Survey

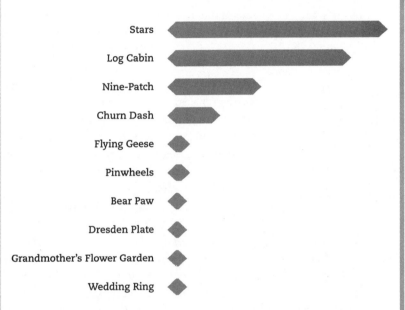

Stars	
Log Cabin	
Nine-Patch	
Churn Dash	
Flying Geese	
Pinwheels	
Bear Paw	
Dresden Plate	
Grandmother's Flower Garden	
Wedding Ring	

❖ I just fell in love with the Churn Dash block when I was hunting for an old pine wardrobe. An old Churn Dash quilt was hanging behind my find. At the time, I knew nothing about quilts, but I was captivated by all the tiny pieces in that design and wanted to know how to do that. *Kit Willey, Niagara-on-the-Lake, Ontario*

⓯ Remove selvages before ironing or cutting, as they can shrink at a different rate than the rest of the fabric.

Christine Baxter, Gordon, Australia

⓰ Buy the best iron you can, and then treat it well! Never use tap water in your iron. This is especially true if you have hard water; the minerals will build up inside your iron, which will lead to spots on the fabric when the minerals eventually find their way out. Instead, use distilled water, because the minerals have been removed.   *Celeste Collier, Guntersville, AL*

17 I have an iron that steams so well that you don't need to use fabric sizing. The name of the iron is Eurosteam. A little pricey, but it has lasted longer than any other iron I've ever had. I purchased it at a quilt show.   *Nannette Konstant, Flourtown, PA*

While quilting, I utilize a small wand type iron to press seams as I go along.

18 While quilting, I utilize a small wand type iron purchased in a fabric store to press seams as I go along. I have a piece of toweling on my sewing table to protect the wood, and I press each seam as pieces are joined. This eliminates numerous trips to the ironing board and assures a smooth finished block.

Carol Mottola, Mineola, NY

19 If the fabric seems quite wrinkled and does not press out quickly using Mary Ellen's Best Press or plain water, I will spray my pieces with water and roll them up and put them in the freezer for a couple days before pressing again. Sometimes I will press both sides. I like my fabric to be nicely pressed!   *Carole Wilder, Hastings, MN*

20 I like to start with all the fabric on my side of the ironing board, pressing and pushing the ironed fabric away from me onto a table, into a laundry basket, or whatever I can find to keep it from puddling on the floor.   *Carolynn Thornton, Seguin, TX*

21 Ricky Tims recommends using a "non-steam" iron because you don't get those little bumps from the indentations in the bottom of a spray iron. I finally found a non-steam iron which I use to press my quilting fabric. I use a spray bottle if I need moisture on the fabric.   *Charlotte Kewish, Gibsonia, PA*

22 If any seams will be on bias edges, then starch the heck out of the fabric before cutting it.   *BJ Chadwick, Marmora, NJ*

㉓ I use light steam when ironing. Mary Ellen's Best Press starch alternative is wonderful for quilters. I buy it by the gallon! It's especially good for getting wrinkles out of batiks.

Kathleen (Kathi) Miller, Vancouver, WA

㉔ I have a room with a queen-size bed in it that I use to stage material and iron. I spread my fabric out on the bed and drape it over my ironing board then turn it before it gets to the floor right in front of me. It helps to keep it smooth after ironing. Then I hang it on a very large, Amish-made hanging rack until time to use it (I have two of these racks I bought at Lapp Coach Shop near The Old Country Store). *Diana Marilla, Glen Allen, VA*

㉕ Before I cut fabric into quilting pieces, I iron the fabric and use Magic Sizing aerosol spray to give it body. Another option is to use a "magic pressing agent" consisting of an ounce of vodka, a gallon of purified water, a splash of scent such as lavender, and just a drop of blue food coloring. Put this mixture in a small spray bottle, and then spray and press. The finish will be slightly crisp, but not as much as if Magic Sizing were used.

Marti Blankenship, Pleasant Valley, MO

㉖ When pressing uncut pieces of fabric, iron with the grain, either from selvage to selvage or from one cut edge to the other. Never iron in a circular motion as you will be distorting the threads in the fabric, making it harder to cut pieces on the grain.

Rosemarie Garone, West Islip, NY

㉗ Those huge backings are terrible to iron. I do the middle section on my big ironing board, and then fold it in half and iron both sides back and front folded—no wrinkles or creases that way.

Ann Roadarmel, Elysburg, PA

㉘ If you have a lot of fabric to iron at one time, set aside some time and put on a good movie to get you through a sometimes laborious chore. *Jennifer Padden, Austin, TX*

㉙ I like to roll the fabric into a tube after pressing, as opposed to folding it. I then place the fabric tubes into a plastic tote. The fabric unrolls flat and free of any creases when I am ready to begin cutting.　　　　　　　　　　　*Sharon Sutton, Lindsey, OH*

㉚ Sometimes, instead of ironing fabric, I tumble it in the dryer on high heat with a wet towel.　　　　　*Beth Miller, Arena, WI*

G. Squaring Up

❶ Squaring up is probably one of the most important early steps. I square up before I iron and then after I iron, being careful to not distort the weave.　　　　　　*Anne Jackson, Prior Lake, MN*

❷ Before I begin cutting my fabric, I square it up by making a small snip and then tearing my fabric. I will then make my first cut about ¼" from the torn edge, making sure that no pulled threads will show on my blocks.　　　*Marcia Porcelli, Forsyth, GA*

> *An easy way to test the fabric grain is to fold a piece of fabric in half lengthwise and pin the selvage edges together. If the fabric lies perfectly flat, the grain is perfect.*

❸ Make sure you check the fabric grain. An easy way to test the fabric grain is to fold a piece of fabric in half lengthwise and pin the selvage edges together. If the fabric lies perfectly flat, the grain is perfect. When you purchase fabric, it is important to lay it out and be sure that it is perfectly flat. Adjust the cut ends, not the selvage ends.　　　*Rosemarie Garone, West Islip, NY*

❹ I learned to sew clothing before I was a quilter, so I try to cut my pieces parallel to the selvage (with the grain) as much as I can.　　　*Laurie Mosley, Mount Holly, NJ*

⑤ I was in Texas a few years ago and was delighted to find that some shops there tear rather than cut their fabric. It annoys me to lose fabric trying to "square it up" with the grain. Where I live now, they only cut fabric, so I usually buy a little extra.

Charlotte Kewish, Gibsonia, PA

⑥ Sometimes, even when the fabric has been torn to get an edge that follows the grain, the fabric may still hang crooked. If you have that problem after washing and pressing; take the opposite corners of the fabric and gently pull to re-align or straighten it. If it is worse after you do that, perform this operation on the opposing corners.

Annemarie (Nancy) Poorbaugh, Montgomery, AL

⑦ Tearing fabric makes me cringe a little. You still have to trim the edges because they're stretched and distorted from the force required to tear the fabric. A little fabric loss during squaring up is inevitable—just buy extra fabric to allow for it.

Marcia Nissley, Ronks, PA

⑧ Do some carpentry to learn about precision, and then be grateful that fabric is a forgiving medium in which to make your works of art!

Sharon Mountford, Canoga Park, CA

CHAPTER 4

Managing Templates

A. *Methods for Making Templates*

❶ I use heat-resistant template material so that way, if I accidentally iron it, it still is in the shape I started with. If I need a bunch of fabric cut from a single template, I go to my local window dealer and he will cut the template out of acrylic for me, and will mark any lines I need on it. He is awesome. *Annette Jordan, Portville, NY*

❷ Templates are expensive, and if you only use them for one quilt, it is a waste to purchase them. So creating my own templates has served me well so far. *Margaret (Peg) Parsons, New Castle, DE*

❸ A lightweight plexiglass works well for many templates. My husband cuts them for me with his bandsaw. Plexiglass can be purchased at many craft stores since it is often used in picture frames.

Delores McDevitt, Evansville, IN

❹ You can also take a children's coloring book and copy the pictures, trace them onto the plastic, and use them as new templates.

Robin Levine, Wantagh, NY

❺ When I use templates in my quilting books or a pattern, I always trace them on my transparent plastic and write the size of the template on it with a Sharpie pen. In this way I don't destroy my quilt books and always will have the template if I need to trace it again.   *Debbie McAdam, Holbrook, NY*

❻ I always mark grainline on any templates that I make.

Carol Keskimaki, Prescott Valley, AZ

❼ Be careful with templates that are directional. A pattern might use the same template but the direction might be reversed. It is good to mark your template with any special directions. Also mark the templates with any corresponding letters that are used in the diagram of the pattern. It will make it much easier to coordinate the fabrics and pattern pieces that way.   *Susan Louis, Briarwood, NY*

❽ I recently purchased a stencil/template-making kit from Genesis Creations. It includes an electric stencil burner which, for my money, leaves other template-making techniques for dead.

Sue Sacchero, Safety Bay, Australia

❾ I use indelible marking pens to draw the template on a margarine or ice cream tub lid that I would be sending to recycle. Then I apply 3M First Aid Tape to the back side so that the template doesn't slide around while I trace it on fabric. I don't recommend these templates for rotary cutting, though, as they're not thick enough to be sturdy.   *Colleen Gander, Prescott, Ontario*

10 Remember to use good scissors and make smooth, clean cuts in the template when using template plastic. I use an emery board to sand out any burrs, as they can cause bumps in the fabric piece.

Cathie Shelton, Montgomery Village, MD

11 Back before I retired, I used a lot of manila file folders that were being tossed because I just couldn't stand to see them thrown away. I recycled them by tracing my patterns on the inside of the folders while on my lunch break and brought them home with the entire block drawn out inside the folder. I could then file these away until I was ready to cut them out and use them. I usually ate lunch at my desk, so this was a perfect time to work on my quilting projects.

Nora Manley, Athens, AL

Large pattern pieces can have the centers cut out to use for other patterns.

12 Large pattern pieces can have the centers cut out to use for other patterns.

Lisa Hughes, Richland, NY

13 I find file folders and postcards, depending on the size of the template needed, to be excellent template material. I simply trace the template with a very fine mechanical pencil so as not to distort the original template design and cut just to the inside of my drawn line.

Candace Pekich, Walla Walla, WA

14 I've learned that fine grit sandpaper under the fabric keeps it from slipping when marking around a template. That is a very old-fashioned trick from long ago!

Carol Keskimaki, Prescott Valley, AZ

15 I like to use my printer and print out the design on paper. Then I use my sewing machine with no thread to sew over the lines and create holes. After that, I use a pounce to mark the design on the quilt.

Allison Evrard, Coopersburg, PA

16 I copy the shapes using my scanner/printer onto the matte/paper side of freezer paper sheets (not off-the-roll stuff) or onto regular paper. Using a glue stick or rubber cement, I glue the shape onto template plastic and then cut out on the line. This eliminates the tedious tracing.   *Annemarie (Nancy) Poorbaugh, Montgomery, AL*

⑰ Since I am old-fashioned, I like to mark around my templates with a ballpoint pen and cut out the pieces with scissors. It would be more efficient to use a die-cutting machine or cut strips with a rotary cutter, but I just like to play with the fabric.

Netta Pyron, Rolla, MO

⑱ If you can budget a die-cutting machine, by all means, get one! These great machines are real time savers.   *Linda Ferguson, Jackson, TN*

⑲ I tend to make new templates for each new project started even if I have made that project before. Accuracy is so important and templates tend to get worn out from use.

Daniela Durham, Greenwich, NJ

B. Template Materials

❶ I enjoy using the precut wooden shapes found at Walmart in the crafting department; every time I trace them, the shape is consistent and does not shift or distort.   *Linda Needham, The Villages, FL*

❷ You can buy template plastic, but you will save money for more fabric if you use what you are throwing away instead: cereal boxes, margarine container lids, etc.   *Rebecca O'Dell, Clayton, NC*

❸ I use freezer paper for templates. You can buy sheets that will go through the printer, saving time tracing the pattern. I have tried using template plastic, but I can never cut it smooth enough.

Coreen Burnett, Damascus, MD

4 I use No Melt Mylar or freezer paper a lot. The freezer paper will stick to the fabric several times and you can cut around it or use your rotary cutter.   *Debbie Westerman, The Colony, TX*

5 I use just about anything made of plastic for a template. Plexiglass is excellent and thick, so you can use your rotary cutter with it. I use my Dremmel Tool to cut a nice straight line when forming it.   *Victoria Page, Amarillo, TX*

6 I will buy clear plastic placemats to use for my templates. I shop through thrift stores looking for clear plastic anything; if it is flat and can be reused, I'll buy it.   *Kathleen Van Orsdel, Talbott, TN*

7 I find that "Shrinky Dink" plastic is the best for making templates. The reason I like it is because it has a coarse side that pencil adheres to well, yet erases from cleanly, but does not smudge over time. Additionally, if you are not concerned about the reversibility of the template, the rough side does not slip on the fabric when you are tracing around it. If you have to reverse the template, as long as you have a firm surface to work on and apply even pressure with one finger of your non-dominant hand upon the template while you are tracing around it, the smooth side won't slip either.

Deborah DeLuca, Wayne, NJ

8 I like heavy plastic with a graph paper grid on it to make it easier to get the sizes right. Don't buy the kind on a roll—it will never lay flat and makes the template hard to use.

Carol Moll, Schnecksville, PA

9 I am a big fan of stacking several sheets of freezer paper and ironing them together before cutting out the templates. This gives me a stiff template that I can then use to turn edges under with starch, a stiletto and an iron without the expense of mylar sheets which can get pricey.   *Stephanie Greenberg, Lawrenceville, NJ*

Best Time of Day to Sew, According to Our Survey

JUST FOR FUN

Early Morning
21%

Morning
30%

Late Morning
5%

Afternoon
20%

Late Afternoon
4%

Evening
11%

Night
9%

❖ I sew early in the morning before I get ready for work. It is quiet and I sip a cup of tea with soft music on while I sew. It's a great way to wake up.
Karel Umble, New Holland, PA

❖ I do better in the morning because my mind and body is well-rested and fresh. The later it gets, the more mistakes I make.
Jenn Martin, Prattville, AL

❖ My favorite time is right after lunch. I'm not really a morning person, so I do boring stuff like laundry when I'm still not firing on all cylinders and save quilting for when I have warmed up for the day!
Sally Eshelman, York, PA

❖ Because of my overly busy work schedule, I begin, believe it or not, sometime after midnight, maybe starting around 1 am and ending around 3 am.
Deborah DeLuca, Wayne, NJ

10 You can use cardboard for templates, but it is much easier to use a transparent material so you can position the template where you want it, especially handy for fussy cutting. My favorite way to cut is without a template: using AccuQuilt GO!

Debbie Henry, Lucinda, PA

11 Instead of buying acetate at the craft store to make plastic templates, I recycle the acetate covers from used notebooks or plastic file folders. It is thin enough to cut easily with scissors or an Exacto knife and metal ruler, and sturdy enough for accurate marking. If the template I plan to make is small, I have even cut templates from plastic gallon milk containers. The ones available to me are translucent, which is useful to see the fabric through.

Kathy Wiedmann, Fairfax, VA

If you can get them, old x-rays make excellent templates.

12 If you can get them, old x-rays make excellent templates. A local vet may be willing to give you a few from patients that are no longer with them.

Jeanette Lyon, Bedford, VA

13 If I need templates, I usually use old x-rays that I ask my doctor for. They are free, and I don't hesitate to throw them away when the project is finished. I have very limited space in my home for my quilting projects, and if I decide to save the templates, old x-rays don't take up much room at all!

Barbara Johnson, Dallas, OR

14 I use tracing paper so I can pin it to the fabric. I do appliqué and usually draw my own patterns free hand.

Patricia A. Ensey, Duluth, MN

15 I do t-shirt quilts, so I use plexiglass template in four different squares which include the seam allowance and are completely clear so I can see what I'm doing.

Shannon Gittermann, Bartlett, TN

16 My grandmother used large index cards and old birthday cards to make her templates. I find that they are easy to use and when they start to fall apart, they are easily replaced. There are template sheets in the store, but they can be costly for the beginner or someone on a tight budget.   *Deborah Kelderman, Lexington, SC*

17 I have used contact paper when I wanted to do machine-quilted leaves and did not want them to be exactly alike. I could stick it down and move it several times before the stickiness was used up.
    Susan Eaglaton, Maryville, TN

18 Used x-ray film with an x-ray light box makes copying shapes and figures easy. Transparency sheets used with overhead projectors are also useful and heavy enough to provide stability when tracing.   *Carol Tunin, Joppa, MD*

c. Adjusting Template Sizes

1 I worked in the graphics/printing field for many years. I have a proportion wheel which is great for sizing things up and down. I would suggest anyone that re-sizes a lot of their patterns purchase one. It's a great investment, and they're not that expensive.
    Amy Mayo, Havre de Grace, MD

2 I use a Reduction Wheel to get the exact percentage needed. The Wheel also works perfectly for accurately determining any size manipulation desired.   *Carol Keskimaki, Prescott Valley, AZ*

3 I use Golden Threads Proportional Scale. Just match up the actual size to the size you want, and it will give you a resizing percentage. Increase or decrease on your computer by that number, or take it to a office supply store and let them do it for you.
    Daniela Durham, Greenwich, NJ

4 I use a ¼" ruler to adjust the template if I need to adjust by that size. For appliqués that need adjusting, I'll either reduce it on a copier, or even eyeball the design, especially for folk-art type work

Patricia Grimm, New Windsor, NY

5 A great tip I learned is easy enough if using your calculator. For example, if you want an 8" block and have a 12", you first enter the number 8 into your calculator and press the division key, then enter your 12" and press the equal key. You should get 0.66666667. Move your decimal point over to the right 2 spaces. You now know you need to reduce your pattern to 66.6% to make your 8" block.

Debbie McAdam, Holbrook, NY

6 Nowadays most of us have desktop printers that also scan and copy. I determine how much I want to reduce or enlarge my template and simply ask the printer to copy or reduce to the percentage I need. If the template is too large, I can always go to my local self-copy shop and use a larger machine.

Candace Pekich, Walla Walla, WA

7 If the image cannot be enlarged on the scanner/printer, I use an overhead projector to make the images any size I want. Just pin a piece of freezer paper to the felt wall and trace, then transfer to template material.

Noelle Clesceri, Oakwood Hills, IL

8 I use a free Photoshop-like software called Gimp to resize any templates I have. You simply scale the size of the template and print at actual size.

Amanda Kei Andrews, Vero Beach, FL

Any time I adjust the size of the template I will make a sample block to test the templates out.

9 Any time I adjust the size of the template I will make a sample block to test the templates out.

Kim Clark, Lakewood, CO

10 I think the best way to adjust my cardboard templates is to cut it down the center and spread it out to the desired length with more cardboard and tape. Double and triple check the size with your ruler, as precision is the key to quilting.   *Annette Crain, Spanish Fork, UT*

⓫ I usually try to just chart them on graph paper. I know there are all kinds of ways to make copy machines do the work, but I just love drafting my own.   *Nancy Swanwick, Fort Scott, KS*

⓬ I use my Electric Quilt software. No math involved. I'm going brain dead after 50.   *Kathleen Santos, New Port Richey, FL*

D. Organizing and Storing Templates

❶ I store templates according to size and type. All squares are stored in graduated sizes, all triangles are stored in graduated sizes, etc. I keep each shape on separate large rings which can be hung on hooks in my sewing room. I store my rulers in graduated sizes by placing them in a long wooden block with slots—one size per slot.
          Cyndy Spiker, New Castle, PA

❷ I have a portfolio, the kind an artist would use; the templates are stored flat, and there is a zipper so they won't fall out.
          Barbara Porter, Arroyo Grande, CA

❸ I keep my pouncing pad and white and yellow markers on the same shelf as my quilting templates. It means I usually have more than one white and yellow marker. I like them to be available at the same time and place as quilting templates.
          Marti Blankenship, Pleasant Valley, MO

❹ I have an old-fashioned letter holder with slots where I organize my templates. It works great.   *Cathy Jolley, Fillmore, UT*

❺ My heavy templates and rulers that I use for my longarm I have hung on an interior cabinet door on a pot lid rack.

Nannette Konstant, Flourtown, PA

❻ I have wire shelving all around my sewing room. I take an "S" hook bought from the hardware store and hook it through the hole in the template, and then on the shelf wire. I can see every shape and size, and they are not in the way.   *Victoria Page, Amarillo, TX*

❼ I keep very long border templates under clear plastic on my quilt machine table.   *Karen Martin, Breezy Point, MN*

❽ I tend to do something fairly simple and portable. I don't have a formal quilting or sewing room and need to be able to move my quilting with me, as I love to hand quilt and take it with me when I can. If I have a pattern that has smaller pieces that could be easily lost, once I've prepared them, I place them within a labeled zipper bag. I then put the labeled zipper bag with the pattern into an 8½ × 11" polypropylene sheet and put the sheet into a 3-ring binder on my bookshelf. All of my patterns are kept alphabetically within the binders, although I don't drive myself insane re-alphabetizing each set of binders as I add new patterns. Instead, I've devised a numbering system for the binders and an indexing system in a list form which I keep in the first binder on my shelf, so that I can easily find any pattern if I have to. When I have template pieces that are larger than my zipper bags, I put them into the polypropylene sheets directly with the pattern sheet(s) and put that again into the appropriate binder for storage, unless I'm using it. Labeling everything is the most important part—the zipper bags, the pattern sheets if they are not already clearly labeled and the template pieces in some form so that if any part is separated from the rest, they can easily be put back where they belong. I use

> *All of my patterns are kept alphabetically within the binders, although I don't drive myself insane re-alphabetizing each set of binders as I add new patterns.*

indelible ink markers to do the labeling on most items; that prevents smudging.   *Deborah DeLuca, Wayne, NJ*

9 I use rubbing alcohol to remove the stains left from the fabric markers and Sharpies.   *Brenda Rice, Nicholasville, KY*

10 For large templates, I punch a hole in the top of it about ¾" in from the side and hang it from a peg board on hooks.
                                               Carol Sands, Tampa, FL

11 I punch a small hole near the edge of the template and string it onto a small beaded chain. I can add more templates to the same chain. Removing them for use is easy, and it is just as easy to return them to the chain for storage. I like to hang the chain with the templates on my bulletin board using a push pin.
                                       Sandra Darlington, Philadelphia, PA

12 I generally only make a project once, so I toss any templates I've made at the end of a project. This is also why I use only inexpensive materials such as file folders and postcards. I dislike using plastic templates as they are hard to cut and can warp in our hot summers.   *Candace Pekich, Walla Walla, WA*

13 I hang templates on clip-style clothes hangers in the closet. They stay flat and are out of the way when I'm not using them.
                                             Jennifer Padden, Austin, TX

14 I hang my quilting templates on a belt hanger in my closet.
                                               Margo Ellis, Key West, FL

15 I have a vinyl-covered metal rack with a basket in the front. It was part of a store display that had been discarded. My large rulers are stacked on the tall rack against the back, and smaller rulers, templates and rotary cutters are in the basket with all instructions underneath on the bottom.   *Nancy Chase, Columbus, MT*

16 I store my templates in a large, flat cardboard box. I have a drawing of each design on a piece of paper which I take along when

I want to purchase a new pattern to make sure I don't buy the same one I already own.   *Sally Petersheim, Gap, PA*

> *I have so many templates that I decided to build a spreadsheet so I don't purchase duplicates.*

17 I have so many templates that I decided to build a spreadsheet so I don't purchase duplicates. I store my most-used templates in a vertical rack near my cutting table and the rest according to size in three drawers. My spreadsheet is organized so I know which template is in each drawer.

Candace Pekich, Walla Walla, WA

18 I store my templates in multiple file folders in hanging file folders in a file cabinet. I sort them by type of figure: birds, flowers, shapes, etc.   *Carol Tunin, Joppa, MD*

19 I store templates in separate plastic sandwich bags that I label with the pattern name, completed block size, number of different fabrics that I used, and anything else that I consider pertinent at the time. If I found the pattern in a magazine or book, I note the title, issue if appropriate, and the page number.

Deborah Gross, Willow Grove, PA

20 I use a CD storage case to store the templates. The pages are see-through so I can identify the templates right away, and the case zips closed to transport to a class.   *Colleen Gander, Prescott, Ontario*

21 I permanently mark every template with source of template and my initials so I can loan them and they're returned. I also measure a 1" measure and a ¼" measure on every template for quick reference.

Carol Tunin, Joppa, MD

22 I hang templates on a nail on the side of my bookcase that holds my quilting supplies.   *Amy Kentera, Highland Mills, NY*

23 I use a three-ring binder with pocket folders. I label each folder with the name of the project and all of the templates go in it. For the Farmer's Wife blocks that I'm working on, I actually use baseball card inserts and put the templates in numerical order in each pocket. It's a great help!   *Twila Sikkink, Clear Lake, WI*

24 I place templates in a ziplocking baggie with a piece of cardboard in the baggie to ensure that they stay flat. It's very important to store them in a dry area out of direct sunlight!

Linda Needham, The Villages, FL

25 Templates stay with a project until the quilt is finished, then I discard them. It's much easier to remake a template than use an old one that might not be the correct size after lots of use.

Carole Brown, Ephrata, PA

26 I will often include a photo of the quilt I made with the templates and any notes about the templates in the zippy bag.

Susan Vargo, Avondale, PA

E. Other Template Tips

1 Several of my friends and I share templates. Whenever we need a template, we raid each others' collections.

Barbara Clarke, Woodbridge, CA

2 I look for quilting templates in thrift shops. They often end up there, and many can be purchased very reasonably.

Louise Bem, Indiana, PA

3 Mark which side is right side up. When fussy cutting, I also draw around items in the design, marking edges and reference points on the template to aid in placement for creating identical cuts. I have used AccuQuilt and Sizzix die-cutting machines to create templates from clear plastic.   *Debbie Henry, Lucinda, PA*

❹ I try to avoid templates for piecing and use them just for appliqué. I have found rulers can be used many times in the place of templates and marked with glow-line tape.

Mary Beth Schrader, Cameron, MO

❺ I don't always just use quilting templates. I find that there are many templates that can be multi-purpose, and can be used for anything from quilting to painting, sewing, etc.

Carolyn McCord, Vancouver, WA

❻ I don't like templates because there is usually a way to rotary cut the same thing. You just need to research another way of doing what the pattern suggests. An example of this is the triangular roof of a school house block.   *Barbara Augustine, Woodbridge, VA*

CHAPTER 5

Marking
Quilting
Lines

A. Choosing a Quilting Design

❶ The quilting design should enhance but not overpower the quilt top. Designs often have a "flavor": for example, oriental, whimsical, formal, elegant, juvenile, etc. Pick the "flavor" that coordinates with the quilt.   *Annemarie (Nancy) Poorbaugh, Montgomery, AL*

2 If unsure or feeling a little insecure for quilting lines, start with something simple. Shadow the quilt blocks by marking a quilting line ¼" on each side of the seams. Or mark simple diagonal lines through the blocks.   *Anna Osborn, Omaha, NE*

3 Remember the denser the quilting, the firmer, less cuddly the quilt.   *Dorothy Thayer, Haliburton, Ontario*

4 When I hand quilt, I generally stick to echoing shapes, in-the-ditch, or random quilt lines, depending on a project. For example, sky fabric *asks* for the cloud shapes to be outlines, or sometimes you want to give the feeling of swirling wind.

> *I often think of the quilting as adding the movement to the quilt.*

With longarm quilting, I generally prefer an overall design like a meandering line. The exception is when I have a pictorial quilt. The quilter works with me to do a custom design that will enhance the shapes and movements in the quilt.

I often think of the quilting as adding the movement to the quilt.   *Nancy Henry, Rochester, NH*

5 The design of the quilt always dictates the areas which should be quilted. I prefer organic patterns—stems, leaves, vines—for hand quilting in asymmetric areas. Geometric patterns fit regular areas; meander quilting is frequently most appropriate in small areas.   *Sharon Mountford, Canoga Park, CA*

6 I choose a quilting design for handquilting by laying different quilting stencils that fit within the individual blocks. I consider the overall lines of the quilt and what blends with the overall look I want to create. Sometimes I choose bigger quilting stencils that will cover several blocks if that blends better. I try to choose a border stencil that blends or coordinates with the block stencil as well and doesn't clash with the blocks within the quilt. Simplicity is usually my best choice.   *Geralyn McClarren, Harrisburg, PA*

7 Take pictures of the area that you want to quilt, then print out the pictures on 8½ × 11 sheets of paper and then draw the quilting

pattern on the picture to help you decide if this is what you want. You can also use transparency sheets and dry erase markers.
Darlene Gerber, Geneva, OH

8 I plan the top design to accommodate the quilting. I try to minimize the number of seams I have to hand quilt across.
Janet Atkins, Athens, NY

9 If you think ahead of time, pick a background fabric that has drawn lines and follow that line. You will look at background fabric differently from now on for sure. No marking! What could be easier? Once I used a leaf from the pattern and drew them all over the background. It turned out great.   *Mary Andra Holmes, Prescott, AZ*

10 I hang the quilt top up on my design board or table, and it eventually kind of "talks" to me. If I'm still unsure, I'll draw the design on a clear plastic overlay using a wet-erase pen to see if it works.   *Ruth Anglin, Tijeras, NM*

11 Frequently I quilt just ¼" from the seam lines. I like the look of straight lines.   *Nancy Stevens, Glenside, PA*

12 I like to have a large photo of the quilt. Sometimes I take a picture of the pattern to an office supply store and have it blown up 300 or 400 percent and I get 3–6 copies. I use the copies to experiment with sketching possible designs such as cross hatching, diagonal stitching, outline stitching, echo stitching around appliqué, or in other ways determine from my sketches what pattern (s) I will use when quilting. I study my quilt to see if there are large open places that need a secondary pattern of stitches—or whether the quilt piecing stands on its own and I should focus on stitch-in-the-ditch and outline stitches.   *Marti Blankenship, Pleasant Valley, MO*

13 The best book for inspiration is the *Encyclopedia of Quilting Designs* by Phyllis Miller.   *Shelia Smith, Goldthwaite, TX*

14 Sometimes I will choose a pattern from one of my white-on-white fabrics, if there are any in the quilt I'm working on, and quilt a larger version of that pattern. It's a great way to tie a design together.   *Amanda Kei Andrews, Vero Beach, FL*

15 I usually lay out my quilt top on the guest bed for a few days and keep walking by it. I will mark a block or two with either water soluble marker or Frixion pen. I'll look at the blocks for a day or two to see if the quilt talks to me. If I like a design, then I will mark the whole quilt and load it to my hand quilting floor frame.

Karen Nick, Lutz, FL

16 As many of my quilts are for babies and young children, I like to use fabric with pictures in it. I outline-quilt around the pictures, especially faces.   *Dorothy Thayer, Haliburton, Ontario*

17 I love traditional grid backgrounds for appliquéd quilts. Most of all, I love feathers in borders.   *Amy DeCesare, Delmont, PA*

18 I like old-fashioned quilting patterns, some of which have historical stories with them. I save my quilting magazines because some things become more attractive after they have been around awhile.   *Carol Baruschke, Dunedin, FL*

19 I base my quilting design (hand quilting) on the finished piecing style. Appliqué and patchwork blocks are outlined stitched. Open spaces include blocks of feathered quilting and cross hatching. Log Cabin blocks are always quilted stitch-in-the-ditch. If the piecing design is busy, I will use all-over cross hatch or a diamond design and may even quilt from the back. My favorite sashing and border quilting designs are cable, pumpkin, feather and straight line stitching.   *Ellen Harris, Huntsville, AL*

20 I like to hide in little elements that go with the theme of the quilt: eagle feathers within a quilt about rainforest flora and fauna, bugs and butterflies in a garden quilt. With the very simple quilting I do, if someone takes the time to really look at the quilting, they will get a nice visual reward.   *LynDee Lombardo, Olympia, WA*

㉑ I tend to do geometric quilts, and my favorite way to quilt is to emphasize the shapes. I usually quilt ¼" from seams, repeating in more echoes if necessary. I like to do patterns with lots of small pieces, but in areas like borders, I sometimes follow the prints or stripes instead of marking a design.   *Nancy Swanwick, Fort Scott, KS*

㉒ When I learn how to use the long-arm at my local quilt shop, my options will be vastly multiplied. Until then I'm limited to my machine at home, and I *hate* wrestling the bulk of a quilt through that, so I grit my teeth and use a simple diagonal grid.
Ellen Mueller, Acton, MA

㉓ Because I love triangles I am drawn to any quilting design using this element. Mixing traditional block patterns with modern quilting lines is one of my favorite things.   *Ellen Corning, McFarland, WI*

> *Mixing traditional block patterns with modern quilting lines is one of my favorite things.*

㉔ I love swirls and paisleys, so they show up in just about every quilt.
Trudy McKinnon, Redcliff, Alberta

㉕ I've come across a design from my mother or grandmother's era and I use it to honor them.   *Eileen D. Wenger, Lancaster, PA*

㉖ In hand quilting, if I have a border or plain block that will show off my quilting stitch, then I will sometimes use a stencil for a "fancy" design. Sometimes less is more, and all that is required is an allover cross hatch design.   *Nora Manley, Athens, AL*

㉗ I consider:
    1. who the quilt is for, male/female, young/older.
    2. what the quilt is trying to say, a theme.
    3. how close the stitching will need to be, based on the batting.
    4. is the quilt top busy, or does it need to have a design element added?
    5. is it intended for the quilting to blend with the quilt, or is it to be readily seen?   *Anna Osborn, Omaha, NE*

28 I have a PC Quilter and a design program for it. I buy designs from designers online. I decide which design would look best on a given quilt and use it. The designs I use on my PC Quilter are simple edge to edge designs.   *Charlotte Kewish, Gibsonia, PA*

29 For machine quilting, I do stitch in the ditch, grid and stipple/ meander. For hand quilting, I do echo and outline quilting.
Valerie Turer, Brooklyn, NY

30 When quilting multiple, same-size squares on a quilt, develop a basic shape and then use variations in each square. Try freeform botanic patterns. No plants are really ever identical. Variation is good.   *Sharon Mountford, Canoga Park, CA*

31 I'm not a fancy quilter. My main concern is to have an all-over even consistency of quilting throughout my quilts. I hate any big unquilted areas.   *Francis Stanley, Slidell, LA*

32 If the quilt top has straight lines, I try to put something with curves on it. If the quilt top has curved lines, I will use something with straight lines.   *Shirley Rouse, Havre de Grace, MD*

B. *Preferred Marking Tools*

1 I prefer Roxanne white and silver pencils because they last longer than most markers.   *Ellen Volker, Lancaster, NY*

2 I love the Hera marker, because it leaves no actual mark, just an indent in the fabric.   *C.L. Schoon, Delfgauw, Netherlands*

3 I have just started using the tip of a wooden "orange" stick (used for fingernails) to indent the quilt and I think I like that best of all: no chemicals in the fabric.   *Valerie Turer, Brooklyn, NY*

❹ The Bohin mechanical pencils with white lead make thin, precise lines that stay in place, even on a vibrating long-arm machine. They come out easily with water or a microfiber cloth. The Chaco liners are also easy to erase with a microfiber cloth, although the line is less precise and not as easy to see.   *Diane Linker, Scarsdale, NY*

❺ I love Sewline pencils in gray and white. They make a fine line and if your thread doesn't cover it, you can erase them. I also use painter's tape for grids as you can get it in several widths and it leaves no goo.   *Dee Johnson, Mankato, MN*

❻ I swear I have every marking tool known to man, but I always go back to the mechanical lead pencil. The lead is very fine. It washes off. I can use it to mark from very light to much darker, and I can refill it.   *Evelyn Horn, Yakima, WA*

> *I swear I have every marking tool known to man, but I always go back to the mechanical lead pencil.*

❼ For darker fabrics I still like the old red chalk markers, the ones that seamstresses use. I've even used slivers of soap, which work well if they are very thin.   *Patricia Grimm, New Windsor, NY*

❽ I use chalk pencils because they never damage the fabric, always come out completely, and are easy to re-trace if necessary.   *Diane Bachman, Leola, PA*

❾ I use the new ceramic pencils. They wash out nicely and stay on the fabric until I finish quilting.   *Judith Beach, Vienna, VA*

❿ I like to use chalk because I know it will come out. Marking pens are great, but they all state that if you leave them too long, they may not come out. Unfortunately, we all get distracted from time to time and have to leave a project longer than we would like.   *Karen Lane, Wandong, Australia*

⓫ I use tailors' chalk for dark fabrics and air-soluble pen for light fabrics. The tailors' chalk lasts and lasts, so I can mark it up and then go back to it days later. Air soluble pen is ideal for light colors, but only lasts for minutes so I can't mark up everything at once.

Deb Spencer, Greenwith, Australia

⑫ I am wary of any marking tools that are ink-based. Call me old-fashioned, but I would be afraid that the ink would change over time and create a stain or some unsightly vision in the fabric. I use a Chaco marker. It is a little vial of chalk that is applied with a tiny little wheel. I can brush it off and remark if necessary. I also use Sewline's pencils, especially if I am marking on light fabric. The marks are easily removed with a damp cloth.

Janice Simmons, Fresno, CA

⑬ I use a yard stick and a Chaco-liner because it's fast and easy. It washes out. But mostly because I love that clickety-click sound it makes.

Ellen Mueller, Acton, MA

⑭ I prefer not to mark as much as possible. I have used chalk pencils and been very frustrated by the chalk breaking and having to sharpen all the time.

Elizabeth Beardsley, Boulder, CO

⑮ I like to trace my quilting design onto tracing paper and pin the tracing paper to the top of the quilt. I stitch through the paper and the quilt sandwich. By the time I'm done, the paper is usually in shreds so the paper removal is not a big deal. I don't have to worry about markings not washing out of the top and get exactly the size I need in exactly the place I need.

Jennifer Padden, Austin, TX

⑯ I use a product called Golden Threads, a tissue-type roll of yellow paper where the design can be drawn on the paper and pinned or temporarily sprayed to the quilt top. The paper is thin and is easy to rip off once the design is quilted to the top.

Marcy Leland, Afton, MN

⑰ I love the Frixion marking pens because they do not rub off during the quilting process and yet will dissolve with the heat of my iron.

Donna Hill, Brimley, MI

JUST FOR FUN

Top 10 Quilting Snacks,
According to Our Survey

2nd — **TEA**

1st — **CHOCOLATE**

3rd — **PRETZELS**

4. M&M'S	8. SODA
5. NUTS	9. FRUIT
6. HARD CANDY	10. COOKIES
7. SNACK MIX	11. POPCORN

❖ I have various healthy snacks stashed in my sewing quarters at all times—because I just hate to stop once I'm in the zone on a project. Nature Valley Protein bars, almonds, dry cereal, almonds ... and yes, some chocolate now and then. Plenty of water on hand also.   *Nancee McCann, Wilmington, DE*

18 I prefer water- or iron-erasable fine point pens. I don't like pencils because they seem to pull the fabric, and trying to erase the marks definitely pulls at the fabric.   *Margaret Ward, Sugar Land, TX*

19 I like to use Crayola washable markers, but I prewash all my fabrics, and wash my quilts when they are done. I use a chalky, waxy white pencil for dark fabric that markers won't show up on.
Barbara Porter, Arroyo Grande, CA

I wash my quilts that are marked with a lead pencil with several white bath towels. The nap of the towels creates a mild abrasive that helps remove the lead pencil.

20 I generally use a Clover white marker on dark fabrics that is easily removed after the quilt top is complete by ironing over the markings. I prefer the marker to a white chalk-type pencil because when I hand quilt, my quilt is handled quite a bit and the chalk wears off the blocks before I get to quilt them. I use the Ultimate lead pencil for lighter fabrics because it is relatively easy to remove after the quilt is complete.

I generally wash my quilts that are marked with a lead pencil with several very lightly colored or white bath towels. The nap of the towels creates a mild abrasive that helps remove the lead pencil.
Geralyn McClarren, Harrisburg, PA

21 My favorite marking tool now is a Frixion pen that you can iron off the marks. Prior to that I used chalk lines. I liked the chalk lines because I could just brush the chalk off, but with the pens you can mark the whole quilt at one time with no worry about losing the lines until you are ready to have them gone.
Catharine Drevniok, Combermere, Ontario

22 Never use cinnamon as it will stain your quilt. I know this from experience.   *Diane Mickel, Woolwich Township, NJ*

23 I trace my pattern on Press'n Seal with a permanent Sharpie, (Press'n Seal is usually used in the kitchen) place the sticky side to my quilt, and quilt around it. Pull the Press'n Seal off when finished.   *Carole Wilder, Hastings, MN*

㉔ I try to avoid using anything that must be washed. I don't usually have any issue with this because I use the ribbon/pin method.
                    Deb Spencer, Greenwith, Australia

C. Achieving Accuracy When Marking Quilting Lines

❶ The best way to ensure accuracy while marking is to do it before layering the quilt top with the batting and backing. If you have to mark after the quilt is layered, some templates can be pinned to secure in place through the little registration holes.
                    Karen Martin, Breezy Point, MN

❷ Take breaks, because marking is tedious and demanding of the vision.   *Kevin Kern, Paradise Valley, NV*

❸ A good flat surface is necessary to lay out your quilt. Good lighting helps a lot. Don't drink a lot of coffee that day!
                    Lorraine Frederick, Perkasie, PA

❹ Have the quilt top on a surface large enough to allow the quilt to lay flat with none hanging over an edge. Secure top with tape like painters' removable tape so it does not shift/move during marking process. Use the same marking tools throughout the entire quilt.
                    Anna Osborn, Omaha, NE

❺ I tend to be somewhat relaxed in the placement of the quilting. I feel this gives the quilt a more natural appearance.
                    Nancy Koyanik, Troy, VA

❻ I try to plan a design that requires as little marking as possible. I use stencils with gridded lines to allow me to make free motion designs that are even-sized and correctly placed. If I am doing a design that requires complete accuracy, I use Golden Threads paper or Press-n-Seal and quilt through it. When using Golden Threads or Press-n-Seal, I make sure that I am using a washable marker because the machine can transfer the ink through the paper to the quilt top.   *Diane Linker, Scarsdale, NY*

❼ For crosshatching quilting, measure the size of the finished quilt block that you are working with. Make sure it can be divided evenly by a number (for example: a 10″ block can be divided by 5, so every line is 2″ apart, an 8″ block can be divided by 2 or 4, thus 4″ apart or 2″ apart). This gives a balanced appearance to the cross hatching. Then start in the center of the quilt, lay the quilt top flat on a table with the edges as square as possible. Work out from the center, using the blocks themselves as a guide to keep everything as straight as possible.   *Sandy Howell, Highland, UT*

❽ I like to use an Alvin drafting compass. It lets you do circles up to 24″ in diameter. It has a mechanical pencil which I love because you get a much thinner line, reducing error due to ever-widening pencil lines with standard pencils.

Rosemarie Garone, West Islip, NY

❾ For hand quilting only: in the main quilt area, I usually quilt in the ditch from seam to seam, so that's easy, but putting cross hatch or slanted lines on a plain border is sometimes difficult. I mark the middle of each border for reference and start at each corner, marking lines heading toward the middle. When you get to the center, adjust the lines to fit.   *Nora Manley, Athens, AL*

❿ Sharpen your chalk pencil often to keep a narrow dense line that is easier to see and more accurate; it can be hard to tell exactly where a thicker, softer line should be.   *Diane Bachman, Leola, PA*

⑪ Measure, measure, measure for things like cross hatching. I often cross hatch in widths that are the width of a ruler.

Most of the other quilting I do is echoing (as in Hawaiian quilts) where I eyeball a ¼" (or larger) space between echos. The quilting is so dense that small variations are not really noticeable.

Nancy Henry, Rochester, NH

> *I often cross hatch in widths that are the width of a ruler.*

⑫ Painter's tape works well for straight lines. Rather than trying to draw lines that are straight and evenly spaced, just sew along both sides of the tape. The tape provides proper spacing and is easily removed when you are finished.   *Denece Turner, Evans, GA*

⑬ I do two things before I mark the quilt: first, iron the top with starch so I won't get folds in the fabric and second, I place a fine sandpaper under the area I am marking. The sandpaper holds the area I want to mark and I am able to mark it lightly (and enough to be able to see with these eyes!).   *Deanna Davis, Dover, AR*

⑭ I like to use background fabrics that have a stripe to them; they require little marking as I can use the stripe as a guide for the quilting.   *Linda Gabrielse, Kentwood, MI*

⑮ I match my quilting lines to the blocks, not to any angle measurement. The eye will make it look right.

Kristi Wilson, Irving, TX

⑯ Ensure that vertical and horizontal lines are aligned with the top and edges of the quilt.   *Shirley Rouse, Havre de Grace, MD*

⑰ I spray a bit of basting spray to the side of the template to be laid onto the fabric. This is a big help to keep it from slipping.

Bobbie Haynes, Shepherdsville, KY

⑱ I match quilting lines up with seams and lines in the print of the fabric and really try to not stress too much. My quilting teacher taught me to enjoy quilting more (and possibly make some small mistakes) and obsess less.   *Krista Schwabe, Lakeland, FL*

⑲ If I'm using a stencil, I either pin or tape it in place since the stencil will move around as you are marking lines.

Catharine Drevniok, Combermere, Ontario

D. *Removing Marked Lines*

I use a special mixture of Clorox 2 and Ivory dish soap that has never let me down.

❶ I usually remove markings with a spritz of water, but if that does not work, I use a special mixture of Clorox 2 and Ivory dish soap that has never let me down.

Barbara Eisenrauch, Grasonville, MD

❷ I remove my marked lines with a toothbrush dipped in water after I quilt a section. Upon completion of my quilt, I wash the quilt in cold water with a gentle cycle. *Ellen Harris, Huntsville, AL*

❸ If you do freehand quilting, you don't need to worry about the marking lines needing to be removed!   *Barbara Johnson, Dallas, OR*

❹ Chalk I blow off with canned air, water soluble I mist with water, and I let pencil wear off.   *Colleen Potts, Pottsville, PA*

❺ Those blue or purple evaporating pens have to be soaked to come out of the finished quilt. The color does go away, but the pen mark stays and when the quilt gets warm for any reason, a brown stain will come back. When that happens, it doesn't go away.

Patti Goggio, Broadlands, VA

6 An artgum eraser is also good for removing pencil lines.
Marti Blankenship, Pleasant Valley, MO

7 I am able to erase the pencil marks with an eraser as long as I don't press too hard.   *Denise Rosbicki, South Prince George, VA*

8 I have a pet hair remover that I use to remove chalk marks. If I ever use any other marker, I soak the finished quilt overnight, then dry the quilt.   *Patti Goggio, Broadlands, VA*

9 I use Mark-Be-Gone, and spritz a little water on it when I'm finished.   *Victoria Page, Amarillo, TX*

10 Sew Clean, a product promoted by Pam Clarke, is the very best product to use for pencil marks, chalk, etc. It is made from oranges and is organic and safe. It doesn't leave any residue on the quilt. It works like a miracle. You wet a sponge and spray some Sew Clean on the sponge. No scrubbing is needed. If I am only removing a loose chalk, I will wipe it with a microfiber cloth first and only use the Sew Clean on any recalcitrant spots.
Diane Linker, Scarsdale, NY

11 I only use bottled distilled water to erase markings, not tap water. Tap water has too many minerals and could leave brown marks on light-colored fabrics   *Lorraine Frederick, Perkasie, PA*

12 I make two pads from white paper towels. One goes in my left hand beneath the quilt and one is dipped into water and then I dab at the quilt top until the marks disappear.
Patricia Grimm, New Windsor, NY

13 If I do use a marking pen, I use the kind that water erases. I use a sponge-topped bottle that is meant for sealing envelopes.
Ann Hay, Carlisle, PA

⓮ Do not mark the Golden Threads quilting paper with a regular graphite pencil. I have had the graphite transfer to polyester thread when quilting on the line and it is difficult to remove.

Georgia Pierce, Seattle, WA

> *Be careful about marking tools. Some of them will come off the quilt top easily enough but will stubbornly adhere to the glaze on the hand quilting thread.*

⓯ Be careful about marking tools. Some of them will come off the quilt top easily enough but will stubbornly adhere to the glaze on the hand quilting thread.

Diane Linker, Scarsdale, NY

⓰ Do not use colored chalk and then stitch over it with white thread. You will not be able to get the color of the chalk out of the thread easily.   *Amy Kentera, Highland Mills, NY*

⓱ I don't remove markings. I make sure the marks are light and sew right over them. That's how vintage quilts were made.

Rosemarie Garone, West Islip, NY

E. Consideration for Machine Quilting Lines

❶ I like to take some element from the quilt and then duplicate it in the quilting pattern. I use a long arm machine to quilt with, so I am usually not marking the quilt but using a laser guide to quilt with, or free handing it.   *Sandy Howell, Highland, UT*

2 If quilting on a domestic machine without a stitch regulator, it is easier for most to quilt straight lines rather than curved lines, although with practice, lovely rounded patterns can be achieved.

Barbara Gentner, West Seneca, NY

3 The thin tissue paper, Golden Threads, that you can transfer quilting designs onto works well for machine quilting applications. It tears away easily and allows you to copy a design accurately without marking up the actual quilt.   *Jan Mast, Lancaster, PA*

4 I have taught machine quilting, and have machine quilted for many years. I find that once quilters are confident, they need to mark less. Unless you are making a quilt to be judged, a little bump here or there, to me, is worth not having to mark the quilt.

Sally Eshelman, York, PA

5 I have an embroidery feature with my Bernina 830, and I can choose to use the designs in my library (which is extensive), or I choose from a book of continuous line quilting designs.

Deborah Gross, Willow Grove, PA

6 Sometimes I use a small cookie cutter and trace with a Frixion pen. Sometimes I go free hand. I try to match the quilting with the theme of the quilt.   *J. Duda, East Amherst, NY*

7 I try to use continuous stitching designs in machine quilting.

Jan Mast, Lancaster, PA

8 I use straight lines when I machine quilt. In the ditch mostly.

Janet Olmstead, Calgary, Alberta

9 As I am now a confident machine quilter, I try to mark as little as possible, because a neat flowing machine stitch line looks much nicer than one that's forced by trying to keep on the marked line.

Ellen Boes-Smit, The Hague, Netherlands

❿ If a stencil is not a continuous design, I try to redraw it so that I can quilt in continuous lines without stopping.

Annemarie (Nancy) Poorbaugh, Montgomery, AL

⓫ I hate marking, so I try to use seam lines and edge of presser foot as a quilting pattern guide.   *Joanne Scott, Peotone, IL*

⓬ If I have a really good backing fabric with an interesting, easy to follow design that complements the front, I quilt it from the back.

Dorothy T. Harrison, Snow Hill, NC

⓭ I only do cross-hatching on a small quilt. I use the bar on the walking foot to measure where the next row goes. I do not mark the quilt top.   *Barbara Augustine, Woodbridge, VA*

⓮ Less is more. Just mark the spines of feathers for instance, and let the brain and machine do the rest. I especially like the stencils that just grid the area and go from there.

Mary Beth Schrader, Cameron, MO

⓯ I rarely mark for machine quilting because meandering is my first choice. If I am doing feathers, I mark key spots I need to hit.

Nancy Chase, Columbus, MT

CHAPTER 6

Cutting Fabric

A. Cutting Fabric Efficiently and Accurately

❶ If you have washed your fabric, do a light spritz with Mary Ellen's Best Press and iron it. The fabric will have a bit more body and be more stable for cutting. Like a carpenter: measure twice and cut once! *Eileen D. Wenger, Lancaster, PA*

❷ Do not cut all the fabric at one time for a complete quilt. Make a test block first. You may hate the block or find an error. Better to test first, cut once. *Shelia Smith, Goldthwaite, TX*

❸ Cut all the pieces from one fabric at a time in the order the fabrics are listed in the pattern. Always cut the larger pieces out first, then do the smaller ones.   *Denece Turner, Evans, GA*

❹ I tend to check the pieces I need, and sketch out a cutting diagram to make sure I can cut all the pieces I need from the least amount of fabric. Then it's off to the self-healing cutting board and the rotary cutter. If the fabric is not cut precisely, the rest of the project is in trouble.   *Barbara Falkner, Wellard, WA*

❺ If I'm working with a large amount of fabric, say for borders, and I know I have plenty of what I need, I'll rip it by hand with about 2" extra, press it again, then fold it up to cut. It's a lot easier than trying to fold the entire width selvage to selvage and trying to cut accurately.   *Patricia Grimm, New Windsor, NY*

Keep a pad of Post-Its nearby to mark your pieces as you cut them. Any interruption, phone, doorbell, etc., will test your memory any number of ways.

❻ Keep a pad of Post-Its nearby to mark your pieces as you cut them. Any interruption, phone, doorbell, etc., will test your memory any number of ways.   *Barbara Miller, Flushing, MI*

❼ I use templates for cutting fabric for most of my quilts. However, I have also taken advantage of the services of a laser cutting service, which was amazing. I have also used dies for cutting curved quilting pieces.   *Kathy McEnearney, McLean, VA*

❽ AccuQuilt GO! is the most efficient way to cut. You can spend 54 minutes of every hour sewing instead of cutting with an AccuQuilt system. In addition to being quick, it's accurate, easy on hands and joints, and can cut multiple layers of fabric at the same time.   *Debbie Henry, Lucinda, PA*

❾ When fussy cutting to get a particular design on the fabric where I want it in the block, I make a picture frame the size I need for the project. I use that to line up the portion of the design on the fabric that I want to cut around. The picture frame is usually cardboard from a cereal box: cheap, easy to cut out, and it starts as a rectangular shape. *Peggy Schaff, Vadnais Heights, MN*

❿ If you have difficulty seeing the one-eighth or other lines for correct cutting, place a strip of masking tape along the line on the ruler that is the correct size for your cutting requirements. It's easier to see, which makes the cutting more accurate and faster.

H. Gail Schwier, Kingston, Ontario

⓫ If I am really having to skimp in piecing, I have even sewed together two scraps and cut out the shape from that. I think it's charming to find pieced shapes in antique quilts.

Ann Lineberger, Allentown, PA

⓬ I am right-handed, so I start with my fabric as far to the right as it will go on my cutting mat. That way I can pick up my cut pieces or strips and continue cutting without having to move the fabric on the cutting mat. *Mardelle Tanner, Sodus, NY*

⓭ I always fold my washed fabric selvage to selvage, then line the ruler up on the single fold at the bottom and line it up on the right hand side to trim the edge. Then I turn my cutting mat 180° to cut from the left hand side so I don't disturb the fabric. After three strip cuts, I check to make sure the end is squaring with the bottom fold, and if not, I turn the mat again to trim the edge just enough.

Karla Santoro, Stanley, NY

⓮ For squares, I went to a stainless steel manufacturer and got them to make me steel squares in sizes from 2″ up to 12″, including the ½″ sizes. This means I can cut squares in almost any size quickly and easily.

Charlotte Cameron, Christchurch, New Zealand

⑮ If it's a big print, notice where you are placing the ruler. If possible, you don't want to have, say, a bird's tail in the middle of a block and the rest of him missing! If you have a directional pattern, be sure you are cutting pieces so they will look right when your block is pieced together.   *Gail Hosmer, Westminster, MD*

⑯ I cut multiple layers at one time. Usually a minimum of four layers, sometimes more. I teach beginning quilters and strongly encourage them to cut two layers at one time. It's a great time saver, and they're always pleased at how easy it can be.

H. Gail Schwier, Kingston, Ontario

⑰ For strip cutting, the June Tailor Shape Cutter Pro ruler is wonderful. There's probably less waste with this method of cutting of fabric than there is, say, with Accuquilt or Sizzix strip-cutting dies. It may be a toss up with the die strip-cutting method as regards time.

The die methods win, hands down, if you are cutting shapes for appliqué. An alternative to the dies worthy of consideration for appliqué and for pieced block quilts is the Inklingo system of printing shapes on fabric using an inkjet printer that can then be cut very efficiently with your rotary cutter.

When all else is exhausted, an 8 × 24" ruler and a rotary cutter with a sharp blade can work wonders, and so can your scissors, if it comes to that.   *Fran Hill, Oakland, CA*

⑱ To keep templates from slipping and sliding when you are using them, attach a product called Invisigrip to the back or flat little rubber or sand paper dots.

Annemarie (Nancy) Poorbaugh, Montgomery, AL

⑲ If I'm cutting multiple strips, I use one of the June Tailor slotted rulers; I can make multiple cuts without moving the fabric or ruler.

Sally Zimmer, Bark River, MI

⑳ I use a dry erase board and write the size of the piece I am cutting so there are no mistakes.   *Elizabeth Merkle, Levittown, PA*

㉑ Often when starting to cut fabric for a large quilt, the thought comes to mind, "Oh, what if I cut wrong?" So I tell myself, something will work out!   *Eileen D. Wenger, Lancaster, PA*

㉒ I cut the largest pieces first, working down to the smaller pieces. I like to have a very sharp rotary cutter and layer up to six layers.   *Karen Martin, Breezy Point, MN*

㉓ I don't always follow the pattern cutting directions, because many times they are not efficiently using the fabric. For example, a pattern may have you cut a 6½" strip and then just cut one 6½" square from it. Then it will have you cut an 8½" strip only to cut one 8½" square from it. With a little forethought, you could just cut one 8½" strip and cut both squares from it.

Sue Hurley, Princeton, NJ

I don't always follow the pattern cutting directions, because many times they are not efficiently using the fabric.

㉔ Scrutinize your pattern to make sure the instructions are clear and without mistakes. Make a dry run of the block to see if the math provided is correct because printed patterns do have mistakes.   *Joanne Picicci, Spokane, WA*

㉕ If I need several cuts of the same size (e.g., 50 2½" squares), I first cut strips 2½" wide, stack those strips, and then turn my ruler around so I can cut 2½" increments by just moving the ruler—not the fabric. I slide my ruler along the length of my strip so that when I'm finished, I have cut all fabric into 2½" squares. This will work with any size shape you need—just use a calculator to help you with the math.   *Erin Crank, Independence, MO*

㉖ I like to have my cutting surface lower than most people. Like kneading bread dough, it helps to be able to get your shoulders into the work. It's tiring cutting when your arms are too high.

Beth Miller, Arena, WI

27 I use at least 100 different fabrics in each quilt I make. I like to cut fat quarters and half-yard cuts completely the first time, so I don't have to re-fold and handle the fabric later. Like this:

- 1″ strips can sometimes be cut from what you would ordinarily throw away as unusable. These 1″ strips can be used in miniature quilts and small block quilts.
- 1¼″ strips for Log Cabin blocks
- 1½″ strips for 9 Patches, Pineapple Log Cabin, and various other quilt units
- 2″ strips for 4 patches and miscellaneous
- 2½″ strips for Half Square Triangles (HSTs) and various other quilt units
- 3″ strips and squares for Hourglass, HSTs and various other units
- 3½″ strips for various units
- 4″ squares
- 5″ squares
- I cut selvages off to be used in making hand bags, etc.
- I pick out any fabric that would be good for appliquéd leaves and flowers and store them together in my appliqué bin.

Nora Manley, Athens, AL

28 Give yourself enough room to cut with precision. If you have a large piece of fabric and a small cutting area, try cutting it somewhere else. The kitchen table is a nice alternative.

Patti Gorman, Kingston, MA

I took a foldable banquet table and put it up on the plastic bed risers that you can purchase at Target or Walmart. My own cutting table, for cheap!

29 I like to stand up while cutting my fabric. Finding a table the right height can be a problem, and cutting tables are expensive. However, I took a foldable banquet table and put it up on the plastic bed risers that you can purchase at Target or Walmart. These are the same bed risers that college students use to have a bed up for more storage. My own cutting table, for cheap! *Shannon Gittermann, Bartlett, TN*

30 I'm not an efficient cutter, but I use scraps for other projects.

Patricia Mason, Virginia Beach, VA

31 A large, flat smooth surface is the best for cutting. I love my ping pong tabletop on top of the billiards table.

Sandra Pavletich, Oakville, MO

32 I keep all project cuts on a flat cardboard take-out tray after the cut so I can carry the strips or pieces to my sewing area from my cutting area. Sometimes I use the tray to carry the pieces to my ironing station. Everything stays organized by size and color. There is also the bonus of being able to see the unfinished pieces disappear as I sew the project together.   *Jo Yawn, Jonesboro, AR*

33 This is just my way, but I find it boring to sew or chain piece all units for a block. That means I cut out a few blocks to construct at a time. I don't get the satisfaction of seeing all the blocks come together at once, but I enjoy my time constructing each block a little at a time and seeing progress little by little and enjoying the process more.   *Sarah Francis, Greenville, TX*

34 If I have something tedious to do, like squaring up triangles, I try to save the task to take along to a sew-in. Things like that are more fun when you are doing them with friends.

Karen Martin, Breezy Point, MN

B. Using Bias and Straight of Grain

1 There are 3 directions to fabric: the lengthwise or straight of grain (follows the selvage edge), the crosswise grain (90° angle to the selvage edge), and the bias (45° angle to the selvage edge). The lengthwise has the least stretch, the crosswise a little stretch, and the bias a lot of stretch.

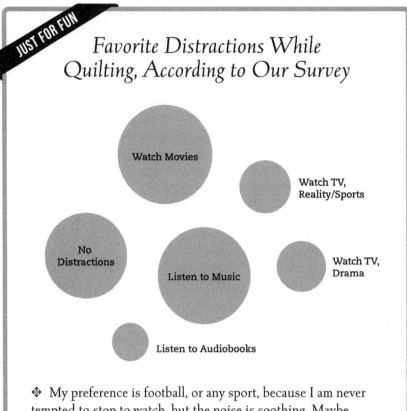

Favorite Distractions While Quilting, According to Our Survey

Watch Movies

Watch TV, Reality/Sports

No Distractions

Listen to Music

Watch TV, Drama

Listen to Audiobooks

❖ My preference is football, or any sport, because I am never tempted to stop to watch, but the noise is soothing. Maybe because I grew up with 4 brothers and a dad who all loved sports.

Barbara Miller, Flushing, MI

I use the lengthwise and crosswise grain for most projects. During quilt construction, however, a piece may be cut such that you end up having to sew on the bias. A good example of this is half-square triangles and Flying Geese. There are ways to make these without fearing the stretch. The bias cut is commonly used when making binding. Curves in the quilt edge (like a scallop border) would indicate use of a bias cut binding.

Anna Osborn, Omaha, NE

② There are three grains to every woven fabric: the straight grain consists of warp and weft. The warp is the threads that were on the loom before the weaving began. They are the long threads that run the length of the fabric parallel to the selvage. The warp does not stretch. The weft threads are the ones that are woven in and out of the warp. They go across the fabric and wrap around the edges to create the selvage; they will stretch very little. The bias is the 45° diagonal to warp and weft, and it is very stretchy.

Diane Bachman, Leola, PA

③ When I sewed clothes, years ago, I was taught to pull a thread to find the straight of grain. I still do that if I can't readily see it in the weave. To do this, make a small clip near the end on the selvage. Fray a few strands, then pull one slowly and carefully. When I want bias cuts, I use the 45° line on my cutting guide. I align it with the straight of grain of the fabric, then make my cuts.

Miki Willa, Renton, WA

④ Sometimes the design is printed on the surface of the fabric and it is a geometric design and it does not line up with the grain of the fabric. You will need to make an executive decision about going with the grain or going with the design on the surface of the fabric.

Deborah Vivrette, Hidden Valley Lake, CA

⑤ Grain line is important even in small pieces because they can twist when the quilt is washed. The grain is important because an off-grain patch will fray and pull apart easier than one that is on grain.

Laroletta Petty, Breckenridge, CO

⑥ Depending on the use of the bias-cut material, you may also want to use some fusible interfacing to keep it from stretching.

Jo Anne Kani-Miller, Kissimmee, FL

⑦ If you are cutting triangles, try to have two edges on the straight of grain. Look at how your blocks go together and avoid having two bias edges to sew together. One straight of grain will stabilize the bias of the other.

Nancy Henry, Rochester, NH

8 If you're going to work with a lot of bias, heavily starch your fabric. Instead of pinning, use double-sided tape. It will help prevent the stretching that usually occurs with sewing on the bias.

Ruth Anglin, Tijeras, NM

9 If making half square triangles, I use squares as a base, (slightly larger than the intended triangle, the finished size of the square of two triangles sewn together plus ⅞"). I draw a line diagonally through the square, then sew ¼" on either side of the line. I cut along the drawn line to produce two triangles with stitching that stabilizes the bias edges.   *Barbara Falkner, Wellard, WA*

10 I never cut fabric lengthwise, not even for borders, as most of the experts recommend. It has no "give" and will not hang correctly.

Nora Manley, Athens, AL

11 Always cut your outside borders on the length of grain of your fabric, even if you have to buy an extra half yard of fabric. Your quilt will be so much better because the borders do not stretch and stand up and wave at you. Very few designers will tell you this in their patterns: they must not quilt their own quilts. Wavy borders are the biggest problem for your long arm quilter. Ugh!

Carole Wilder, Hastings, MN

I use spray starch when necessary to stabilize bias edges.

12 I use the Shape Cut Pro to cut strips or squares and even use it on the bias as it holds the fabric securely and avoids stretching the bias edges. I use spray starch when necessary to stabilize bias edges.   *Doris Gould, Johnstown, NY*

13 Some time ago I found an easy way to cut bias binding. Open fabric flat, selvages top/bottom with no folds. Fold bottom selvage up to cut-side to form a 45° angle. Rotate fabric so fold is now on your left and fold up on top of the 1st fold. Finally fold down, leaving a triangle over-lapping the bottom. Cut off the left fold which should be a thin strip. You can now cut your binding in strips whatever width you want and you will only be left with a triangle on the right as waste. Sounds way more complicated than it is—once you have done it, it is a snap!   *Brenda Seth, Waterford, PA*

c. Rotary Cutting

❶ Three standard sizes of rotary cutters are 28mm, 45mm, and 60mm. I would recommend having at least one of each. The 28mm is the smallest and is great for making small cuts or using in tight areas. The 45mm will be the most used. It's able to make most cuts you will need to make. The 60mm is good for cutting through multiple layers of fabric, like in a Stack-n-Whack type pattern. I also use the 60mm when trimming the quilt sandwich after it has been quilted.   *Anna Osborn, Omaha, NE*

❷ Always cut away from your body with the cutter in your dominant hand and the ruler to the opposite side. If you're right handed, position the fabric to your right and the ruler to the left so you can work left to right, making continuous cuts without needing to reposition the fabric.   *Jan Mast, Lancaster, PA*

❸ When I am cutting, I always walk my hand down the ruler so the ruler doesn't move.   *Karen Nick, Lutz, FL*

❹ I angle the cutter toward the ruler a bit. I try to keep the cutting pressure on the fabric, not on the ruler.
    Jenifer Aragon, Bloomington, CA

❺ When you're starting a long cut, cut 1″ towards yourself with the rotary cutter, then proceed away from yourself to the finish. This helps prevent pushing the fabric and having it shift.
    Eileen D. Wenger, Lancaster, PA

6 There are small ridges along the top edge of all rotary cutters with which I'm familiar. This is meant for your "peter pointer" finger to help add leverage strength when cutting fabrics.

H. Gail Schwier, Kingston, Ontario

> *Position a ruler over the piece you want to keep. If the rotary cutter strays, it will stray into the excess and not your piece.*

7 Position a ruler over the piece you want to keep. If the rotary cutter strays, it will stray into the excess and not your piece.

Karen Renninger, Punta Gorda, FL

8 Buy the largest cutting mat you have space for. I love my 30 × 58" mat because it gives me enough room to cut width-of-fabric strips from even the widest fabrics.

Linda Jedlicka, Freeland, WA

9 A rotating mat is my biggest helper. I am not a great cutter—awkward is a better description—but the rotating mat allows me so much more flexibility.   *Brenda Seth, Waterford, PA*

10 I use the *blank*, not *ruled* side of the cutting mat. Therefore, the ruler lines are creating the measurement.

Barbara Hutton, Carolina Shores, NC

11 Your cutting mat shouldn't be too worn. A good quality mat with no wear works wonders. Sometimes I think the blade is dull, when actually the mat is worn.   *Joan Norfolk, Kilmore, Australia*

12 Cutting with a dull blade makes me press down harder to make my cuts, leading to strain on my wrists, arms, and shoulders. I like to break out a new blade when I start a new project. I love the way a really sharp blade slices through the fabric, and it leads to less stress on my wrist and arm.   *Rosemarie Garone, West Islip, NY*

13 If you feel like you are pressing down too hard, or there is a skipped part that you have to go back over, you need to change your blade. You will be amazed how much easier it is to cut.

Lori Fitzpatrick, Havertown, PA

14 Get into the habit of closing and locking the blade every time you put the rotary cutter down, especially if you have children or pets. Someone mentioned that rotary cutters might look like popsicles to a child.

Rosemarie Garone, West Islip, NY

15 After teaching sewing classes in our local high school for many years, my main comment on rotary cutters is to *never lay a cutter down with the blade exposed.* Stand while you cut so you'll have more control of the ruler/ straight edge, and always cut away from yourself to keep from giving yourself another belly button.

Nancy Swanwick, Fort Scott, KS

16 Always use a sharp blade. A dull blade slows down cutting and is harder work for your hands. We only get one set of hands. There are plenty of blades for sale. Take care of your hands!

Virginia Bissen, Rose Creek, MN

17 To remind me to lock the rotary cutter, I wear a hair scrunchy on my wrist. When I wear it on my wrist, the ruler

---

JUST FOR FUN

Some of Your Favorite Movies to Quilt to, According to Our Survey

- Pride and Prejudice
- Gone With the Wind
- Pretty Woman
- Mamma Mia
- The Sound of Music
- How to Make an American Quilt
- Sleepless in Seattle
- Steel Magnolias
- You've Got Mail
- Singing in the Rain
- An Affair to Remember
- Doctor Zhivago
- Sense and Sensibility
- Fried Green Tomatoes
- Notting Hill
- McLintock!
- The Wizard of Oz

❖ Pride and Prejudice—the Colin Firth version, of course! I know the dialogue so well that I don't need to keep my eyes on the TV, hence the sewing and/or quilting will actually be completed.

H. Gail Schwier, Kingston, Ontario

should be in my hand. When not, the scrunchy should be around the cutter.

Peggy Schaff, Vadnais Heights, MN

18 Always put a pair of closed-toe shoes on before using your rotary cutter. This can save a trip to the ER or urgent care if your cutter slips out of your hand and lands on your foot.

Erin Crank, Independence, MO

19 Keep blades separate for cutting paper (such as foundation piecing and crafts) and fabric.

Louise Lott, Healesville, Australia

20 Make sure you only have *one* blade in the cutter— the blades like to stick together when I change them, and two blades cutting make a mess!

Sheila Beins, Seward, NE

21 The rulers I use are all outfitted with slide-resistant circles on the bottom, as well as a finger guard. I did have one serious mishap with my fingers and a rotary cutter early on and that was enough.

Susan Chandler, Solon Springs, WI

22 Always use a sharp blade. I bought an electric blade sharpener for this reason. I also take my cutter apart frequently and clean it with a soft cloth or brush. Sometimes I put a tiny dab of silicone or sewing machine oil on the blade.

Emily Galea, Boca Raton, FL

> *When the blade is just a little dull, run the blade through fine grit sandpaper or aluminum foil several times.*

23 Sometimes when the blade is just a little dull, I will run the blade through fine grit sandpaper or aluminum foil several times. Just cut through it like you would fabric.

Betty Charlebois, Brownfield, TX

24 I usually write on the blade with a permanent marker the date the blade was changed.

Barbara Hill, Huntsville, AL

25 I use a Klutz glove to change my blades. I also use a pencil box when I bring it to class or a workshop along with extra blades. I've seen and heard of way too many accidents. *Susan Walters, Newark, DE*

26 Keep the package instructions when you buy a rotary cutter so that you will recognize all the pieces and can take it apart and put it back together, as well as adjust the tightness of the blade as you use it. *Laurie Eason, Voorhees, NJ*

27 I use a type of rotary cutter that does not expose its blade until pressure is exerted, and then the blade automatically retracts when done. *Helenruth Schuette, Bemidji, MN*

28 I'm left handed and my favorite rotary cutter is Martelli's. It keeps my hand and wrist in proper alignment. *Cathie Shelton, Montgomery Village, MD*

29 I love my Olfa that can be used easily by left and right handers by just sliding a lever back as I teach people to sew and am a leftie. *Robyn Waite, Cherrybrook, Australia*

30 Dressmaker weights work well to anchor and support fabric on the cutting mat. The edge along which you cut must be stable. I find a draftsman t-square the best tool for stable rotary cutting. *Sharon Mountford, Canoga Park, CA*

31 Since my hands shake a lot from Parkinsons Disease, I was afraid to use rotary cutters until I got a "Shape Cut" guide, which has slits in ½" increments on a heavy plastic square of about 15". It does a great job of controlling the rotary cutters. *Netta Pyron, Rolla, MO*

32 I like using my wavy-edge (pinking) rotary cutter. If I cut my blocks with it, they do not ravel, which is good since I handle them a lot while I am appliquéing them. *Karen Nick, Lutz, FL*

D. Cutting Rulers

❶ I have loads of rulers, from my 1 × 6" ruler with the ¼" lip that I use to get an exact ¼" seam for paper piecing, up to the longest ruler that fits completely across the width of my cutting table. If I need to cut several seam allowances, I put a strip of painters' tape to the ruler to mark the cutting width; it's easy to see since painter's tape comes in colors and doesn't leave any residue on the ruler.

I also have a collection of different sized squares from 4" to 12" I find being able to use the best length, width or square shortens my cutting time. I think these rulers are a good investment, like good scissors.   *Marion Eggers, Winter Park, FL*

❷ I do have a favorite size of ruler—the 6" by 12". It is quite versatile. If I were permitted only one ruler, that would be it.
Gloria Clark, Wayne, PA

❸ I like the 8½" Creative Grid for cutting strips. It is easy for me to see the lines and I like the extra 2" width for more options. Another favorite ruler is Deb Tucker's Tucker Trimmer for cutting squares accurately.   *Annie Morgan, Johnson, VT*

> *I use the smallest ruler possible to get the size patch I need. Smaller rulers are usually easier to manage so there are fewer mistakes or slips when cutting.*

❹ Mostly I'll use Creative Grid rulers. They have gripper dots on the underside to prevent slippage, thin black lines, and are very accurate. If a fabric is very dark, I'll use the Omnigrid ruler because the yellow lines are more visible.   *Eileen D. Wenger, Lancaster, PA*

❺ I use the smallest ruler possible to get the size patch I need. Smaller rulers are usually easier to manage so there are fewer mistakes or slips when cutting.   *Jennifer Padden, Austin, TX*

❻ Woodcraft, a store that my carpenter husband shops at, has a heavy, very accurate ruler that does not shift easily on fabric. The weight helps to hold it down. On one side the center mark is O and I can center that O on a motif that I want in the middle of a quilt piece. I then mark and cut.

Nancy Powell, Coatesville, PA

7 I use the June Tailor Shape Cut Pro, Shape Cut Plus, and Exact Eighths often when cutting lots of pieces of the same size. I hate cutting something 3⅞". With the Exact Eighths ruler, cutting is a breeze.

Frances Courson, Maryville, TN

8 If my ruler is not an Omnigrip, then I put the little sandpaper discs on it. Those seem to work the best for me. I have tried Invisigrip and the silicone circles and was not impressed.

Marti Walkup Rajotte, Mount Juliet, TN

9 My first ruler was 3 × 18. I don't use it very often anymore. I like my 6 × 24 for cutting strips, and I have a 9½" and 14½" square which I could not live without. I use them for squaring up blocks and corners. Invaluable.

Olivia Kuebler, Kansas City, MO

10 I love the green line Birch Craft Rulers. It doesn't matter what fabric it is on I can always see the line to cut. The line looks like it is fluorescent. My favorite one is my 6½ × 12".

Deb Williams, Burra, Australia

11 I use Salem rulers. They're sturdy and relatively straightforward without a lot of distracting lines that I normally don't need!

Amanda Kei Andrews, Vero Beach, FL

12 I use a draftsman T-square which has a notch which just fits over the edge of the mat and grips the right end while I apply pressure to the left end. I use no special rulers and have never found the need for any.

Sharon Mountford, Canoga Park, CA

13 I like the ones that have the lines laser-cut in them. They do not wear off. My favorite company, Rob's Rulers, is no longer in business because of a hurricane. I'm hoping that when I need some new rulers, someone else will start manufacturing them again. They were green, easy to read, and the company would engrave your name on them if you ordered directly. No more lost rulers at quilting retreats!   *Carole Wilder, Hastings, MN*

If I could have only one ruler, I would use a 12½" square ruler. It is especially valuable for squaring blocks.

⑭ If I could have only one ruler, I would use a 12½" square ruler. It is especially valuable for squaring blocks.

Gail Hurn, Highland Haven, TX

⑮ I use Eleanor Burns' rulers because they are easy to understand. Basically all her rulers have the same principle of the 45° angle and the instructions, if you should lose them, are on her website.

Kellie Hewitt, Marion, VA

⑯ I make lots of small reproduction quilts and *love* the yellow Omnigrid rulers that are marked in ⅛" increments. I also prefer to use shorter rulers, even for width-of-fabric cuts, because I can control them better.   *Jo Ann Disbro, Dillsboro, IN*

⑰ I love Quilter's Rule rulers of any kind or shape. They have deep ridges that nestle into the fabric and don't slip. The one I use the most is the 6½ × 24".   *Pat Smith, Sidney, NY*

⑱ I have a 5" square which I use as a template to quickly cut leftover fabric into charm squares. I make layer cakes from my stash with a 10½" ruler, especially if I am going to make a stack-and-whack quilt. It's much easier and more accurate to trim down several at a time to 10" rather than lining up those already cut at 10".

Nancee McCann, Wilmington, DE

⑲ There are several products to apply to the ruler to reduce slippage, but what works best for me is piece of rubbery shelf liner. It serves the same purpose, is dirt cheap and what I like best —is not permanent. Using something designed for non-slippage reduces the need to press so hard to stabilize the fabric. As a retired physical therapist assistant, I also suggest using body weight through your palm flat on the ruler. That's a far better alternative to the traditional spread hand, fingers only pressing on the ruler. Palm flat is far less stressful to the wimpy hand muscles.

Nancee McCann, Wilmington, DE

20 I use the Easy Angle and Companion Angle rulers for cutting triangles. I took classes from Bonnie Hunter and like her method of cutting triangles using these rulers.   *Janet Bland, Smyrna, GA*

21 I have the Lazy Geese x 4 ruler that I love to use to make Flying Geese super easy! I make 4 at a time which saves time, plus there's no bias sewing.   *Amy Mayo, Havre de Grace, MD*

22 I love the Gypsy Gripper on the rulers I use to cut strips and smaller shapes with my rotary cutters. The smallest size is especially helpful when cutting fabric using plastic templates.

Linda Jedlicka, Freeland, WA

23 I use the Alto cutting system because I have arthritis in my hands. It helps me keep the ruler straight and it doesn't move.

Sherrie Mazzocchi, Annandale, NJ

24 Currently, I'm using the Martelli system. One ruler has ½" cuts across the entire ruler. You put your cutter into a slot and cut. It makes perfect cuts every time.   *Melanie Truesdale, Russellville, TN*

25 If I'm cutting large pieces of fabric across the grain, I'll use my 8½ × 24" ruler, as it neatly fits across the fabric. If you have to use more than one ruler to make a single cut, either one can shift or slip a bit. For smaller cutting jobs or subcutting the large width-of-fabric strips, I always use my 6 × 12" ruler. This one seems to be the most useful and is less cumbersome to use than many others.

H. Gail Schwier, Kingston, Ontario

26 I always use the same brand of rulers (Omnigrid) for my quilt projects. This guarantees the measurements are all the same.

Annette Crain, Spanish Fork, UT

27 I love the Olfa frosted rulers because they are easy to read on both light and dark fabrics. With the frosted back, they do not slip, and they stay flat rather than wobbly if you add non-skid items to the back.   *Patricia Boyle, Bedford, TX*

28 I enjoy the Log Cabin ruler set; it takes all the guesswork out of lengths, and I can cut the whole quilt top with just one ruler.   *Diane Bachman, Leola, PA*

29 I have found a Sullivan's "The Cutting Edge" clear ruler. The measurements are clear, and the bonus is the rotary cutter blade can be sharpened whilst you are cutting because of the abrasive edge on one side.   *Barbara Falkner, Wellard, WA*

E. Selvages

Remember to cut off the selvages before you cut. The weave on that portion of the fabric is different than the rest so it won't behave the way the rest of the fabric will.

1 Remember to cut off the selvages before you cut. The reason you do this is because the weave on that portion of the fabric is different than the rest so it won't behave the way the rest of the fabric will. You can save the selvage in case you need to know what you bought. Or you can use them to tie up various bundles, or you can take them fabric shopping with you to choose harmonizing colors with the dots on your selvage.

E. Anne Hendrickson, Toledo, OR

2 I always like to cut off the selvage before cutting out pieces. There is the temptation to creep into the selvage as I cut pieces, and the thicker edge could make a difference to your quilt.   *Barbara Falkner, Wellard, WA*

❸ Keep the selvages after you remove them. There are some nice patterns for strip piecing using these selvages.

Nancy Miller, Sun Lakes, AZ

❹ I usually cut the edge off that has the name of the fabric and manufacturer and keep that until I am done with the quilt. That way if I need more fabric, I know what I used and can look for it at the quilt store or online. I also use these strips to tie up my garden plants, like tomato plants, when they start to fall to the ground. I pound a stick in the ground and tie the plant with the strips. They are environmentally safe, and after I am done with them, the birds like to pick them up and use for their nests.

Judy McLeod, Alexandria, MN

❺ I like to cut off the selvages, plus ½". I save them, roll them into a ball, and use the selvages to tie up items, plants, fabric bundles, etc.   *Nannette Konstant, Flourtown, PA*

F. *What To Do With Scraps*

❶ I keep 4½" squares and matching 2½" squares cut from scrap fabric. It makes it easy to throw together a scrap star whenever I need a fast gift.   *Kathryn Wright, Gales Ferry, CT*

❷ I think before I cut. I don't leave much space, if any, between pieces. And after I've cut everything for one project, I save the fabric for something else. I don't throw much away, and the scraps I can't sew with, I use for starting a line of chain piecing or testing seam width or stitches.   *Gail Hosmer, Westminster, MD*

❸ I collect small pieces and cut them into three sizes per Joan Ford's book of using scraps. She sorts them into three sizes: 5", 3½" and 2" pieces. All of her patterns use these sizes of blocks. It takes time to sort the different categories, but I am well on my way to having enough to make a quilt.

Very small pieces are sorted for a friend who uses them to stuff dog beds for the local animal shelter. Nothing is wasted!

Margaret (Peg) Parsons, New Castle, DE

❹ Sometimes we end up with just a narrow strip of fabric. Find yourself a nice Log Cabin quilt pattern. Cut those narrow strips into the width needed for the Log Cabin quilt (i.e. 1½"). Of course the lengths will vary. Put them in a box marked "Save for Log Cabin Quilt". If you do a lot of quilting, in no time you will be well on your way to making a Log Cabin quilt with a lot of cutting already done. *Virginia Bissen, Rose Creek, MN*

❺ I love string quilts for using up scraps.

Lucy Esposito, Granbury, TX

❻ I save leftover binding strips to make a scrappy binding for a scrappy quilt or use to tie up pretty packages.

Brenda Rice, Nicholasville, KY

❼ Place a container near your work area for fabric scraps. Save them—if you don't use scraps, give them to a quilting buddy.

Linda Ahn, Mohrsville, PA

❽ The threads and cut off ends and any small pieces that I don't believe I can work into a scrappy quilt somewhere, I use to stuff pillows, or I may throw them outside for the birds to use for nests.

Kellie Hewitt, Marion, VA

CHAPTER 7

Piecing

A. Accurate, Efficient Piecing

❶ Accuracy and consistency are the key to successful piecing. You want each block to be able to match in size. Almost all quilt patterns call for ¼" seam allowances. To check to see if your seam allowances are accurate, you can do a test. For example, you want to make a 6" finished Four Patch block. Cut four 3½" squares and sew two of them together, using a ¼" seam allowance and the same thread you plan to use to make all blocks in your quilt. Press the seam over to one side and measure those two pieces. They should measure 3½ × 6½". If your measurements are smaller or larger, adjust your needle position and re-sew until you have an accurate measurement. If your machine doesn't have the capability to adjust positions, you can lay a small ruler underneath your sewing foot and manually bring down your needle to the ¼" line. Then place a piece of painter's tape next to the edge of your ruler to give you a guideline. *Francis Stanley, Slidell, LA*

❷ Use a "leader" and a "follower" so you never have to pick up the presser foot. Start with the leader fabric (a small scrap about ½ × 1½") and then proceed to sew your seams. At the end of the seam, just sew off onto the follower fabric, which becomes the leader for the next seam. This is to make sure that the bobbin thread does not pull the seam down into the machine or cause a wad of thread to appear on the back of the seam.   *Mary Heidemann, Daykin, NE*

❸ An important step if you're machine piecing is to put a light to the right of your needle instead of the left. This eliminates the shadow that can throw off your ¼"!   *Ruth Anglin, Tijeras, NM*

❹ I find that folding pieces in half and creasing the centers for alignment has greatly helped in the accuracy of my piecing.
Janet Bland, Smyrna, GA

❺ If I'm using a lighter weight fabric line along with a heavier fabric, I may use some light interfacing in order to keep the lighter one from stretching while sewing. Starch is another alternative.
Kathie Wilson, Camarillo, CA

❻ I love to work with small pieces. I will cut them larger, sew them, and then trim them to a small, perfect size.
Barbara Clarke, Woodbridge, CA

❼ It never hurts to make some extra blocks, whether as practice blocks or as extras to audition in a quilt design. These are fun to incorporate into the quilt backing or to use as a signature block on the back. They can also be the starting point for matching pillows.
Jan Mast, Lancaster, PA

❽ Make a sample block first. Even after many, many years of quilting, I still do that. Sometimes I will use the fabric from the quilt I'm making, but most often I will use scraps to be sure that the cutting and piecing instructions are correct. Very often I will find that I need to tweak a size, or prefer a different method of construction. Sometimes, I've make a block and realized I really didn't like it and have changed the quilt plan because of it.   *Sally Eshelman, York, PA*

❾ I achieve accuracy by sewing slowly; I have to make myself slow down sometimes.   *Vicki DiFrancesco, Conowingo, MD*

10 I piece my quilts with pins, lots and lots of pins. I find that fork pins work well with 90° angle piecing (such as Four Patches or Nine Patches). In all other piecing, I like to use flat-head quilting pins.

Steaming the seams is also another important factor in keeping my seams straight and in place as I am piecing a block into the whole quilt.   *Lisa Hughes, Richland, NY*

11 I keep a notebook of the stitch length, width, and, if necessary, foot used, and needle placement. This record-keeping really helps with reproduce-ability and consistent block sizes.

LynDee Lombardo, Olympia, WA

12 I *always* use pins. I also sew over pins. I admit that I bend a lot of pins, and break an occasional needle, but my piecing is very accurate.   *Carol Lattimore, Ozark, AL*

I keep a notebook of the stitch length, width, and, if necessary, foot used, and needle placement.

13 When pinning, I place my pins perpendicular to the edge that needs to be sewn with the point of the pin pointing towards that edge. That way, if I put down the pinned piece and come back to it later, I know the edge that needs to be sewn: my pins are pointing to it!   *Sue Hurley, Princeton, NJ*

14 I use the thinnest pins I can buy (yellow/blue glass heads by Clover) and take the smallest bite with the pin. Also, my pin heads are on the outside of the seam, pulling them out onto the bed as I approach the needle, which creates less shifting. I also nestle the seams together, pin at a seam, then pin in between seams, too. I'm a pinner!   *Michele Rutolo, Sinking Spring, PA*

15 I set my scant ¼" seam by using the Perfect Piecing Seam Guide by Perkins Dry Goods to mark the throat plate on my machine with several layers of masking tape. I find that strip piecing is the most efficient way to assemble parts of a quilt.

Alice O'Dwyer, Wilmington, NC

JUST FOR FUN

Top 10 Must-Have Sewing Room Items, According to Our Survey

#1
Sharp Rotary Cutter

#2
Various Sizes of Accurate Rulers

#3
Cutting Mat

#4
Well-Maintained Machine

#5
Sharp Scissors of Various Sizes

#6
Good Iron that Doesn't Spit

#7
Good Lighting

#8
Variety of Quality Thread

#9
Seam Ripper

#10
Comfortable Sewing Chair

❖ ... An iPad or laptop for inspiration, tutorials, free patterns and chatting. A camera so you can take pictures of your project to share online with your quilting buddies. A furry friend so you don't get lonely.

Karen Martin, Breezy Point, MN

🔞 Make sure you have an accurate ¼" seam. Don't judge the seam by markings on the sewing machine. The seam is from the edge of the fabric to the needle.   *Janet Bland, Smyrna, GA*

17 I love Aurifil thread for piecing. It takes up less space in a seam and makes it easier to get a ¼" seam without having to sew such a scant ¼" seam.   *Frances Courson, Maryville, TN*

18 I drew a line with a fine-tip Sharpie on the right side of my presser foot to show the ¼" mark.   *Gail Hosmer, Westminster, MD*

19 A precise and consistent seam allowance goes a long way toward guaranteeing accurate piecework. Adjusting the needle one position to the right or left to compensate for a presser foot that's not accurate is a great way to assure a precise ¼" seam.

Jan Mast, Lancaster, PA

20 I pin and I am careful to match my seams. I have also put a drop of Elmer's white glue on the seam if it is a small piece and pressed it—thus no distortion of the seam from pins.

Dee Johnson, Mankato, MN

21 I use a permanent fine-tipped marker and draw the ¼" sewing lines around each piece (tedious to others but a step I do enjoy). Next, I use tiny bites of a running stitch from each end of the seam, leaving the ¼" seam allowance open. Following these steps ensures perfect points and junctures.   *Joanne Picicci, Spokane, WA*

22 Another trick I just learned is that, since your machine's upper and lower feeds feed at a slightly different rate, it can create an "arc" or bowing over the length of a strip when you are strip piecing. The trick is to alternate which end you start sewing from. That way you are alternating which fabric is on the bottom. For example, if you are joining sets of two strips, when you join two *pairs* together, start sewing at the other end. I use a pin at the end of each set to remind me where I started sewing. This makes the seams' natural tendency to bow get spread evenly in both directions.

Nancy Henry, Rochester, NH

23 I found my best trick is when I add the borders. I find the center of the quilt and make a small crease there. Then I find the center of the border and put a small crease—however, I crease the fabric so they nest. If I press the quilt right sides together, then I crease the border wrong sides together so the little crease will nest nicely and then I pin on each side of the crease.

Coreen Burnett, Damascus, MD

24 I make sure that all seams butt together exactly by pressing all seams in opposite directions and pinning them so they do not shift. I also measure for accuracy every step of the way so any wonky pieces can be corrected right away. *Iva Burroughs, Newark, DE*

25 I piece accurately by using exact seam allowances and making sure they are consistent throughout a quilt.

I piece efficiently by chain piecing: I will send many pieces through the machine and keep them hooked together, moving them to the ironing board to press. I press them and then snip them apart and place them in appropriate piles. I use trays to stack pieces. If there are too many for a stack, I may use a bowl or larger box to keep them separated. This tray or box is then moved back to the machine for quick transportation and further piecing.

Kris Ranck, Indianapolis, IN

26 When you piece a quilt, press as you go. By the time you finish a block, it is pressed.

The same is true when putting the blocks together. Press each seam as you go and when you are finished sewing, you are also finished pressing. *Marti Blankenship, Pleasant Valley, MO*

Instead of using your finger to finger press when piecing, try using a wallpaper seam roller—it works great.

27 Instead of using your finger to finger press when piecing, try using a wallpaper seam roller—it works great.

Barbara Kolb, Red Bank, NJ

28 Ironing is very important for a project. One unique benefit is that it gives you exercise! If you put your ironing board on the other side of the room or somewhere you have to walk to, it makes you get up and move around, which is beneficial mentally as well as physically. *Marlys Wiens, Edina, MN*

29 Once I completed a geometric patterned top and had started the quilting on it when I noticed that one piece was not sewn in the right place. I was sick about it and wondered how I could fix it. I hand appliquéd the correct size and piece right over the mistake. I showed that quilt as a show-and-tell project in a club meeting, and not one person could notice a mistake or even tell that I had appliquéd over a spot! Not perfect, but it worked.

Wanda Beach, Gold River, CA

30 I am not much of a perfectionist, so I don't worry if the points are not perfect. I make mostly art quilts, and the piecing is more free form. *Margo Ellis, Key West, FL*

B. Machine vs. Hand Piecing

1 I do English paper piece specifically for a Grandmother's Flower Garden. All my other piecing is done by machine.

Debbie McNeely, Enon, OH

2 I've only pieced one quilt by hand using a hexagon shape. I did it in bed at nighttime when my children were small and that was the only peace and quiet time I had. And, also, I could not set up my sewing machine and keep it out of way of my children.

Lorraine Frederick, Perkasie, PA

3 If I have a lot of intersecting seams that create too much bulk, I will elect to hand piece. *Teresa Caldwell, Long Valley, NJ*

4 I am making a Tumbling Block charm quilt by hand. The y-seams are easier to do by hand than machine. I work on this quilt

only when we are going down the road in the motor home or car.
I will hand quilt it when it is pieced. I call it Tumbling Down the
Road. This started as a lap size and got a bit out of hand, so it is
now planned to be for my antique full-size bed.

Susan Eaglaton, Maryville, TN

5 I've only done hexies by hand. They make a great portable
project. All other piecing I do by machine. Bernina makes a great
¼" foot, that has markings to help you stop/start ¼" from the edges,
so set-in seams are not a problem.   *Ila Kool, Brookings, SD*

6 The one exception I make to machine piecing is when stubborn
mitered corners don't line up properly. Then I hand sew them.

Anne Hollenbach, Hudson, WI

7 I belong to a small group of quilters that meet once a week at
each other's homes. This is the best time to do hand piecing for my
heirloom quilts and to keep alive my love of traditional quilting.
The rest of the time, I machine piece, especially when doing quilts
for others, which are mostly charity quilts.

Janet Miller, Winchester, VA

8 Most of my piecing is done on the machine: straight lines,
gentle curves, block assembly, etc. It's faster, and I want to see parts
going up on the design wall quickly. I've found, though, that set-in
pieces (Y's and 90° set-ins) are more accurately done by hand.

Libbie Ellis, Tarpon Springs, FL

*I think that I can hand
piece as fast as doing it
by machine. I love the feel
of fabric and the sense of
accomplishment I receive
from hand piecing.*

9 I think that I can hand piece
as fast as doing it by machine.
I love the feel of fabric and
the sense of accomplishment I
receive from hand piecing. I'm
addicted to hand piecing!

Nancy Fairchild, Crossville, TN

10 I have pieced by hand when I
have worked on vintage fabric or

antique feed sacks, as the fabric era warrants doing so. I have also repaired two vintage quilts that were originally hand pieced, so I repaired both quilts by hand. *Jan Dunn, Hudson, WI*

11 I piece by hand if I'm working on something miniature. I find it easier when sewing something tiny. Otherwise, I always piece by machine. *Brenda Radzinski, Albion, NY*

12 Generally, I piece by machine for speed, of course. However, I always have some type of hand piecing project ready to do on the go. When I'm traveling, I take this project with me. *Marsha Hunt, Glenside, PA*

13 When I travel, I will piece by hand. I do not have to bring a sewing machine. I have a Cathedral Window quilt I have been working on for 4 years now. Maybe I need to travel more! Otherwise I machine piece. *Barb Thomas, Wantage, NJ*

14 I do not piece by hand. I have a lovely old Singer Featherweight on which I do all my piecing. It stitches far more consistently than I can. *Alice O'Dwyer, Wilmington, NC*

c. Strip Piecing

1 Strip piecing can be used on quilts for efficiency where there are a number of units that are the same. Some of these quilts have the added advantage that the ¼" seam isn't so important. What is important is a uniform seam allowance and straight sewing. *Joan Oldham, Panama City, FL*

2 If you have a pattern that uses Nine-Patch blocks, strip piecing is a fast and easy way to do Nine Patches. *Patricia Henseler, Maple Grove, MN*

❸ Strip piecing works very well for a scrap quilt, such as Fence Rail, Amish diagonal designs, Log Cabin, and Broken Dishes. Strip piecing is easily cut with a rotary cutter and pieced quickly.

Julie Jaquith, Lunenburg, VT

❹ I find the Tumbling Block pattern and Bargello are good examples of patterns for strip piecing because you can avoid y-seams and with the Bargello, you get a good amount of design freedom.

Teresa Caldwell, Long Valley, NJ

> *I love taking a pattern with large, solid blocks and substituting strip-pieced blocks for them. It gives the quilt a little pizzazz.*

❺ I love taking a pattern with large, solid blocks and substituting strip-pieced blocks for them. It gives the quilt a little pizzazz.

Janet Bland, Smyrna, GA

❻ I am working on circular patterns that use strip piecing . The strips are cut in wedges and re-sewn, creating the most unusual and interesting designs.

Janet Keen, Medicine Hat, Alberta

❼ Strip piecing is a great stash buster. It is time consuming, but you don't have to be real exact. You just cut different widths of strips.

Mary Heidemann, Daykin, NE

❽ You must pay attention to the level of thread in your bobbin because if the machine doesn't alert you and you pick up the pile behind your machine, beaming with pride at how much you have accomplished. . . then, zap, you realize they are not sewn together.

Gale Priesmeyer, Bellville, TX

❾ Recently, I learned that reversing sewing direction from one strip to the next keeps unwanted curves from developing.

Valerie Turer, Brooklyn, NY

❿ Strip piecing works great for any pattern where you want repeat color progressions. I have found the set-up process (sewing the strips together) to be excruciatingly boring, though, and really prefer a more random, scrappy look.　　*Libbie Ellis, Tarpon Springs, FL*

⑪ When I get bored with making lots of the same units over and over, I find it helps to keep a picture of the quilt in front of me. Often it's a photo from a magazine, sometimes just a colored graph paper design, but it helps keep me focused on the end result.

Cathie Shelton, Montgomery Village, MD

D. Paper Piecing

❶ Paper piecing works best for patterns that have odd-shaped elements. Pieces that can't be cut in multiples are more suited to paper piecing.　　*Sharon Genners, Omaha, NE*

❷ Paper piecing liberates the block design by allowing much more complicated shapes to be accurately sewn together. Anything with odd angles, small shapes or a lot of bias edges is great for paper piecing. It helps with odd angles by enabling more accurate piecing than with templates. Small shapes are more accurate as well. It also stabilizes the fabric. For that reason, it is best not to tear away the paper until the blocks have all been sewn together.

Kari Vojtechovsky, Centennial, CO

❸ Lots of angles and triangles and bias edges can be tamed by paper piecing. Also, blocks like New York Beauty that combine curves and triangles can't be done easily without paper piecing.

Valerie Turer, Brooklyn, NY

❹ When accuracy is a must for the finished block, as in Mariner's Compass, stars, and New York Beauty, and you do not like hand piecing, paper piecing is your answer.

Mary Andra Holmes, Prescott, AZ

5 When paper piecing, you don't have to cut accurately, you just need to be able to sew on the line. As long as you can sew on the line and follow the pattern, your points won't get cut off and your blocks will be consistent. *Louise Lott, Healesville, Australia*

Paper piecing allows quilters to use all of their bits and pieces of expensive fabric.

6 Paper piecing allows quilters to use all of their bits and pieces of expensive fabric.
Geraldine Whitley, Washington, DC

7 Anything that has tiny pieces and points work well for paper piecing. Small pieces are very difficult to piece, and it's easy to cut off points if you don't use paper piecing.
Michele Haberer, Zurich, Ontario

8 Paper piecing is a wonderful way to be creative. However, instead of using paper which sometimes is difficult to detach from the design, I use gauze, dryer sheets, or muslin. These fabrics can remain with the design through the quilting process. In many cases, the middle layer (batting) can be omitted from the quilting process because the muslin, gauze, and dryer sheets are substantial enough. *Geraldine Whitley, Washington, DC*

9 Remember to shorten your stitch length when you're paper piecing so there's less chance of distorting the block when you remove the paper, or else use the AQ paper that stays in.
Jana Pratt, Barnegat, NJ

10 One of the great things about English paper piecing is that you just grab a piece of fabric and do not have to worry about bias edges. Paper piecing works best when you are using smaller scraps that may or may not be cut on the straight of grain. You get a better result, and it won't be so distorted since you do not know how it came off the bolt. *Olivia Kuebler, Kansas City, MO*

11 I make a lot of miniature quilts of 1 to 3" finished blocks. I am constantly asked if I achieve my accuracy via paper piecing. Fact is, my construction technique is the same as for larger blocks: rotary cut, stitch, press, trim. I find paper piecing wasteful. Though I have done paper piecing, I am not a great fan. I often think I am not dyslexic enough to grasp this "backward" technique.

Nancee McCann, Wilmington, DE

E. Keeping Order with Small Pieces

❶ Mark the pieces after you have cut them. I like the 2" Wonder Clips to hold the cut pieces together. You can mark them with a dry-erase pen so you know what you have in hand.

Karen Benke, Medina, OH

❷ I sort colors in clear plastic sandwich bags and tack them up on a cork board, lining them up in the order I will use them.

Norma Gehman, Ephrata, PA

❸ I use index cards and zip-lock bags. I write on the index card the step from the pattern, size of the square and how many for each block after I cut them. When I start to sew, I just look for step 1 and all the pieces are together. *Jill Armstrong, Bradenton, FL*

❹ I put the separate pieces in small plastic bags and label them with a magic marker. I then put all the small plastic bags into a larger plastic bag and mark it for each block.

Nancy Fairchild, Crossville, TN

❺ When I have to number rows, instead of using small scraps of paper, I use pins to make the Roman numerals, as they can all be done with straight lines. *Marsha Hunt, Glenside, PA*

6 For each quilt that I start, I place the pieces in a large bag with handles so that I can keep them together and work on several quilts at the same time. When I watch TV, I have the bag near me to pin the pieces together for sewing. I often get the bags from places like Olive Garden, Panera Bread, or Bath and Body works.

Donna Dickinson, Harrington, DE

7 I use an old, rimmed cookie sheet to line up my pieces in order. I tape a label for each piece across the edge before placing the pieces on the tray. I slide the tray into a large plastic bag in between sewing sessions to keep the pieces in order.

When I am "kitting" a quilt (making a kit) for future piecing, I separate the pieces into labeled sandwich bags for each block.

Barbara Merritt, Brackney, PA

I doubt that I have ever made a quilt that did not have a tray involved.

8 I like to use low-cut boxes such as the ones canned goods arrive in at the store to organize cut pieces. I also use lots of trays. I doubt that I have ever made a quilt that did not have a tray involved.

Susan Eaglaton, Maryville, TN

9 I have used clean pizza boxes with a layer of batting to keep cut pieces from shifting. *Charda Seuferer, Des Moines, IA*

10 I use cupcake tins as a great way to organize small pieces. I can label each section. *Kathie Wilson, Camarillo, CA*

11 I save the boxes that prewashed salad greens come in. They are a nice big size and they are clear plastic. The boxes stack nicely, I can see contents at a glance, and they are free.

Emily Galea, Boca Raton, FL

12 As I am cutting pieces out, if there are not too many, I place them on paper plates and stack them on top of each other. If there are lots and lots of pieces, I have plastic containers that I label with the specific piece information. If I have to put stacks of several shapes in the same container, then I will label the top shape on

each stack with an office dot that has the identifying information
on it.   *Juanita Brandt, Huntsville, AL*

⓭ Lori Holt of Bee in my Bonnet shows how to make small
project boards. The board is covered with batting or flannel, so the
pieces stay put, and I can move them from the cutting table to my
machine. I have several of these boards, and I love them.
       Twila Sikkink, Clear Lake, WI

⓮ Sometimes I pin the pieces to a block of styrofoam to keep
them organized.   *E. Anne Hendrickson, Toledo, OR*

⓯ To organize strips, I often use a clothes-hanger-type rack for
men's ties.   *Marsha Hunt, Glenside, PA*

⓰ I hang a flannel-backed vinyl tablecloth on my wall with the
flannel side out as a design wall. It can be taken down and folded
up with the project on it if it needs to be moved, taken to class and
brought home intact. I have a couple tablecloths and can change
out when necessary.   *Martha Ethridge, Rolla, MO*

⓱ If the pieces are small, I cut as I go so I don't lose anything.
       J. Duda, East Amherst, NY

CHAPTER 8

Appliqué

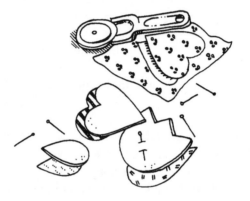

A. Preparing Pieces for Appliqué

❶ I think for appliqué you need to be skillful with *all* the methods as each pattern, dependent on piece size and difficulty, has different skill needs. I try to be versatile. I find needle-turn relaxing, English paper piecing perfect, and freezer paper good for tiny pieces. I like my finished work to be strong and well done, and this figures into my choices. *Elaine Nixon, Abbotsford, British Columbia*

❷ To prepare my fabric for appliqué, I wash out the factory chemicals and finishes. Then I carefully iron it with steam. I want the fabric soft enough to needle-turn into gentle curves without any "pointy-s" that may show up in stiff fabric.

Jennifer Padden, Austin, TX

❸ Once the fabric is pressed and I am certain it is on grain, I use spray starch on it and press with a dry iron. This adds body, prevents stretching while handling the fabric, and makes lining up my appliqué piece a snap. I do not turn under my appliqué edges, preferring to either hand or machine finish the edges. I add a light-weight fusible bonding product slightly larger than the appliqué. I like Lite Steam-A-Seam2.

I add cross-hairs in water soluble pencil to mark the grain on the fabric before I bond it. I draw vertical and horizontal lines on my tracing pattern so that I can make sure it will be on grain with the fabric when I trace it. I then trace my appliqué design in reverse on one of the paper liners.

I am now ready to cut out my appliqué, remove the final piece of paper, and fuse it to my fabric, being very careful to line up my cross hairs (grain marks). I prefer to prepare several pieces of fabric for appliqué at once, so that when the time comes to bond the pieces to my blocks, I'm ready to go.   *Jan Roach, Anderson, CA*

❹ Another method is to put the freezer paper shiny-side up on the back of the fabric, trim, allowing for the seam, and then turn the fabric over the freezer paper with an iron. Go carefully around the edge of the fabric with the point of the dry iron, then "painting" sizing on the turned seam allowance and ironing it dry. Pull out the paper when you're halfway through stitching the piece onto the background fabric.   *Marie White, Waiuku, New Zealand*

❺ Take your time when cutting out the fused pieces, and use small, sharp scissors. Turn the fabric piece, not the scissors, when cutting, so the edges come out smoother and accurate.   *Kathy Gooden, Tallahassee, FL*

❻ I copy my pattern design on an inkjet printer with freezer paper sheets in it. It saves hours of tracing. I make a clear overlay using a special film paper made for an inkjet printer

Turn the fabric piece, not the scissors, when cutting, so the edges come out smoother and accurate.

that I purchase in a office supply store. This is a huge time saver. I
never mark my background fabric.

Stephanie Greenberg, Lawrenceville, NJ

7 I love to do needleturn appliqué, and I do mine a little bit
differently than anyone I have ever known. I trace or draw each
appliqué piece on freezer paper, labeling it with a letter or name so
that I know where it will be positioned on the background fabric.
I cut each shape out on the line where the fabric will be turned
under. I then iron that piece of freezer paper onto the front of the
fabric I have chosen. I draw around the freezer paper onto the
fabric with an erasable pen and cut it out, leaving a scant ¼" seam
allowance. I number all of my appliqué pieces in the order that I
will be sewing them onto the background fabric.

Marcia Porcelli, Forsyth, GA

8 I trace each design on freezer paper, cut out the actual design,
and iron to the back of my fabric. I then cut it again, allowing about
a ¼" seam allowance. I lay out the pieces, pin, and baste stitch them
on with the sewing machine. After you wash your quilt, you will not
be able to see the sewing marks left by machine stitching. This is
faster than hand basting and makes your appliqué portable so that
you can take it with you to doctor's appointments or other places.
Also, you will not have to worry about losing any of your pieces.

Nora Manley, Athens, AL

9 I do back-baste appliqué, so I trace my pattern on freezer paper,
iron it to the front side of my background and trace it on the fabric.
I mark my pattern with colors for each piece, then look for items
that need to go on first. Using a light box in my lap, I position my
fabric on the piece to be applied.   *Wilma Scholl, Kaufman, TX*

10 With back basting, I do not have pieces floating around to keep
track of.   *Annie Morgan, Johnson, VT*

11 On simple shapes, I cut the piece ¼" larger all the way around,
sew it to a used dryer sheet with right sides together with a ¼"

seam. Cut a slit in the lining and turn it right side out and press.
No raw edges.   *Marsha Nelson, Clinton, UT*

⑫ I always use Steam-a-Seam. So basically, I only have to draw
the design onto the paper, cut it out, and iron it on. If it is a wall
hanging, I stop there. If it is on a bed quilt that's going to be
washed, then I also sew around the design.

Joan Hagan, St. Marys, PA

B. Organizing Appliqué Pieces

❶ To keep track of the pieces that must be appliquéd, I always
do what I call a "mock up" of the entire block, and then the entire
quilt on graph paper. I assign my fabrics numbers, snipping off a
piece and adding it to my chart on the mock up. Then I make up
a full-size pattern piece that depicts the entire pattern that is to
be appliquéd on each individual block. Each individual part is
numbered and/or color coded. As pieces are prepared, I number
them on the bonding paper and attach the appropriate piece with
a quilting pin to the full-sized mock up of the block. I found this
keeps me on track and I can catch any mistakes quickly before a
total disaster happens.   *Jan Roach, Anderson, CA*

❷ I make a second copy of my pattern and pin it to a foam core
board. As I prepare my pieces, I pin them to the foam core board.

Barbara Cascelli, Murrieta, CA

❸ I like to string my appliqué pieces onto a heavy piece of thread
in the order in which they will be applied to the background fabric.
They travel nicely with no chance of being lost or mixed up.

Jean Post, Santa Cruz, CA

4 I use Ziploc bags with labels inside the bag. I don't write on the outside so I can use the bag again and again—saves money and the environment. *Janice Bayers, Dartmouth, Nova Scotia*

5 I stack the appliqué pieces into numbered piles on a small cookie sheet. When I am done for the day, I cover the cookie sheet with a sheet of foil or plastic wrap so that they stay in place. The pieces are kept clean, with no danger of being blown off and onto the floor, never to be seen again. *Sharon Sutton, Lindsey, OH*

6 I number the appliqué pieces by which go first. I use blue painter's tape because it removes easily and doesn't leave any residue behind. *Joyce Carey, Waterford, MI*

7 I usually lay them out on the background fabric on a spare bed near my sewing room. When I get the right look, I will take a photo to make sure I get the same look after I remove the pieces when I start sewing. When there are really small pieces, I like to put them in a shallow plastic container so they don't get lost, giving me easy access to the pieces. *Carolyn Haggerty, Advance, NC*

8 Using the starch method, I can glue baste all of the block pieces to the background at once and don't have to worry about losing any of them. *Karen Martin, Breezy Point, MN*

9 I have about 12 squares of flannel-backed vinyl. Once the pieces are cut for a block, I lay them on the flannel side and store them in a pizza box. This holds them in place until I'm ready to sew them on. I can also roll the vinyl up quickly for a quick "to go" project. *Ruth Anglin, Tijeras, NM*

10 If it's a large quilt with many blocks, I use a notebook and top-loading protector sheets to keep my pieces for each block, along with a picture of that block in the protector sheet. I organize a protector sheet for each block. *Rebecca Hoffmann, Plant City, FL*

c. Appliqué Tools

❶ Any fusible web will adhere to your needle, so it's important to keep a clean needle. I periodically take out my needle and clean it with Goo Off, Goo Gone, or WD-40.   *Elizabeth Merkle, Levittown, PA*

❷ I have recently been using the Trolley Needle Thread Controller to try the needle turn technique. You can feel the edge of the piece right where it needs to fold over! You can then use a glue stick to hold the fabric over.   *Jessica Brinkerhoff, Bountiful, UT*

❸ Use a fiberglass appliqué cloth so your ironing surface and iron remain clean.   *Elizabeth Merkle, Levittown, PA*

❹ Use the smaller pins that are made for appliqué. They make life much easier.   *Deborah Gross, Willow Grove, PA*

❺ For circles, I love the yo-yo method using Karen K. Buckley's perfect circles, coins or washers for the template. Perfect circles, every time.   *Louise Lott, Healesville, Australia*

❻ For hand appliqué, take small stitches with good matching thread, using a size 11 straw or a Roxanne appliqué needle for best results. The thread should match the appliqué, not the background; I use DMC or Masterpiece thread. I use tiny dots of Elmer's white washable school glue to place the appliqués, and then take them with me so I can sit and sew anywhere.   *Linda Noble, Colorado Springs, CO*

The thread should match the appliqué, not the background.

❼ I have outlined the edges of appliquéd pieces with a permanent Pigma pen or Sharpie to make the pieces stand out.   *Jenn Martin, Prattville, AL*

8 Soft-fuse is the best product out there. It is light weight, and I can appliqué through it easily without my needle sticking.

Doris Caldwell, Friedens, PA

9 I always have a wooden chopstick in hand to push and fix a pointed piece in place as needed when I'm machine appliquéing. Never a metal ripper or any other metal tool, because my needle could break on those.   *Joke Dingemans, Amersfoort, Netherlands*

10 Always start with a new needle. Old needles and appliqué aren't friends. If you're not careful, you will end up with a snag and be forced to rip your piece out and start anew— that is, if it didn't snag the background fabric, too, which is what happened to me. Trust me, it's easier to just reach for a new needle.

Elizabeth Rogers, New Port Richey, FL

D. Pros and Cons of Appliqué Methods

1 Needle turn is my favorite method of appliqué. I find I can get sharper points, better curves, and smaller stitches.

Roberta Bland, Milton, FL

2 Once I made a very elaborate appliquéd quilt, using needleturn appliqué with the starch technique and freezer paper. The results were beautiful, but I think a lot of the effort was lost once the quilting was done. I chose to quilt around the edges of many of the pieces and loved the results, but in the end you couldn't really even tell I'd done all of that handwork!   *Amy DeCesare, Delmont, PA*

3 I like needle turn because the fusible that comes on pre-fused pieces sticks terribly to my needle and causes all sorts of issues.

Denise Rosbicki, South Prince George, VA

Your Favorite Quilting Magazines, According to Our Survey

JUST FOR FUN

Fons & Porter's Love of Quilting

American Patchwork and Quilting

McCall's Quilting

Quilters Newsletter

Quiltmaker

Quiltmania

Better Homes and Gardens

Primitive Quilts

Quilter's World

The Quilt Life

Easy Quilts

Quilt

Quilting Arts

The Quilter

Quilt Sampler

Quilt Trends

❖ I like the issue that talks about the different stores. I love to go on shop hops, so I like to plan trips around shop hops in different areas. *Mary Wojtkiewicz, Santa Ana, CA*

❹ I like needleturn appliqué. I find it has the most control, and I can sew anywhere. I tried the glue/starch/ironing method and found it too constricting and also time consuming. It usually only

worked with large templates and not the small pieces that I work
with now.   *Judy Craddock, Babylon, NY*

5 I love needle turn appliqué because I can prepare the pieces
ahead of time and take my appliqué with me to quilt bees, or watch
TV with my hubby and appliqué. Needle turn is something I can do
with other people, rather than being in my sewing room by myself.
                                    Patricia Dews, Gainesville, VA

6 I like needle turn appliqué because it gives me clean edges,
and it also gives sort of a 3-D effect. However, I love wool appliqué
because it is simpler than needle turn. I can just iron my wool piece
onto the background and then do the blanket stitch on its edges
because wool edges will not fray.   *Patricia Henseler, Maple Grove, MN*

7 I prefer the freezer paper method so that I can see what the shape
looks like ahead of time. I've tried needle turn and it works well, but
by using the freezer paper, I can control difficult shapes ahead of
time and avoid having to re-do curves.   *Jill Bowman, Jamestown, NC*

8 I use the toothpick turn method of appliqué. I find the toothpick grabs the fabric and makes it easier to turn the seam allowance
under. I then appliqué the piece in place by hand.
                                    Mary Andra Holmes, Prescott, AZ

9 I like to do machine-turned edge appliqué. My pieces are prepared and glued to the background, and then I sit and sew with an
invisible stitch. My results look as good or even better than hand
needle-turned. I like this because it is faster for me to complete a
project. I also now have arthritic hands, so it is difficult for me to
hand stitch.   *Rebecca Hoffmann, Plant City, FL*

10 I prefer to hand sew appliqué because it's easier to work on
curves, and I can ensure all edges are sewn.   *Jenn Martin, Prattville, AL*

11 On wool, I prefer hand appliqué which gives a slightly more
primitive or hand work appearance than using my machine.
                                    Marsha Brasky, Algonquin, IL

⑫ I like to do freezer paper appliqué because I get better points and curves. I also like the choice of sewing them down by hand or machine, whatever suits me at the time.   *Carol Lewin, Hay Springs, NE*

⑬ I like machine appliqué because it is stronger and holds better. My appliqués are for kids, and they are tough on clothes and blankies.   *Joyce Carey, Waterford, MI*

> *I like machine appliqué because it is stronger and holds better.*

⑭ I prefer back basting. I do not like having pins in my way, and I know the appliqué piece is secured as I want it to look when finished.

Jeanne DeHart, Livingston, MT

⑮ I prefer to use the mylar templates, starch, and hand appliqué. These steps ensure my pieces are always exactly the correct size and have a wonderful finished edge, which will remain as beautiful as the day I stitched it for many years to come.

Elizabeth Rogers, New Port Richey, FL

⑯ I like a portable project, so I use the starch method with the paper removed and pieces glue basted to the background. I can easily work on it in the car or at a meeting and not have to dig around for pieces. I like to thread up all the colors I will need and carry them in a domed needle keeper.   *Karen Martin, Breezy Point, MN*

E. *Machine Appliqué*

❶ Take it slow. I get the worst results when I rush machine appliqué. If you don't want your piece to be stiff because of the fusible web, you can use fabric glue or a glue stick to keep it in place. Or you can trim out the middle parts of the fusible web after you trace

your design (but before you fuse it), removing up to ½" inside the
traced design.   *Kari Vojtechovsky, Centennial, CO*

❷ Thin fusible batting can really work wonders with machine
appliqué, especially with animals on baby quilts. It makes them pop
out more.   *Amanda Kei Andrews, Vero Beach, FL*

❸ Cut away the fusible in the center of large appliqué pieces,
which is called windowing. It's best to use this technique for things
that won't be washed often.   *Lisa England, Ashland, KY*

❹ Make sure you stabilize the area to be stitched before you
machine appliqué. Do this even if your shapes are fused on
because it helps your stitching to be smooth with no pull on the
background. Use a tear-away stabilizer.   *Marianne Udell, Santa Fe, NM*

❺ The most common machine appliqué is to use narrow zig-zag
to catch the edge of the appliqué with the zig and the foundation of
the quilt with the zag, very close to the edge of the appliqué.
    You can use either polyester monofilament thread which goes
with anything, or match your thread to the appliqué. Many stitch-
ers like to use silk thread because it blends in so well, but others
may want to use a contrasting thread with a more obvious stitch to
add another design element in the quilt.   *Jennifer Padden, Austin, TX*

❻ I prefer to use a narrow blanket stitch when machine appliquéing. This stitch reminds me of a dance step: forward back, left
back, forward again, so it is easy to watch for the perfect moment to
pivot. On concave curve intersections, stop with your needle down
inside of the appliqué piece, then pivot. In convex curve joints,
stop with your needle down in the background fabric. Pivot/turn
and stitch some more. On straight line intersections and corners,
always come up to the intersection, stop with your needle down in
the background fabric, then pivot before sewing some more.
                              Elizabeth Rogers, New Port Richey, FL

7 Satin stitch is another way to hold the appliquéd pieces. This is lovely if the pieces are larger, as satin stitch gives texture to the work.   *Barbara Falkner, Wellard, WA*

8 When coming to a point in my work, I slowly decrease the satin stitch width and at the end, plant the needle and then pivot. I continue with the smaller stitch, gradually increasing the width to where I started.   *Gayle Baxley, Dalton Gardens, ID*

9 I use the buttonhole stitch as well as the zig-zag stitch and try to use as narrow a stitch as possible while touching just on the edge of the piece to attach it to the background. Satin stitch is time consuming and eats thread up quickly. I prefer a lighter stitch for most of the pieces I do.   *Margaret (Peg) Parsons, New Castle, DE*

> *Satin stitch is time consuming and eats thread up quickly.*

10 I like to use the satin stitch rather than the blanket stitch. I don't like any fray on the edges of the appliqué which can happen with the blanket stitch.   *Gayle Baxley, Dalton Gardens, ID*

11 I like to use the hem stitch on my machine at a very short length and width. My machine does what they call a "lift and pivot." Every time I stop sewing, my presser foot raises enough to move the fabric. This comes in very handy when doing appliqué.   *Patti Goggio, Broadlands, VA*

12 I used to use a satin stitch, but since I got my machine with the blanket stitch, I use that to sew around the edges. Sometimes I will do a free motion stitch around the edges to give some texture, especially if I want a fuzzy look for animals or a more natural edge for leaves and flowers.   *Sally Eshelman, York, PA*

13 I have used the buttonhole stitch for machine appliqué, but you must make the stitches very small, or corners and points are difficult.   *Stephanie Leuthesser, San Ysidro, CA*

14 I am partial to the machine blanket stitch for my fusible appliqué, but have also used some of my decorative stitches where the particular piece might appropriately call for it. I was doing a block with a mom and baby walrus sitting on an iceberg, and I used a deep sea blue decorative up and down stitch with my 30wt Sulky Blendables, which gave the iceberg some dimension.

Barbara Theriault, Brooksville, FL

15 I find the use of an open-toe foot wonderful for machine appliqué. You can see exactly where you are going, and it is easy to see the cut edge of the fabric. I love those open-toed feet!

Joan Norfolk, Kilmore, Australia

I always program my needle to finish in the down position. I can pivot easily, and I don't leave any gaps in my sewing.

16 I always program my needle to finish in the down position. I can pivot easily, and I don't leave any gaps in my sewing.

Kerilee Corrie, Ross, Australia

17 Using transparent thread allows you to see the pieces and not the thread, avoiding errors if you are new to machine appliqué.

Lynn Dyck, Barrie, Ontario

18 I like to use a thread color that matches the fabric and stitch over the shape 2–3 times each. For pieces that I want to pop, I use a contrasting thread.

Louise Lott, Healesville, Australia

19 Practice first to warm up *every* new session. Chances are good you forgot to set something on your machine.

Ellen Mueller, Acton, MA

20 I always do a sample of the pieces for stitch length and width to see how the stitches lay. I also write down the stitch length and width for future reference. *Mary Ellen Larson, Mary Esther, FL*

㉑ Being able to regulate your speed is really important for machine appliqué. I also find my knee-lift quite helpful with the needle-down option on my machine.   *Nancy Swanwick, Fort Scott, KS*

㉒ I like Celtic appliqué: cut strips on the bias, sew a seam and tuck it to the back. This method is good for stems and open design work.   *Sharon Kelly, Hollywood, FL*

F. Raw-Edge Appliqué

❶ When using the zigzag stitch for machine appliqué, be sure the stitch is wide enough and close enough to catch and hide all loose threads.   *Jeanne Bartleson, North Augusta, SC*

❷ If the raw edge of the appliqué is supposed to fray, stitch ¼" inside the appliqué. If a smooth edge is desired, use an iron on fusible on the appliqué, and keep the stitches quite close together on the very edge of the appliquéd shape.   *Marsha Nelson, Clinton, UT*

❸ Starch and press, starch and press, and starch and press. Sometimes I will run a line of large stitches along the edge of the fabric, just to keep it from fraying, then pull the stitching out after I'm finished with the project.   *Joyce Carey, Waterford, MI*

❹ If it is something that will be laundered often and you are not going to satin stitch the edges, use fusible web on the back. Then take a toothpick or a fine artist's paint brush and lightly edge the appliqué with fray check. Let it dry. Fuse to the quilt with an appliqué pressing sheet, and stitch as desired.
    Debbie Henry, Lucinda, PA

❺ For raw edge appliqué, I use either the open-toe embroidery foot or the free motion foot, stitching very close to the edge of the appliqué piece with a straight stitch. It takes patience. Pivot frequently and use a stitch length of 1½–2".

Diana Miller, Barrie, Ontario

I use a layer of tulle over the entire top when it is completed and quilt through the tulle. It anchors all the raw edges, and they will never come loose.

❻ I use a layer of tulle over the entire top when it is completed and quilt through the tulle. It anchors all the raw edges, and they will never come loose. Tulle is fabulous. It is cheap and comes in so many colors, so you can lighten or darken the quilt depending on the color you choose. I anchor the tulle in the borders because I apply the borders to the tulle-covered quilt top.

Nancy Henry, Rochester, NH

❼ If a frayed, ragged edge is desired, after washing, use a toothbrush to soften the edges of the appliqué.

If you have a lot of raw edge appliqué, such as flannel on top of denim, take the quilt to a laundromat to wash in an oversized machine. A home machine cannot handle the amount of lint that will wash out. *Marti Blankenship, Pleasant Valley, MO*

❽ Use a narrow piece of Heat n Bond around the edges of the shape to prevent raveling. *Joan Miller, Richmond, VA*

❾ I cut fabrics on the bias, so I get little fraying in machine appliqué. *Barbara Porter, Arroyo Grande, CA*

G. Other Appliqué Tips

1 Read a lot, research on the internet, and start small. By that I do *not* mean small pieces, but small appliqué projects. Make one block. If you like it, turn it into a medallion style wall hanging and move on to something more complex. Many top designers put out books that have a one block project or a good entry level design.

Michelle Harrison, Morganton, GA

2 While doing hand appliqué, be sure to wax your thread. It will save lots of headaches from tangled thread!

Peggy Nelson, Janesville, WI

3 Use a needle and a thread to match its size. If your needle eye is big and you are using thin thread, then you will have lots of tiny holes in your fabric you'll be able to see through. If your needle eye is small and your thread is thicker, then there will be pulling on the fabric and a chance your thread will weaken by being forced through the fabric many times.   *Mary Andra Holmes, Prescott, AZ*

4 A blanket stitch done by hand around the edge of a fused piece of fabric looks very special, especially if done with perle cotton.

Valerie Turer, Brooklyn, NY

5 If you are using a light piece of fabric on a patterned or darker background fabric, cut a lining of muslin and insert it behind your appliqué piece.   *Diane Linker, Scarsdale, NY*

6 Find a needle that is comfortable for you. I use 11 straw needles. As you make your appliqué stitches, keep your needle parallel to the edge of the fabric.   *Candy Hargrove, Kansas City, MO*

7 If you're having difficulty removing the backing paper from fusible web adhesive, try scoring the center of the paper with a needle. This slight cut will make it peel off much more easily.

Jan Mast, Lancaster, PA

8 If accuracy is not your thing, do primitive/folk art appliqué, not Baltimore Album.   *Annemarie (Nancy) Poorbaugh, Montgomery, AL*

9 If you want to enhance your appliqué, be willing to pay for custom quilting or quilt your own. An overall edge to edge or pantograph pattern in machine quilting does not enhance the appliqué. I have seen very nice quilts that would have been beautiful if they had been custom quilted instead of an overall pattern.

Mary Beth Schrader, Cameron, MO

10 One of the best tips given to me in an appliqué class by Sue Garman is to try using the opposite hand if the one you are using doesn't feel right.   *Shelia Smith, Goldthwaite, TX*

CHAPTER 9

Batting

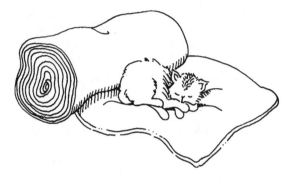

A. Preparing Batting

❶ There is a grain-line to batting. Just like fabric, batting has a warp and weft, and stretches one way more than the other. This is important to know for wall hangings, clothing, and decorative items.   *Sharon Mominee, Alpine, CA*

❷ I sometimes run the batting through a gentle cycle in the washing machine, and then into the dryer. That generally takes care of some of the shrinkage. If I don't have time for the wash cycle, I'll put it in the dryer on air-fluff, just to loosen it up and get some of the wrinkles out.   *Karen Renninger, Punta Gorda, FL*

❸ If I am planning to hand quilt a project, I soak the batting in cool water, gently roll it in a towel to remove the excess water and lay it flat to dry. It makes needling much easier.
                    Karen Martin, Breezy Point, MN

4 Always unwrap your batting and let it relax before you use it. Sometimes I put it in the dryer on air fluff for a few minutes. If I don't want any shrinkage, I put it in the washing machine and let it soak with no agitation for 5 minutes, then spin it, and put it in the dryer on low.   *Roxie Fitzgerald, Cerritos, CA*

5 To eliminate wrinkles in my batting before I make the quilt sandwich, I found putting a dampened light towel, like a kitchen towel, in the dryer with the batting and a dryer sheet, makes the work of putting the quilt together much simpler. The batting feels fluffy but not thick. I formerly just spread out the batting and let it rest out of the packaging, but it is nicer out of the dryer.

Joan Trautwein, Belle Mead, NJ

6 Always remember to cut batting about 4" larger than your quilt top and backing.   *Jean Taylor, Edmond, OK*

B. Preferred Battings by Brand Name

1 I prefer Warm & Natural needled cotton batting. I love that it doesn't bunch up, that you can quilt or tie it up to 10" apart, and it doesn't contain any glues or resins. And I love that I can use it on the outside too. I have a couple projects where I've used this batting on the outside in appliqué and it's given a great effect!

Amy Mayo, Havre de Grace, MD

2 I am a longarm quilter and the batting that I use most often is Hobbs 80/20 which is 80% cotton and 20% polyester. It quilts beautifully, has a nice drape, is breathable and with the added strength of the polyester, it doesn't bunch and shift within the quilt. It has the look and feel of a traditional cotton batting and washes and dries wonderfully. *Barbara Gentner, West Seneca, NY*

3 I prefer either Warm & Natural 100% cotton batting or Quilters Dream mid-weight 100% cotton batting. My personal taste is a more traditional look to a quilt and not the more poofy look created by higher loft polyester batting. Also, I've found that cotton batting tends to hold up better wash after wash and doesn't tend to separate like polyester batting can. I make my quilts to be used, so they will be washed. *Geralyn McClarren, Harrisburg, PA*

> *I've found that cotton batting tends to hold up better wash after wash and doesn't tend to separate like polyester batting can.*

4 For charity quilts, I use poly. For baby gifts, I use Quilters Dream Angel for its flame deterrence. Often for adult gifts, I use wool for its lightness and warmth. *Leah Groenwald, Glasgow, KY*

5 Currently I am using Dream Select cotton and Hobbs Heirloom Wool together in my quilts. They permit me to get a faux trapunto look that accentuates the quilting stitches.
Georgia Pierce, Seattle, WA

6 I use Quilters Dream. All of the products they sell are awesome quality. They have four lofts and sell cotton, wool and poly batts. They even have recycled green batting that is made 100% from recycled bottles. *Karen Benke, Medina, OH*

7 I prefer Quilters Dream Select. I like the weight of the finished quilt using this. It's not too heavy, but warm. It's so easy to use and to trim to size because of how it is folded. It clings to the quilt top and is easy to smooth out any wrinkles. *Colleen Coffman, Mulino, OR*

8 I prefer 100% cotton batting such as Heirloom or Dream Cotton. It is easy to control under the walking foot, safe for baby items, washes without moving and bunching, and leaves less debris on my machine. *Karen Farnsworth, Hallam, PA*

9 I like Quilters Dream Cotton when I send my quilts out for long arm quilting. It has a good drape to it and feels more like a hand quilted quilt. It is also a good batting for hand quilting.

Nora Manley, Athens, AL

JUST FOR FUN

Your Favorite Quilting Websites, According to Our Survey

- OldCountryStoreFabrics.com
- MissouriQuiltCo.com
- QuiltingBoard.com
- FonsAndPorter.com
- YouTube.com
- Pinterest.com
- TheQuiltShow.com
- AllPeopleQuilt.com
- Quiltville.com
- QnnTV.com
- Craftsy.com
- QuiltInADay.com
- Hancocks-Paducah.com
- UnitedNotions.com
- AmericanQuilter.com
- JoMortonQuilts.com
- SewMamaSew.com
- LeahDay.com
- CupcakesNDaisies.com

❖ I go to the websites of my local quilt shops to see what classes are offered, what's new, and check for specials.

Leslie O'Brien, Exton, PA

10 I use Warm & Natural Cotton Batting almost exclusively. I buy queen size and cut it to the size I need.

June Bryant, Rochester, NY

11 I prefer cotton batting, and I usually get Warm & White or Warm & Natural. I find these are soft and they don't leave a lot of fluff around. When I used Quilters Dream Orient, my machine had a lot of fibers, and I was sneezing as I sewed.

Kathie Wilson, Camarillo, CA

12 I prefer Fusible Fleece (Pellon) for small wall hangings or table runners that I'm not going to handquilt. It gives stability to the layers.

Ruth Ann Gingrich, New Holland, PA

13 My new go-to batting is Pellon wool batting. For years, I used Warm & Natural cotton batting. I thought that the thick and thin spots were just how batting was made. A friend recommended Pellon wool batting, and I found that it did not stretch and pull apart like the cheap cotton batting. It gives a lovely loft in the finished quilt. It is warm in the winter and cool in the summer. *Janice Simmons, Fresno, CA*

c. Preferred Battings by Fiber Content

❶ The easiest batting for hand quilting is polyester, but I try not to use it because sometimes the batting migrates through the quilt when it's washed, and I end up with little knots on top of my quilt.

Nora Manley, Athens, AL

❷ I use a poly/cotton blend batting for charity work because I think it holds up well to excessive use. I use cotton for my personal quilts as I like the crinkled look after washing. Cotton batting clings to the quilt fabric so well during quilting, and the whole quilt feels great. I'll use either cotton or poly for wall hangings and lap quilts and leftovers of either in placemats.

Nancee McCann, Wilmington, DE

❸ For baby quilts or quilts for young children, I like to use polyester fleece rather than batting. Fleece stands up to repeated washing and resists pulling on the quilting. *Katherine Schaffer, Lima, NY*

❹ I prefer polyester batting because it gives a slightly puffy look which looks so cozy to me. *Sally Petersheim, Gap, PA*

❺ I prefer to use a cotton/poly blend batting. I get the softness of cotton plus the stability from the polyester. This batting is also easier to hand quilt than an all-cotton batting.

Tammy Jones, Vienna, MD

6 I love a wool/poly blend batting. It washes well, and the more you wash, the softer the quilts become. It's warm enough to be the only thing we use on our bed through spring and summer, and it doesn't require dense quilting.   *Louise Lott, Healesville, Australia*

7 I prefer a wool batting as we live in a region of cold winters and super-hot summers. Wool is perfect for the extremes. It is also wonderfully soft and easy to quilt.   *Julie Hinks, Pine Mountain, Australia*

8 For hand quilting, I like 100% wool or 100% silk. It is like quilting through butter. For machine quilting, I use 100% cotton as it doesn't slip or beard.   *Barbara Porter, Arroyo Grande, CA*

I just converted to bamboo batting. It's so soft, especially as I make many baby quilts, and it's environmentally friendly.

9 I just converted to bamboo batting. It's so soft, especially as I make many baby quilts, and it's environmentally friendly.   *Robyn Waite, Cherrybrook, Australia*

10 I have used bamboo on my last two quilts and have been amazed by how well this performs as a really good batting. It quilts very well, and washing is so easy on gentle cycle. The quilt comes out looking amazing. I will be using bamboo batting more often, if I can source more of it.   *Anne Ryves, Thornlands, Australia*

11 I prefer natural types of batting, cotton being the cheaper natural one. I do love the soy and bamboo batting which are more expensive. They are better for the environment, lie flatter and breathe. I like the feel of the batting and the look of the quilt after it has been quilted. It gives the quilt a more old-fashioned look.   *Susan Louis, Briarwood, NY*

12 I have been using a pure cotton fusible batting on both the quilt top and the backing. It is light, soft, and very easy to apply, especially on larger quilts. It makes quilting so much easier that I can now do it myself and don't need to send away for quilting.

Miffy Smith, Hastings, Australia

13 I like thin and soft cotton batting. Sometimes I use flannel for that antique look that I love. Tiny stitches are also easier with thin batting. *Ann Liebner, Pine Grove, PA*

14 If you are quilting a very dark fabric quilt, make sure you purchase black batting. It makes a difference!

Peggy Quinlan-Gee, Salt Lake City, UT

D. Pros and Cons of Natural Battings

1 I have found that natural fibers adhere better to cotton fabrics, making them easier to quilt. Natural fibers have some shrinkage which causes that crinkled, aged look. This is either an advantage or disadvantage, depending on what end result you prefer.

Nancee McCann, Wilmington, DE

2 Natural fibers have stood the test of time. We know that quilts using these fibers last. The newer batting made from bamboo, recycled bottles, etc., do not have this proven track record.

Georgia Pierce, Seattle, WA

3 Cotton batting is soft to the touch, drapes nicely, quilts beautifully, and does not have little fibers that get up your nose like a polyester batting does. The biggest disadvantage is that cotton shows fold and crease lines more than polyester does.

Judy Dowdy, Grandy, NC

4 I'm not keen on bamboo batting. Although it's soft, when I quilt it on the long arm machine, it pops through the stitch holes and brings a lot of fluff around the needle and bobbin.

Louise Lott, Healesville, Australia

5 Natural fiber batting can be stronger. My mother used wool batting made from felt that was previously used to press water out of paper at a paper mill. These battings have outlived their fabric sandwiches and are currently being used in new quilts.

Karen Enslen, Port Republic, VA

6 Natural fibers can breathe, but they are more expensive than poly fibers. Natural fibers burn but do not melt as do poly fibers, making them safer for children's quilts.   *Betty Phelps, Wichita Falls, TX*

7 Polyester battings do hold their shape better and also resist molds and mildew. A polyester-filled quilt will be thicker but weigh less than a quilt with a 100% cotton batting.

Sharon Sutton, Lindsey, OH

8 As a vegan and environmental activist, I prefer fabrics and batting made from natural fibers grown organically. As organic is not always the easiest to find, and there is not as much selection as far as patterns and colors go, this is a definite disadvantage. Some new battings are becoming available made from recycled manmade fibers that are also more environmentally friendly than, say, conventionally grown cotton, which requires immense amounts of water and pesticides.   *Amanda Kei Andrews, Vero Beach, FL*

Wool should only be used on quilts that will get a lot of use as the batting could attract moths in storage.

9 Cotton batting is my favorite. Bamboo seems super linty, and wool should only be used on quilts that will get a lot of use as the batting could attract moths in storage.   *Leigh Spears, San Antonio, TX*

10 Make a sample set for yourself. Get pieces of many types of batting and sew them, wash them, and keep them so that when you need a batting, you have a reference guide of your own. Mark each so you know what it is. Washing lets you know how it will wash as far as shrinking and keeping its shape. A good place to get samples is at quilt shows. Batting companies many times will give a sample pack of their products.

When purchasing a bag of batting, read the bag. It tells you how to care for the product, how close the quilting needs to be and what the content of the product is. I keep these bags until the quilt is finished. If I have any pieces of the batting left over that I intend to keep, I put them back in the bag so that when I go to use that piece, I know what it is. *Patti Goggio, Broadlands, VA*

E. *Different Lofts*

❶ With tied quilts, I use high-loft batting so it is fluffy and airy. With quilted items, I use a low loft because it's easier to sew and creates a more uniform quilted product. For home decor items like placemats, I use interfacing with no loft so my kids' cups don't tip over due to lumpy batting. *Liz Brown, Annapolis, MD*

❷ In baby quilts, the higher loft makes the quilt lightweight and fold-able. I use thinner densities in table runners and placemats because they lie nicely. In larger quilts for beds, the wool batting is nice because it drapes well, yet it's lightweight.

Judy Parmley, Blaine, MN

❸ For heavily quilted projects, a thinner batting is better to show the shadowing. A thick batting would not only be difficult to quilt, but much of the detail in the quilting would be lost. With regard to piecing, the more complex the piecing, the less dense the loft. Once a project with complex piecing is finished, it can become quite heavy, just due to the seams in the fabric.

Kathleen Keough, Berwyn, PA

❹ I use more loft in wall hangings and children's novelty items when I want that "pop out" effect. The cheaper poly or cotton/poly mix gives the amount of lift that I need.   *Karen Farnsworth, Hallam, PA*

Since most battings get thinner as time goes on, I often don't use the low loft.

❺ To create depth, I might use more layers of batting or a different density batting. If I want an area to stand out from the background, I will puff it up more with another layer. I once did this with a sunburst, putting more loft in the center portion of the sun.   *Paula Clark, Ethridge, TN*

❻ Since most battings get thinner as time goes on, I often don't use the low loft.

Kris Newlin, West Chester, PA

F. What To Do With Batting Scraps

❶ Don't throw away your batting scraps. You can zig-zag stitch them together to create larger pieces you can reuse. I have quite a few quilts that are made this way, and there is no difference in washing or drape.   *Liz Brown, Annapolis, MD*

❷ I use pinking shears to cut batting pieces to make it easier to butt them together to make a larger size.   *Terry Miller, Alexandria, VA*

❸ If you have to piece the batting because you didn't have a big enough single piece, be sure to use the same types of pieces together. Don't mix cotton with cotton/poly to create one piece, for example. They have different degrees of shrinkage.

Patsy Shields, Sellersburg, IN

❹ I have made several large quilts that I've quilted in sections. I have found that Hobbs 80/20 batting is very easy to join together with nylon tricot interfacing strips. These joints cannot be detected from the front or back of the finished quilt. It makes quilting a large quilt on a regular sewing machine much easier to handle.

Laroletta Petty, Breckenridge, CO

❺ Save those small batting scraps you don't need for your project. They are good substitutes for pricey floor dusting sheets!

In addition, I find that a 2" wide strip of lightweight fusible interfacing will join two smaller pieces of batting to make a useable piece. I use this method especially for baby quilts.

Susan Bloomfield, Wilder, VT

❻ Save all your batting scraps and use them to stuff little pillows and cloth toys. I also wrap long strips around wooden hangers to pad them well, and then cover them with muslin. Padded hangers are nice for hanging liturgical vestments such as chasubles.

Valerie Turer, Brooklyn, NY

CHAPTER 10

Thread

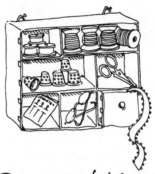

A. Hand Quilting Thread

❶ I like to use a quilting thread color that is 3–4 shades deeper than the fabric on which I am quilting. The quilting itself causes an indentation that is slightly shadowed. By using a deeper color thread, the quilting design is enhanced, and the stitches have the appearance of being more even. Using a thread that is the same shade or lighter than your fabric can cause the stitches to appear as if they are closer to the surface, causing the design to be less apparent. *Linda Gabrielse, Kentwood, MI*

❷ I prefer Coats and Clark Cotton Hand quilting thread. It does not tangle or fray and it is super sturdy. I also love Mettler Cotton Quilting thread for the same reasons. *Nancy Henry, Rochester, NH*

❸ Pay attention to thread weight: the higher the number, the finer the thread. *Carolyn Vidal, Newport, WA*

❹ I like YLI thread that is already waxed. When I use Mettler 40, I wax it either with Heaven-sent or beeswax. *Vicki Strumpf, Osprey, FL*

5 I like, and have used for years, YLI threads. They glide so easily through batting and fabric.   *Leona Briggs, Needham, MA*

6 I prefer 100% cotton hand quilting thread that has a natural shine to show off the stitches. While polyester core threads tend to be stronger, they can be too strong for cotton fabrics and actually damage the fabric.   *Linnette Dowdell, Apopka, FL*

7 I have learned that any thread is fine for hand quilting as long as I heavily wax it.   *Kathy Perry, Sugar Land, TX*

8 When choosing thread for hand quilting, always take into account the backing color of the quilt. I have a friend who is hand quilting with white thread on a quilt with a solid red backing. She is very unhappy with how easily her somewhat irregular stitches are showing. Even a grey or dark tan thread would have shown up less on the red backing and probably made her happier.

Nancy Swanwick, Fort Scott, KS

9 I made a "bug quilt" for my young grandson using bug fabric in a mason jar design. For his favorite jar, I used dark navy solid fabric and embroidered lightning bugs using glow-in-the-dark thread that he can only see at night.   *Nancy Chase, Columbus, MT*

B. Machine Quilting Thread

1 In machine quilting, use a finer thread in the bobbin so you will not have to change the bobbin so often.   *Carole Wilder, Hastings, MN*

2 I prefer Aurifil 100% cotton 50 weight thread for all my machine quilting. It is strong and creates a beautiful subtle stipple. It is also most compatible with my sewing machine and fine needles.

Linda Pace, McDonough, GA

❸ I prefer to use interesting top threads, and Valdani Cottons 35 weight are my very favorite. They come in a great range of colors and variations. I almost always use bobbinfill, an extra-fine thread that won't show on the top of the work. I use "Superior Threads The Bottom Line" by Libby Lehman which has the advantage of matching backing fabrics so well it is sometimes hard to see the stitches. Or I use Gutermann's Skala 240 which comes on 5,000 meter rolls and is therefore very economical.

Sue Sacchero, Safety Bay, Australia

❹ I now use a long-arm for most of my quilting, and I use all trilobal polyester. It is strong and comes in tons of luscious colors. When I machine quilt using my domestic sewing machine, the thread I choose really depends on how dense the quilting will be and if it is going to be a utility quilt or a decorative piece. My regular sewing machine prefers cotton thread, like Aurifil or Prescencia 60 weight.   *Annemarie (Nancy) Poorbaugh, Montgomery, AL*

❺ I typically use cotton 40 weight for basic quilting and polyester 50 weight for denser quilting.   *Keeley Levitsky, Pottstown, PA*

❻ The thread I choose for machine quilting depends on how much I want it to show. Silk or extra fine for high density quilting, Isacord poly for texture but not too much statement, and King Tut by Superior if I want the thread to make its own statement.

Patty Gertz, Ringoes, NJ

❼ If I find that my thread is breaking in either the bobbin or needle, I know I have not got the same weight in each. Also, finer threads tend to break more easily if there is too much lint in and around the bobbin case. I find it best to clean and dust my machine before every project.   *Linda Pace, McDonough, GA*

❽ Water-soluble thread is great for basting the quilt together or doing trapunto. Don't wet your fingers to thread the needle—the saliva will dissolve the end of the thread! Wet your fingers and rub the needle, then thread. A white plastic bread-bag tab works great as a threading aid when you hold it in back of the needle—works for monofilament thread too! Keep water-soluble thread in a closed Ziploc bag when not using, or it will pick up the room's moisture and start to weaken.

Loosen the top tension considerably, and don't bother using water-soluble thread in the bobbin, because when the top thread dissolves, the bottom thread will just fall away. You don't have to wash the quilt to remove the thread. You can spritz it.

Patty Gertz, Ringoes, NJ

9 Buy some chenille stems and use them to keep thread spools and their matching bobbins together in pairs. You will be able to locate the match-ups quickly.

Michelle Harrison, Morganton, GA

Buy some chenille stems and use them to keep thread spools and their matching bobbins together in pairs.

10 If I want to keep my quilt soft and draping, I use 50 or 60 weight 100% cotton. If I want to make a stiffer quilt, say for a wall quilt, I'll use a heaver 100% cotton in 30 or 40 weight.

Barbara Porter, Arroyo Grande, CA

11 For the spool, I prefer 100% Egyptian-grown long-staple cotton. It sews like a dream. In the bobbin, I use either a fine basting thread if the quilt will be heavily quilted or a regular-weight, all-purpose sewing thread.

Andrea Mitchell, Silver Spring, MD

12 I prefer 40/3ply 100% cotton machine quilting thread with a silk finish because it sews like a dream, doesn't tangle in the machine, has proven to be durable, and doesn't cut the fibers of fabric over time.

Pat Smith, Sidney, NY

13 I prefer Egyptian cotton in a 50 weight for machine quilting. This weight and finish in thread will cause less lint in your sewing machine and take up less room in your seam area, which also allows for more accuracy in the piecing phase. I have used 60 weight in more miniature scale pieces to give even more room in the seam area.

Kim Wiley, Willow Grove, PA

⑭ I prefer 60 weight polyester because it gives the quilting a little sheen, while still not being so "thready." I like to match my thread to the fabric I am sewing on so when I am doing more complicated designs, the thread will not show any mistakes. When I want the quilting to really stand out, I will use a polyester variegated thread or a metallic thread. I will usually stitch over the design about three times to really give it emphasis.

Linda Bridges, Clarksville, TN

⑮ I like Libby Lehman's Bottom Line for bobbins. This is a fine but strong thread that does not pull to the front of the work.

Sally Zimmer, Bark River, MI

⑯ My quilting experience began in the late '90s in Tucson, Arizona. I began with a pair of scissors (also being used for paper and plastic), spools of thread found around the house (one for turkey stitch-up), a very old Montgomery Ward machine (discolored from white to light mustard), all of which I hauled to a quilt class. Since I didn't have to do much more than straight stitching, I managed rather well and tried not to notice the dowdiness of my machine next to those that glistened around me.

I graduated to a used Pfaff within the first year (still happily in love with it) and never looked back! I learned that more had to evolve with it. What was life like before the rotary cutter? I became conscious of thread and fabric quality in the bargain. The better both, the better the quality and beauty of the quilt! So, I early on jumped from the bargain bins of thread at JoAnn's to her Sulkys and Gutermann's in the display cases. Now I regularly shop the specialty quilt shops for top-of-the-line thread.

Jennifer Neighbours, Palmyra, VA

c. Monofilament Thread

1 I only use 100% polyester monofilament thread. Nylon will stretch when heated up as it passes through the tension disk, and relax when in the quilt. So it is difficult to get an even tension with nylon. I also use polyester monofilament in my bobbin. But I never use monofilament for baby quilts, as it can be dangerous, if the baby pulls out stitches, and the monofilament gets wrapped around little fingers or in little mouths.   *Barbara Porter, Arroyo Grande, CA*

2 *Patience* and a new size 90/10 needle helps me. If I'm appliquing with monofilament, my bobbin has regular thread.
Debbie Daugherty-Ball, Salisbury, MD

3 When using monofilament, slow down your quilting speed. Loosen your top and bottom tension, because monofilament is finicky. If you want to use a color thread in the bobbin, use a thin polyester (60 wt or higher bobbin thread). Polyester thread has no fine hairs like cotton and will not catch on the monofilament.
Linda Bridges, Clarksville, TN

4 Working with monofilament can be a challenge. One of the most important things I have learned if I am using it in the bobbin is to wind the bobbin slowly and only fill it half-full. If a bobbin is wound too fast with monofilament, the thread can stretch as it is winding and may cause puckering as you stitch. Winding the bobbin only half-full will prevent "back spin" while sewing.
Linnette Dowdell, Apopka, FL

5 I use the monofilament thread on top and a regular 50 weight cotton thread in the

If a bobbin is wound too fast with monofilament, the thread can stretch as it is winding and may cause puckering as you stitch.

bobbin. I also keep the monofilament in an airtight baggie when not in use so that it does not become stiff.   *Judy Craddock, Babylon, NY*

6 Only use monofilament when making projects that do not require excessive washings, such as a wallhanging, doll quilt or bedrunner. Do not use monofilament thread if the project is going to be washed in hot washers and dryers. It will melt and all the quilting will be destroyed.   *Donna Powers, Tellico Plains, TN*

7 Use a thread net on the spool to keep it from unwinding. Superior Thread even includes a net when you buy the spool.   *Karen Benke, Medina, OH*

8 It helps to see monofilament stitching if you use natural daylight or a black light while quilting. Make sure you tie off well at the beginning and end to prevent your stitches from unraveling.   *Ruth Anglin, Tijeras, NM*

9 I color the end of the thread with a marker to better see it for threading.   *Jennifer Padden, Austin, TX*

10 I only use Superior Monopoly monofilament. I love it and keep a spool of it right next to my sewing machine. I use it mostly for stitching in the ditch around appliqué. In the bobbin, use a thread color that matches the color of your background fabric, the fabric under your appliqué. That way, if your tension is not quite perfect and you're getting porkies (the bobbin thread poking to the top), you won't notice them as much.   *Sue Hurley, Princeton, NJ*

11 I use monofilament for micro background quilting when I do not want the quilting to show, but I just want the textural effect of the quilting.   *Barbara Merritt, Brackney, PA*

12 When machine quilting, try using monofilament thread on the topside of the quilt and traditional thread on the underneath side of the quilt. The results will be amazingly similar to hand-quilting, as only small "stitches" of the underneath thread pull to the surface and resemble neat, even handstitching.   *Jan Mast, Lancaster, PA*

Top 5 Pieces of Advice for Beginners, According to Our Survey

JUST FOR FUN

❶ Measure Twice, Cut Once

❖ Take your time and do not rush on your project. Always measure twice before cutting.   *Sharon Sutton, Lindsey, OH*

❷ Start Small

❖ Make potholders first, lots of potholders, for practice before you use your prettiest or more expensive fabrics.

Barbara Johnson, Dallas, OR

❸ Use The Best Supplies You Can Afford

❖ Use good quality sewing tools including rotary cutter, rulers, a cutting mat, and good sharp scissors. The better your tools, the better your accuracy and the better your finished project.

Linnette Dowdell, Apopka, FL

❹ Mistakes Are Okay

❖ Your quilt does not have to be perfect—nothing is ever perfect. Some of my biggest mistakes have become the unique feature I like best in the finished quilt.   *Mary Marlowe, Hedgesville, WV*

❺ The ¼″ Seam Is Important

❖ Those crazy ¼″ seams are hard at first, and no one is perfect the first time. Put a piece of painters tape on your machine by the presser foot where that seam should be. A couple of layers will help even more. Later, if you really like quilting, get a special foot for your machine. It will make it much easier.

Linda Ladrach, Dover, OH

⓭ I always have problems with straight line stitching with monofilament. It looks great until I hang the piece, and then there is frequently evidence that the monofilament stretched in stitching and is now relaxing and pulling ever so slightly on the line of stitching. I avoid long lines of monofilament stitching.

Sharon Mountford, Canoga Park, CA

⓮ I don't like monofilament. Every quilt I made in the late '80s and early '90s with that product I have had to replace all the quilting. *Kristi Wilson, Irving, TX*

D. *Metallic Thread*

❶ Metallic threads are not as strong as other threads. They are best suited to decorative items that will not be washed or dried very often. Be sure to use a needle specialized for metallic threads as the eye and the scarf of the needle are shaped to prevent fraying. Don't use your needle threader because you can nick the inside of the needle's eye, causing a burr that will shred the metallic thread.

Annemarie (Nancy) Poorbaugh, Montgomery, AL

❷ Metallic threads are great for adding a little extra sparkle, but you need to realize they can be a little scratchy in a quilt.

Judy Minard, Sayre, PA

> *I like metallic thread for free motion thread painting on landscape designs.*

❸ I like metallic thread for free motion thread painting on landscape designs. I also like it for couching larger fibers, like yarn, on thread art projects. *Janet Bland, Smyrna, GA*

❹ When I use most metallic threads, I use a large-eyed needle. A size 90 topstitching needle is my favorite as there is less friction on the thread as it passes through the eye. Using a longer stitch length and sewing slower also helps to keep the delicate metallic thread from breaking. *Linnette Dowdell, Apopka, FL*

5 I use metallic thread only if there are metallic accents on the fabric, or if I am quilting dupioni silk and want a festive look. I think it looks best as straight-line quilting or outline quilting.

Valerie Turer, Brooklyn, NY

6 I've been told that if you put metallic thread in the freezer, it will not fray as much, but I have not tried it.

Brenda Rice, Nicholasville, KY

E. *Perle Cotton*

1 I like the stitching to be a major design/color element in a quilt, so I favor perle cotton because of the range of colors and thicknesses. *Michelle Harrison, Morganton, GA*

2 I enjoy doing "big stitch" embellishments using perle cotton. By that I mean, a running stitch (⅓–¼" in length), a lazy daisy, or big old French knots. I also have done couching over perle cotton. Mark the line you want to embellish and run a line of teensy dots of washable glue along the line. Then apply the perle cotton to the glue and either wait for it to dry or press with a dry iron. Couch over it with a zig-zag that is long and just wide enough to cover. That keeps the focus on the perle cotton.

Andrea Mitchell, Silver Spring, MD

3 I'm hand quilting a 1930s repro quilt with butterflies hand appliquéd on it. I used black perle cotton to embroider the blanket stitch around each one. *Patricia Grimm, New Windsor, NY*

4 I have tied quilts with perle cotton and have utility quilted with bigger stitches for a more primitive look.

Annemarie (Nancy) Poorbaugh, Montgomery, AL

I use the perle cotton when I serge the edge of a fleece baby blanket to finish the edge. This is instead of binding.

5 I use the perle cotton when I serge the edge of a fleece baby blanket to finish the edge. This is instead of binding.　*Susan Walters, Newark, DE*

6 I really like to appliqué washed, felted wool in blanket stitch, using perle cotton.

Barbara Porter, Arroyo Grande, CA

7 On my most recent project, a reversible baby quilt, I used perle cotton to hand stitch the binding. I used large running stitches similar to big stitch hand quilting. It added a very sweet touch to the baby quilt.

Marcia Nissley, Ronks, PA

8 I took a class where we used perle cotton stitching next to the binding which made a nice effect.　*Barb Thomas, Wantage, NJ*

9 Perle cotton can be used in the top thread of the machine. The stitching will show great definition and gives a hand-quilted or rustic feel.　*Janice Simmons, Fresno, CA*

10 My personal preference is No. 8. When using perle cotton to quilt by machine, I wind a bobbin of No. 8 perle cotton and sew from the reverse side so that the perle cotton is on the front of the quilt.　*Linnette Dowdell, Apopka, FL*

F. Caring for Thread

❶ Don't stock more thread than you can use in a year. Thread becomes brittle with age and will break, and you'll have invested in something that you can't use.

Robbin Golden, Summerville, SC

Don't stock more thread than you can use in a year.

❷ Be sure that your thread is fresh. If you have thread that was handed down to you from your great aunt, use it for crafting, but not in that quilt you want to last. Test the strength of your thread by pulling a length out and tugging on it to make sure it doesn't break easily. *Janice Simmons, Fresno, CA*

❸ I used to keep my threads on a thread stand, but now I keep them in plastic drawers to keep them away from dust and light.

Karen Martin, Breezy Point, MN

❹ Using Thread Heaven works great when using thread for hand work. It is a solid silicon that lubricates the thread, so it doesn't get knots or tangles. Beeswax used to be used for this, but it is now suggested that beeswax attracts bugs.

Barbara Porter, Arroyo Grande, CA

CHAPTER 11

Hand Quilting

A. *Pros and Cons of Frames*

❶ I have quilted on all types of frames from large to small. The large frame is not easy for me as I can't quilt in all directions. I have tried a lap frame and it is okay for smaller projects, but it gets heavy. I have settled on a free-standing Grace hoop that rotates in all directions. On my Grace hoop, I have quilted everything from a king-size quilt to a wall hanging.   *Marjorie Polay, Canyon Lake, TX*

❷ Frames can really help to stabilize the quilt layers, but they are awkward to use. They need to be moved a lot. I have small hands and do not use a large frame. I will often hand quilt without a frame, just with the quilt spray basted and safety pinned on a table in front of me. I have had no issues with ripples forming.

Marianne Udell, Santa Fe, NM

❸ Large floor frames hold the layers of the quilt well, but it's only possible to quilt in one direction. It takes a long while to attach the quilt and takes up a lot of space.

Marion Bathe, St. Jean du Bouzet, France

❹ I prefer my floor frame to quilt just because I don't have to baste. I hate basting. With a small hoop or lap frame, the best pro is that you can turn the quilt to quilt towards yourself, which is the easiest direction to quilt. This is not always possible in a floor frame. But I can usually muddle my way through all quilt designs on a floor frame, including quilting 180° away from myself.

Sarah Francis, Greenville, TX

❺ A frame is really handy for basting your quilt —no more getting down on your hands and knees—but frames are expensive and take up a lot of space.   *Joan Martino, Kingman, AZ*

❻ A good reason for using a frame would be to hold a project taut, so that the stitches are more even. But if I am quilting a pattern across the quilt, I need to keep moving the frame, and that can be time consuming.   *Leigh Spears, San Antonio, TX*

❼ In a frame, the quilt is off my lap so I can quilt all summer long. It holds the layers better, and the back of the quilt is flatter. I make better stitches because it's sturdy, and it keeps the cat away from the quilt. The downside is that the frame is as big as a living room sofa.

Janet Atkins, Athens, NY

In a frame, the quilt is off my lap so I can quilt all summer long.

❽ Quilt frames do take up space, but then what looks lovelier than a quilt in progress?   *Nancy Powell, Coatesville, PA*

❾ I did buy a full-size frame when I was hand quilting. The pro side of it is that the quilt was always there ready to go, and I could sit and add a few stitches while I waited for the school bus or had dinner in the oven. I did like to use a hoop on a stand for smaller projects, so I could join the family in the TV room while I quilted.

Lorraine Vignoli, Commack, NY

❿ I find using a folding table gives me the same results as a quilting frame. After I have secured my quilt top with the batting and backing fabric using pins, I lay my quilt on a folding table. I use a 6-foot one, letting the quilt hang down over the sides. I use big clips and clip it down. I start quilting in the middle and then take my pins out. I take the clips off and roll the quilt up from the top until I get to where I want to start my quilting. I move the quilt down as I get further along, re-pinning as needed. This gives me the same tension as using a frame or hoop.

I also have done hand quilting by just laying the quilt on my lap and tucking one side underneath me to pull it taut. Working with the quilt on my lap is a great way to keep warm in the winter.

Debbie McAdam, Holbrook, NY

⓫ I use a lap hoop. I can control the stitches better, and since I have never learned to quilt away from myself, I am not sure I could use a large stand. I can twist the lap hoop so I am always quilting top right to bottom left.   *Joan Oldham, Panama City, FL*

⓬ I learned to hand quilt using a 12" round hoop, and that's the only way I can quilt the way I want. Without a hoop, I feel like I can't get consistent stitches. I need that "third hand" that a hoop provides. I keep turning the hoop so I am always quilting toward myself.   *Nancy Robertson, Scituate, MA*

⓭ A small round hoop allows for ease of movement around the top and can be carried from room to room with little use of space. A rigid frame is useful for group quilting but requires lots of space.

Shelia Smith, Goldthwaite, TX

14 Not using a frame makes for a softer quilt because the quilting is looser.

Joan Miller, Richmond, VA

15 Do not let your quilt sit longer than a day or two in the frame. The tightness of the hoop could stretch the fabric. Quilting will correct this in most cases, but don't chance it. If you baste the quilt sandwich with safety pins, be careful not to catch your pins between the hoops, or the pin holes may pull the fabric or possibly rip it.

Rosemarie Garone, West Islip, NY

> *Do not let your quilt sit longer than a day or two in the frame. The tightness of the hoop could stretch the fabric.*

B. Hand Quilting Needles

1 When you are hand quilting, use the smallest needles (highest number) that you can work with. I am rough on needles, and I do perfectly with #10. When I try to use #11 or #12, they bend and break for me. #9 or #8 (bigger needles) feel like I am sewing with nails.

Nancy Henry, Rochester, NH

2 I use a #12 between. It is very true that the smaller the needle, the smaller the stitch. Needles do bend and break, but the Piecemaker needles are the strongest. Believe me, I've tried all of them.

Ann Roadarmel, Elysburg, PA

3 I use a size 10 straw needle. I like the length and flexibility for loading stitches, and the thin diameter goes through three layers easily.

Leigh Spears, San Antonio, TX

4 I like a large-eye quilt needle because I don't like spending more time trying to thread the needle than actually quilting.

Sally Berry, Virginia Beach, VA

5 For fine threads, I use Dritz #10 Betweens. These needles just slide through the fabric. I use them for all hand sewing. When I use thick thread, I like the skinniest, sharpest embroidery needles that will accept the thread.   *Valerie Turer, Brooklyn, NY*

6 I use #8 or #9 needles because that is the size that best fits my fingers. A very tiny needle gets "lost" in my hand and a longer needle seems awkward as well.   *Ruth Ann Gingrich, New Holland, PA*

7 I use a small quilting needle that has the eye in the middle, so that I have a point on each end.   *Laura Wisenbaugh, Owosso, MI*

If there are seams in the backing as well as the front, I will use a longer needle because it will bend instead of break if I'm applying too much pressure.

8 If there are seams in the backing as well as the front, I will use a longer needle because it will bend instead of break if I'm applying too much pressure. As I am getting older, I need a larger eye with darker threads.

Linda Scheible, Austin, TX

9 I do not like the short needles (betweens) many quilters use. I am simply not comfortable with them, so I use a needle such as a sharp or milliner's needle that I have good control with. It allows me to achieve the nice even stitches I am seeking to make.   *Colleen Froats, Alanson, MI*

10 I have tried a lot of needles, but right now I really prefer Roxanne's. I am a self-taught quilter since age 17, so my method is my own. I quilt pushing the needle with the thimble on my thumb, so I consider myself a "power quilter." I can snap a thin little needle in half with no trouble. The Roxannes are substantial enough not to break, yet small and sharp.   *Nancy Swanwick, Fort Scott, KS*

11 I like Richard Hemming & Son large eye, betweens, size 10. They are easy to thread. They are pointed, not blunt, and don't bend or break too easily.   *Barbara Isaak, Lakeville, MN*

12 I prefer Roxanne's #9 betweens. This needle has a strong smooth shaft with a smooth eye. I do not have difficulty threading this needle and it does not shred my thread. I have had no issues with the needle point breaking off, so that means the needle was made from one piece and the point was not added after the shaft was made.   *Marianne Udell, Santa Fe, NM*

13 I use only John James Gold'n Glide needles. They are teflon-coated, so I find they pass more smoothly through the fabric.   *Rosemarie Garone, West Islip, NY*

14 I use #11 Roxanne needles. The needles are strong, yet fine enough and the right length for me. You need to measure and make sure that the needle is the right length for your finger to avoid stress and pain at the knuckles when quilting for a length of time.   *Marie White, Waiuku, New Zealand*

15 I use John James Gold'n Glide size 11 for hand quilting. It is easy to thread and glides smoothly through the fabric due to its teflon coating. To thread it, I make sure the end of the thread has a fresh cut, and put the needle opening in front of white paper to thread it. If it doesn't work, I try the other side of the needle as it's easier to thread one side than the other. If that still isn't working for me, I resort to a little metal loop needle threader.   *Ceil Jancola, Wallingford, VT*

C. Thimbles

1 I use two different thimbles, depending on the type of quilt I am making and the style of quilting at the time. If I am quilting traditionally with fine hand quilting thread, I use a traditional silver closed-end thimble, but if I am quilting with perle cotton no 8, I use a Clover open-ended thimble. I do try to vary the thimbles I use to alter the way I quilt so I don't put too much a strain on my hands and shoulders.   *Diane Anderson, Auckland, New Zealand*

2 I use the rubber or disposable thimble so that I can feel the work better. Also, being left-handed, it seems easier for me to use.   *Donna Dickinson, Harrington, DE*

3 I use a dimpled metal quilting thimble with a ridge around the top because my finger never gets sweaty and the ridge always catches the needle.   *Kirsten Schmitt, Baldwin, NY*

4 I do not use a traditional thimble because the tips of my fingers are smaller than the first knuckle, so thimbles fall off. I use the sticky bandage fabric that is used to wrap a horse's ankle. I cut a piece 1" wide and 4" long. I wrap it on my finger and squeeze it to make the shape. It stays on all day, and the needle does not penetrate this custom thimble. The bandage is sold at the local feed and grain store. One roll will last a lifetime.   *Karen Benke, Medina, OH*

5 I have a thimble by TJ Lane that she altered to fit my arthritic joints so I could quilt without pain. I even have two: one to use normally and one to use when my hands are swollen. She will repair them for free if anything happens to them. I have quilted holes in mine several times and she has fixed it.   *Teri Weed, Wynnewood, PA*

6 I use a baby spoon on the underside of the quilt and the adhesive-backed leather Thimble Pad for my needle finger. This method gives me more control and feels more natural.   *Ruth Anglin, Tijeras, NM*

7 My favorite thimble is from The Thimble Lady. It has deep dimples that hold the needle well. It was expensive, but I look at it as a life-time investment.   *Joan Martino, Kingman, AZ*

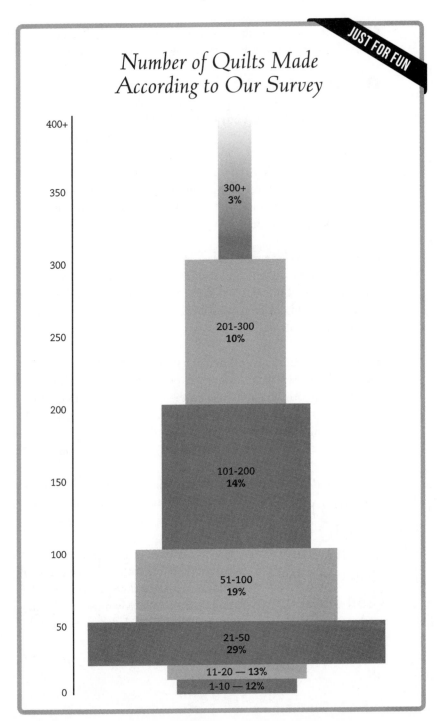

8 I like the "jelly" thimbles made by Clover. I don't like the smell of metal thimbles and leather stretches.   *Valerie Turer, Brooklyn, NY*

9 Nimble Thimble is the only one I use. It is flexible enough for me to feel the needle coming through the quilt, but the metal tip prevents serious pricks. I buy them in bulk!

Nancy Henry, Rochester, NH

10 I've always used a metal thimble until recently. I just bought a silicon thimble with a metal top. The silicon fits easier on my old knobby finger joints, and I still have the protection of the metal cap to push the needle with.   *Jenn Martin, Prattville, AL*

11 I have a tailor's thimble passed down from a great-great-aunt that fits me. It is a silver band that fits around my finger. I have tried the leather thimbles, and the ones that have the solid tops, but I just like my old one best, probably because that is the one that I first got used to using.   *Nancy Powell, Coatesville, PA*

12 I use an antique silver thimble that belonged to my grandmother. We must have the same size fingers because it fits perfectly. It's smooth and well worn on the inside, secure enough to stay on, but not uncomfortably tight. I can put my work down and do something else and forget I even have the thimble on.

Sally Eshelman, York, PA

I use a small wad of ticky-tack (like putty) inside the tip of the thimble. My finger has plenty of room, but I can shake my hand and my thimble won't fall off.

13 I use a beat-up old thimble that my grandmother had, just because it was hers.   *Danette Lockler, Denver, CO*

14 I use a size extra-large metal quilting thimble with a rim. I use a small wad of ticky-tack (like putty) inside the tip of the thimble. My finger has plenty of room, but I can shake my hand and my thimble won't fall off.

Joanne Picicci, Spokane, WA

⓯ I switched from a flat top thimble to an open tip thimble, when I started to have carpal tunnel symptoms. The pain I was experiencing disappeared just by using the ball of my finger, instead of the tip, to push the needle.   *Ann Liebner, Pine Grove, PA*

⓰ After trying several kinds of thimbles, I ended up with a sports medicine Coban elastic bandage. Then it became a hassle since every time I washed my hands, I would have to rewrap and waste the previous wrap. Then I found Cosco medium rubber finger tips. Apparently it is a finger protector from an office supply store to prevent paper cuts. Now it's the only thimble I use. It comes in size 11½, 12 tips in a box, $2.50 a box, which comes out $.21 per piece! They're great for short or long nails, and I have them in my different sewing kits.   *Eugene Diokno, Towson, MD*

⓱ I cannot use a regular thimble; it just is too clumsy. Instead I use self-adhesive wrap or tape around my middle finger. This is more like a second skin, and I have more control over the work.   *Mary Ann Bonne, Ord, NE*

⓲ My favorite thimble is the leather Skin Thimble. It fits completely over my finger and has a small elastic band inside to help hold it in place without restricting flexibility or circulation.   *Marsha Brasky, Algonquin, IL*

⓳ I love a leather thimble. I have tried the metal ones, but find it very uncomfortable with my acrylic nails.   *Mania Wilson, Bloomfield, IN*

⓴ My favorite thimble is the silver dimpled coin thing you stick to your finger. No sweat, no falling off. It is amazing.   *Jennifer Padden, Austin, TX*

㉑ I use a gold thimble that I purchased at a quilt show for around $40. I think it was made by someone special and is sold individually. The finger nail side is open and allows my finger to breathe.   *Margaret (Peg) Parsons, New Castle, DE*

㉒ I have tried many different thimbles, but never found one that works. Now, if I have a lot of hand sewing, such as many bindings, I will apply two band-aids to just the right spot. This works for me.

Karla Santoro, Stanley, NY

㉓ A Roxanne thimble works for me. I actually put a hole in one thimble, and then I tried Roxanne's. I love that you use the thimble on the side of your finger instead of on top. It's better for my arthritis.   *Marjorie Polay, Canyon Lake, TX*

㉔ I use a small stick-on leather patch. I wrap a small piece of bandage tape over it, around my finger. I use the tape many times over, and the little leather stick-on lasts forever.

Lorry Kirschner, Brookville, IN

㉕ I use Clover Protect and Grip. It fits my fat finger and I like the lip around the tip.   *Janet Bland, Smyrna, GA*

㉖ In order to get used to wearing and using the thimble during my early days of quilting, I sometimes wore the thimble all day long while doing my household cleaning chores—it got to be a part of me and now I can't appliqué or even sew a button on a shirt without it.   *Nora Manley, Athens, AL*

D. Sore Fingers

❶ I use a lot of hand cream. I can build up a pretty good area of thick skin on the underside of my quilting finger. I have tried varying ways to protect this finger, but I find my quilting stitch is not as good, so I opt for sore fingers!   *Marjorie Polay, Canyon Lake, TX*

❷ I try to hand quilt a bit every day to build up a callus to protect my fingertips. It is important to keep your quilting fingers clean, and I apply triple antibiotic cream if the tips are sore when I go to bed at night. If they are sore and I will be doing housework or outdoor work, I protect those finger tips with liquid skin, band-aids, or work gloves. I am a nurse and have seen some very nasty infections due to small cuts and abrasions. *Marianne Udell, Santa Fe, NM*

❸ When the fingers on the underside get sore from being pricked too many times, I cut up a Steri-Strip and pop it on the offending area. Because Steri-Strips are thin, I can feel what's going on with my quilting, while offering a degree of protection to my sore finger.
Louise Lott, Healesville, Australia

❹ I use a product called New Skin. It is used by nurses to coat cracked fingers, and it works well. *Rachel Applegate, Slingerlands, NY*

❺ I keep my hands moisturized and give special attention to working moisturizer onto the tips of my fingers. Within a few days, a callus forms and makes quilting much easier.
Marti Blankenship, Pleasant Valley, MO

❻ Use a finger cot from the band-aid department on the index finger of your stitching hand. It helps immensely with gripping the needle. *Karen Renninger, Punta Gorda, FL*

❼ I recommend using Thimble-It, an oval-shaped self-adhesive finger pad. It's a great way to prevent getting those annoying sores and callused fingers. You can use Thimble-Its on any finger and as many as you like.

A great tip someone told me was to use chapstick on sore fingers. It's inexpensive and convenient to take with you anywhere. I also use Vaseline after smoothing out the callused areas on my fingers with a soft pumice stone.
Debbie McAdam, Holbrook, NY

A great tip someone told me was to use chapstick on sore fingers. It's inexpensive and convenient to take with you anywhere.

8 I have used clear finger nail polish on sore fingers. Brush a thin coating over the sore area. It does work and helps to heal quickly.

Ruth Ann Gingrich, New Holland, PA

9 If I have a lot of needle pricks, I use a liquid bandage. It not only protects my fingers, but it seems to speed up the healing too.

Karen Martin, Breezy Point, MN

10 There's cream on the market called Working Hands that's excellent for fingers made sore from quilting or other handwork.

Jan Mast, Lancaster, PA

11 Bag Balm rubbed on fingertips before bed works best for me.

Lisa Clark, South Plymouth, NY

12 Aveeno lotion is my personal favorite for sore fingers. At night, I apply it fairly heavily and cover my hands with socks. A little Vitamin E on a band-aid or under a finger cot also helps throughout the day.

Marsha Brasky, Algonquin, IL

13 I wear a thimble on my underneath finger. It took a while to get used to it, but no more sore fingers.

Barbara Clarke, Woodbridge, CA

14 Rest is the best thing for sore fingers. Skip quilting for a day and machine piece the next quilt top, or work on another project for a day.

Jenn Martin, Prattville, AL

15 I do not have sore fingers as my quilting method is stab-stitch; this is especially good for people with arthritis.

Marilyn Verburgh, Mahone Bay, Nova Scotia

E. Big-Stitch Quilting

❶ Big stitch is just like your regular hand quilting, only using larger stitches, thicker thread, and bigger sewing needles. You can use either an embroidery needle or larger sewing needles. If you don't use the right size, the thread will be difficult to pull through your layers. Besides using bigger needles, you need to use thicker thread, like embroidery or crochet thread. As you do your running stitches, do only 2 or 3 at a time.   *Debbie McAdam, Holbrook, NY*

❷ I do big-stitch embroidery sometimes as an embellishment. For that, I use either three strands of cotton embroidery floss or multiple strands of regular sewing thread (e.g., a strand of blue with a strand of green to create a subtle texture).

Andrea Mitchell, Silver Spring, MD

❸ I love big-stitch quilting. It's fast, easy and decorative. Although I try to make the stitches even, since the overall look is primitive, I don't stress over it. A few wonky stitches here and there just add to the character of the quilt.   *Ann Liebner, Pine Grove, PA*

❹ The most important issue with big-stitch quilting is to use an embroidery needle that is large enough to ease the doubled thread (the thread through the eye) through the layers. If you are having to tug too hard, the needle is too small, and it can be very hard on your hands.

Marianne Udell, Santa Fe, NM

If you are having to tug too hard, the needle is too small, and it can be very hard on your hands.

❺ I like to use perle cotton (size 8 or 12) and use consistently sized stitches top and bottom. My stitches are a little smaller than ¼" long.

Annemarie (Nancy) Poorbaugh, Montgomery, AL

6 Use a heavier thread in a contrasting color because it's part of the design. Don't stitch-in-the-ditch when you're using thicker thread. The stitching will not be seen.   *Marsha Nelson, Clinton, UT*

7 I like to use a size 5 embroidery needle and size 12 or 16 perle cotton. I find having my quilt slightly looser in the hoop also helps.

Joan Martino, Kingman, AZ

To keep your stitches uniform, attach a guide of ¼" tape to your left fingernail.

8 To keep your stitches uniform, attach a guide of ¼" tape to your left fingernail. You can easily measure your stitches in this way.

Donna Magee, Midlothian, TX

9 Sashiko, Japanese embroidery, is fun and produces a special look. A longer needle works better and you don't use a frame.

Sharon Mountford, Canoga Park, CA

10 Use a rubber needle puller for big-stitch quilting. Fons & Porter sells a great one with their wool needles.

Diane Johansen, Naperville, IL

11 Instead of struggling to pull a knot of perle cotton through the fabric, I pull the thread through, leaving about a 1" tail inside the quilt sandwich. I then take a couple of small stitches on top of each other before continuing with the big-stitch hand quilting.

Marti Blankenship, Pleasant Valley, MO

12 When you run out of thread, knot the new thread to the old instead of the traditional burying the knot; this method keeps with the primitive look.   *Ceil Jancola, Wallingford, VT*

F. Starting the Thread in Hand Quilting

❶ I make a knot in the thread, leaving a short tail. Start about ⅜"
away from where you want your first stitch to begin, running the
thread through the batting, taking care not to go through to the
backing. Come up where you wish to start and pop the knot into
the interior of the quilt. Make sure you approach from the direction
you are going to sew so the end doesn't show through.

Jenifer Aragon, Bloomington, CA

❷ I make a quilter's knot and insert the needle about ¾" from
my starting point. Go into the quilt top and batting, and bring the
needle up at the starting point. Your goal is to bury the knot in the
layers. Give a little tug, with your finger over the insertion point, to
bring the knot through the top fabric. If you have trouble getting
the knot to go through your needle hole, take the needle and insert
it into the spot where you're trying to bring the thread/knot in and
wiggle it a bit to enlarge the hole. Keep trying until it works!

Marcia Guza, Brick, NJ

❸ Knot the thread: thread the needle, wrap the long end of the
thread around the tip of the needle three times, then pull the
needle through, holding onto the thread, forming a knot at the
end. Start the needle in the fabric about 1" from the start point and
come up where you want to start. Pull the thread until the knot
"pops" through fabric.   *Carol A. Landis, Quarryville, PA*

❹ Always thread your needle with the thread off the spool and
knot the end that you cut off. This keeps the thread from twisting
and knotting.

For hand work, use medium to short lengths of thread to keep
it from looking tired. Move the tail very often, almost with every
pull of your running stitch, to keep the needle eye from fraying the
thread.   *Joanne Picicci, Spokane, WA*

G. Quilting in Process

❶ I like to wash my hands thoroughly before beginning to quilt to remove any lotions or oils from my hands. I feel it makes it easier to grip the quilt and will leave less on the surface of the quilt that could leave an oil stain later.   *Lisa Hughes, Richland, NY*

❷ Thimble finger at 3 o'clock, thumb at 7 o'clock, so as not to put stress on your wrist.   *Barbara Porter, Arroyo Grande, CA*

❸ I only thread about 18" of thread onto the needle. It takes less time to re-thread a needle than it does to untangle knots in thread that is too long.   *Colleen Froats, Alanson, MI*

❹ If you aim to go up and down as perpendicularly as possible in hand quilting, your stitches will be more even, top and bottom.
          Nancy Henry, Rochester, NH

❺ When changing directions in the quilting design, it is not necessary to end the thread. Instead, pull the thread through the inside, the batting, and exit at the beginning of the next quilting area.   *Susan Louis, Briarwood, NY*

❻ I love the magnetic item that holds on to my quilt so I can put my needle or pins on it so as not to lose them.
          Linda Ramsey, Arnold, MO

Change to a new needle often, about every 4–8 hours of quilting, thus only using sharp needles.

❼ Change to a new needle often, about every 4–8 hours of quilting, thus only using sharp needles.   *Rachel Applegate, Slingerlands, NY*

❽ I change needles if the quilting gets harder, as the oils from your fingers cause needles to oxidize. And don't put too many stitches on your needle. I usually put 3 on my needle with my rocking stitch. With more stitches, the layers get harder to rock and the length of the stitches increases undesirably.   *Sarah Francis, Greenville, TX*

9 I always start quilting in the middle of a quilt and work my way out. That way, all of the lumps and bumps even out by the time I get to the borders.   *Kirsten Schmitt, Baldwin, NY*

10 I usually start in the middle of the quilt and go out to the sides, east and west, then north and south. When I do this route, I find that I do not end up catching the backing to other parts of the quilt and having to rip out a lot of the quilting that I just completed.
     Danette Lockler, Denver, CO

11 Start with an overall big design to cover the entire quilt, then return to areas for more detail. This way if you decide you don't want to quilt anymore, the entire quilt is completed, and not just one block with so much detail that you can't bear the thought of completing the pattern.   *Marla Knappe, Flemington, NJ*

12 Don't start the project with tiny quilting stitches if these are difficult for you to do because you won't keep it up and your stitches will get larger, resulting in an uneven finish. Better to start with a slightly larger stitch that is easier to maintain, resulting in a uniform look for the whole project.   *Fiona Madden, Lilli Pilli, Australia*

13 I machine quilt in the ditch between the blocks, then hand quilt in the open areas. This speeds things up considerably.
     Sandy Helin, Watsonville, CA

14 Three things to keep in your sewing box for hand quilting (note that all pertain to threading the needle!): a sharp scissors for cutting the thread on an angle for easier threading, beeswax for coating the tip of the thread, and a needle threader.
     Ann Liebner, Pine Grove, PA

15 I keep paper and pencil close by to keep track of the yards of quilting thread used. Also, I use a dome threaded needle case to house 10 threaded needles. Remember to have the radio at hand to play beautiful music or books on tape!

Eileen D. Wenger, Lancaster, PA

Avoid dry eyes from hand quilting by consciously blinking and looking away from the quilt routinely.

16 Avoid dry eyes from hand quilting by consciously blinking and looking away from the quilt routinely.   Trudy Hadcock, Webster, NY

17 Invest time and effort to (re)learn how to handquilt. When I saw Jean Brown's video, I decided that was a method that I could grow old with. Of course I had to go through the trouble of learning how to handquilt her way, all over again. But I'm really glad I did: no aches, bad attitudes (bodywise) or any nasty side-effects like sore fingers.

C.L. Schoon, Delfgauw, Netherlands

18 Try quilting a wholecloth project. It is a great training ground for practicing your stitch without being encumbered by seams.

Annie Morgan, Johnson, VT

19 Enjoy the handquilting process. Don't look at how long it is going to take. This gives me time to think about the person I am making the quilt for and pray for them.   Karen Nick, Lutz, FL

20 If you get a drop of blood on your work, rinse your mouth well with water, then rub your saliva into the fresh spot. This has always worked for me.   Valerie Turer, Brooklyn, NY

H. Ending a Thread in Hand Quilting

❶ To end hand quilting, I zig zag the needle into the batting only, pull the thread taut, then clip it.   *Stephanie Greenberg, Lawrenceville, NJ*

❷ I like to be sure and have enough thread left to make this process easy. There is nothing more frustrating than to have to fight the thread because you have taken a few stitches too many. I make a knot to pop through the top fabric and batting. Once it is buried nicely, I travel down through the batting about 1", then come to the top. I pull with the slightest pressure and clip the thread. It then slips back down into the quilt.   *Joan Martino, Kingman, AZ*

❸ I make a small knot and pop the end of the thread back into the quilt, 1" or so away from the stitching line. That way the back of the quilt is as lovely as the front.   *Kirsten Schmitt, Baldwin, NY*

❹ On the back side, I take one tiny stitch, and then take my needle and turn it in different directions between the fabrics three times. I believe this procedure is called Walking to Kansas. My friend from Kansas told me this technique

Carol Baruschke, Dunedin, FL

❺ I have never figured out how to tie a knot in the end of a thread, so I just travel through the batting about 1" from where I ended and then come straight back down to where I stopped. After a little practice, you can almost feel the thread getting caught up in the batting to the point it will not come out.   *Nora Manley, Athens, AL*

I. Storing the Handquilted Quilt in Process

1 I pin the needle in place with a square of contrasting fabric so I can easily find it again. I roll my projects and keep them free of dust and sunlight by storing them in a large tote.

Kirsten Schmitt, Baldwin, NY

2 I store quilts in process between two finished quilts in my spare bedroom. If I don't want to remove the quilt from my 3 × 5′ frame, I cover it with a cotton sheet to protect it until I come back.

Betty Phelps, Wichita Falls, TX

3 I always take the quilt out of the frame, even if I think I'm coming back to it soon (you never know!). I always wash out the markings as soon as I'm done quilting for the night, so I drape it on my chair to dry. *Patricia Grimm, New Windsor, NY*

4 With a hoop frame, I take the outer part of the frame off and leave the quilt draped over the bottom part. *Annie Morgan, Johnson, VT*

5 If I am toting a quilt in process to quilt class, I roll it around a long foam swimmer's tube, a pool noodle. This makes it convenient for putting it in and out of the car with minimum wrinkling. When I'm at home, I lay the quilt as flat as possible.

Irene Kelsey, Plainville, CT

6 I use one of the lightweight tote bags sold for groceries and other items to store a partially completed project. These are generous in size, and since I have quite a few in different colors, I can keep track of each project. I keep the supplies for that quilt (thread, a couple of needles, little scissors, etc.) in the same bag so I can grab and go when there is an opportunity to work on it. *Marcia Guza, Brick, NJ*

CHAPTER 12

Machine Quilting

A. Machine Quilting Feet

❶ Machine quilting requires a walking foot if your machine does not have an accu-feed built in. It keeps the fabrics from slipping.

Denece Turner, Evans, GA

❷ For free motion quilting I use several feet. Sometimes I use the little round embroidery foot that came with my Pfaff 2170. It's especially good for small areas. I also use an open-toe, free motion foot. This is clear plastic and has an open area in the front, just like a regular open-toe foot. I use this when I'm quilting a bigger area. For stitch in the ditch, I use an open-toe foot so I can see where

I'm going. My Pfaff has the integrated upper feed system, so I don't need a walking foot.   *Sally Eshelman, York, PA*

3 I use a walking foot to guarantee equal top and bottom tension in moving the quilt sandwich through the machine and an open hinged darning (free motion quilting) foot to give the flexibility to move the quilt sandwich in any way needed to make any design I want.   *Melody Zimmerman, Lowell, OH*

4 I use a large-holed embroidery foot for free motion quilting. I can go any direction—backwards, side wards, and forward.
                                      Kris Newlin, West Chester, PA

5 I use a stitch-in-the-ditch foot. This is a wonderful guide for staying in the ditch when doing this type of quilting.
                                      Janet Henley, Alvin, TX

B. *Other Machine Quilting Tools*

1 Make sure your needle is new and has a large enough eye to carry the thread correctly. My needle of choice is a 90/14 topstitch needle because it is sharp and has a large eye so there is less wear on the thread. If I use heavier thread than a size 90 needle can accept, then I go up to 100's. Size 100 denim needles work beautifully for heavier threads, and they are sharp.   *Mary Dyer, Flagstaff, AZ*

2 I love the Titanium 80 topstitching needle. I use it because it was recommended by an expert, Bob from Superior Threads, to prevent thread breakage and give a nice stitch.
                                      Maureen Beller, Morris Plains, NJ

3 Use spray adhesive to hold the layers together. I use my rolling pin (which I no longer use for pie crusts!) to ensure good adhesion. Too busy making quilts to bake.   *Kay Hinkelma, Florissant, MO*

4 I use the tips of yellow latex dish-washing gloves on my fingers to help me move the fabric more easily.   *Christina Morris, Newark, DE*

5 I love using Machingers gloves. They help me keep control of the quilt. Any quilting glove will help, but these are by far my favorite of any brand I've tried. I have a hard time machine quilting without them.   *Kari Vojtechovsky, Centennial, CO*

6 I use pet-grooming gloves with the bumps, but I cut out the fingers so that I don't have to take them off when I need to thread the needle or rewind the bobbin.   *Sharon Kelly, Hollywood, FL*

7 I do not use fancy gloves to quilt. I use little squares of rubber mats, bought at the Dollar Store for a buck. I cut them into 3" squares and use them under my hands on the quilt, to guide the quilt while I quilt. They grip beautifully.   *Maggie Ziehl, Kanata, Ontario*

8 If you use a Bernina, try out the BSR (Bernina Stitch Regulator) foot. It makes free motion quilting much easier, and the stitches are all the same size. Use that basting spray that makes the fabric stick so it doesn't shift as you quilt.   *Heidi Siebenlist, Burgsinn, Germany*

9 If you want to machine quilt and can afford it, get a machine with a deeper throat. I use Martelli rings or Sharon Shamber's Halo rings to guide my fabric.
          Judith Putnam, Paris, TN

10 For smaller quilts like wallhangings, I spray baste so I don't have to use pins and start and stop. However, be careful to spray baste the fabric and not the batting as the spray sinks into the batting and you lose all the stickiness.   *Kellie Hewitt, Marion, VA*

Be careful to spray baste the fabric and not the batting as the spray sinks into the batting and you lose all the stickiness.

⓫ When I'm working on a large quilt, I put two-thirds of the batting in. That way I can quilt the middle (the third without the batting is rolled up to my right). Then, I can quilt the outer third with the batting (all the rest is to my left). Then I can attach the rest of the batting with Heat-n-Bond and quilt the rest. This way, I never have the problem of trying to get all that quilt through the open space on my machine.   *Sharon Kelly, Hollywood, FL*

⓬ Pigma markers can be used to change the color of thread—that stitch that went out of the ditch might be disguised with a little color change.   *Georgia Pierce, Seattle, WA*

⓭ Buy a mini-vacuum to remove the dust and debris that accumulates under the stitch plate from the batting fibers and fabric.
                                    Amy Kentera, Highland Mills, NY

c. *Starting and Stopping Machine Quilting*

❶ Always start and stop with the needle down. Newer machines have that option for the "needle down" position.
                                    Mary O'Donnell, Las Vegas, NV

❷ I stitch about 5–10 super tiny stitches to start and stop machine quilting. I find that it holds very well, won't form an unsightly knot, and is super quick.   *Kari Vojtechovsky, Centennial, CO*

❸ I am not making show quilts. I usually just sew a few stitches in place and then cut the thread.   *Debra McDaniel, Valparaiso, IN*

❹ I pull my bobbin thread up to the top. I hold both threads and take about 3 small stitches to secure it. If you just sit in place and stitch 3 stitches, you will get a little ball of thread on the bottom.

Sharon Gregorczyk, Kyle, TX

❺ When I begin machine quilting, I take 3 or 4 tiny stitches. I lower the needle into the quilt sandwich and then raise it again to bring the bobbin thread to the top. I take another 5 or 6 stitches and cut the thread ends. At the end of my stitching, I again take 3 or 4 tiny stitches. Then I pull the top thread so that a loop of the bobbin thread is exposed and I cut both threads. This way I do not have to turn the quilt over to cut the bobbin thread.

Kathleen (Kathi) Miller, Vancouver, WA

❻ When starting and stopping machine quilting, I always take one stitch manually and pull up the bobbin thread from underneath to the top. This helps prevent those bird nests you get when the bobbin thread gets pulled down into the bobbin or tangled up with the top thread. I leave a long tail at both ends and thread it onto a hand sewing needle when the project is completed. I then bury the tail into the quilt and trim as necessary. *Mary Kokoszka, Magnolia, DE*

❼ If I'm doing edge to edge quilting (i.e., cross hatching), I do a backstitch at the beginning and ending edge to be covered by the binding later. *Mary Caldwell, Howell, MI*

❽ If your bobbin runs out while machine quilting, attach a large safety pin where you stop so you can easily see where to start again.

Jan Mast, Lancaster, PA

❾ When I run out of bobbin thread in the middle, I will restart by going over prior stitches with tiny stitching. *Kris Newlin, West Chester, PA*

If your bobbin runs out while machine quilting, attach a large safety pin where you stop so you can easily see where to start again.

D. *Machine Quilting Stitches*

1 I use a straight stitch most of the time because I usually make scrap quilts. I want the fabrics to tell the big story, while the quilting accentuates the fabric and stabilizes the layers of the quilt.

Mary Jane Hollcraft, Indianapolis, IN

2 I prefer straight stitch because I like the look of modern, gridded quilt designs placed all over my quilt top.

Melissa Velik, Kutztown, PA

3 I do like to play with my decorative stitches. I like the zig-zag, the blanket stitch, and the shamrock stitch. I always like to throw the shamrock stitch in and see if anyone can find it—kind of like my hidden signature.

Mary Jo Millonzi, Mt. Prospect, IL

4 I prefer machine quilting using decorative stitches that will show on the back for a very interesting backing as well.

Myrtle Yopp, Shawsville, VA

5 I love using the zigzag and serpentine stitches with the straight stitch to add variety to the quilt.

The leaf stitch, star stitch, and snowflake stitch are special stitches on my machine that I have used, and I love the special look they give to my quilts. I usually use the largest setting for these stitches as they work the best when doing the quilting. I just experiment with them before I actually use them on the quilt.

Fred Ogline, Friedens, PA

6 I have used decorative stitching on quilts assembled by groups when the seams are not quite even; a decorative stitch covers the "oops."

Kris Newlin, West Chester, PA

7 There are times that I use a blanket stitch when I am appliqué-ing through all three layers of the quilt.

Mary Potts, Oxford, PA

8 Sometimes I use a feather stitch and straddle the seam line. Using the feather stitch is easier than stitching in the ditch!

Donna Caldarise, Saint Johns, Florida

9 For straight line quilting, I always increase my stitch size because with the bulk of the quilt, it makes it a smoother process because it doesn't drag as much. When I'm stippling, the feed dogs are down, so the length of the stitch relies on my hand movement; the smoother my hand movement, the more even the quilting.

Maureen Mackie, Endeavour Hills, Australia

10 I set my machine to quilt 8 stitches per inch. It gives the quilt a nice finished look, and it is easier to pick out if I make a mistake.

Mary Marlowe, Hedgesville, WV

11 In machine quilting, 12 to 14 stitches per inch will stay sewn better than fewer stitches per inch.   *Yolande Smith, Titusville, FL*

12 It helps if you can drop the feed dogs when you are machine quilting. If you can't, set your stitch length at zero and you'll get a similar effect.   *Kay Hinkelma, Florissant, MO*

E. Free Motion Quilting

1 Focus on where you're headed with the quilting, and not where the needle is actually sewing, for a smoother, more even stitch.

Jan Mast, Lancaster, PA

2 Find the machine quilting speed where you are most comfortable. You don't have to go fast, but I have found if I go too slow, I have just as many problems as going too fast.

Christina Morris, Newark, DE

❸ Concentrate on an area no bigger than a potholder to quilt. It makes the project easier to quilt and less intimidating.

Maggie Ziehl, Kanata, Ontario

❹ When doing an all-over stippling design, I usually start quilting at a bottom corner and work up in 6" widths. You don' t need to start in the middle like with hand quilting.

Lorraine Vignoli, Commack, NY

❺ I am unable to produce acceptable free-motion quilting without the stitch regulator tool. My machine calls it BSR (Bernina Stitch Regulator). I am still not able to keep my stitches completely uniform, and so I wind up ripping out a section if it doesn't measure up.   *Sharon Mountford, Canoga Park, CA*

Wax the bed of your machine with spray wax before you start free-motion quilting

❻ Wax the bed of your machine with spray wax before you start free-motion quilting, or use a teflon pad. Use a large sewing table with a dropped platform for your machine so the bed of the machine is even with the table. Set up an "L" shaped work area with a second table on your left so the quilt is supported.

Pat Smith, Sidney, NY

❼ Use gloves! I have some crabbing gloves that I bought at a fishing supply store on the coast. They are tacky enough to keep my hands from slipping around and moving the fabric unevenly. They are better than the garden gloves that I used to use.   *Kathi Swindell, Fruitland, ID*

❽ Keep a light touch on the fabric so you do not cause the stitches to become too close and look tight. If the fabric piece is large, I may have penciled my design on the quilt before beginning to stitch.   *Mary Marlowe, Hedgesville, WV*

❾ I like the 3-sided, horseshoe-shaped, rubber bars. I don't have to use gloves and can "steer" my way around the quilt with them. I can move them down or over without stopping. I also like the fact that they are not completely round.   *Patricia Grimm, New Windsor, NY*

⑩ I find that singing when free motion quilting helps me keep a regular rhythm and pace.   *Myra Witmer, Nellysford, VA*

⑪ I like to practice my motif on a small dry erase board. By repeating it a few times, I can develop muscle memory before I move on to the quilt.

Lorraine Vignoli, Commack, NY

I like to practice my motif on a small dry erase board. By repeating it a few times, I can develop muscle memory before I move on to the quilt.

⑫ I keep a spare quilt sandwich handy and practice the stitching and motions I plan to use on my quilt. It helps me get familiar with the feel of the machine and how to move at a pace that keeps even stitching   *Melody Brown, Santa Maria, CA*

⑬ I like to use tracing paper with the stitch motif printed on it to pin on top of the quilt. I do not usually get hung up with any other threads on the top of the quilt, and the paper is so thin that it tears away easily, sometimes before I'm ready for it to tear away. I am able to keep focused on the stitches and not the blocks it's going over.

Jennifer Padden, Austin, TX

⑭ The way to become a good free-motion quilter is practice, practice, practice. I also practice my quilting designs by doodling on paper. I've learned that if I can't draw a design, I won't be able to quilt it.   *Kathleen (Kathi) Miller, Vancouver, WA*

⑮ I pin baste no more than 4" apart. I keep my thumbtips together and only stitch in the U formed by my hands. I wear gloves to help me grip the fabric.   *Jann Dodds, Kenthurst, Australia*

⑯ Don't try anything too big on your regular machine because it gets very cumbersome. It's much easier on your body if you use a

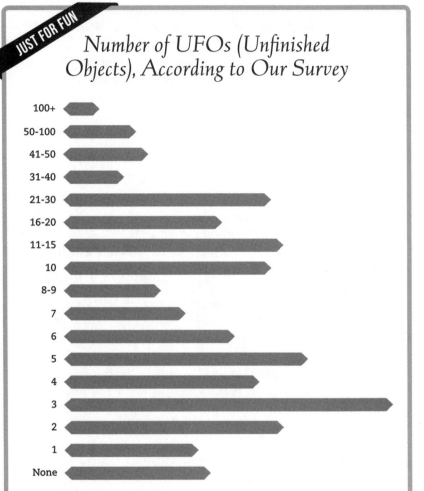

JUST FOR FUN

Number of UFOs (Unfinished Objects), According to Our Survey

100+
50-100
41-50
31-40
21-30
16-20
11-15
10
8-9
7
6
5
4
3
2
1
None

❖ Thanks to my mother's good training, I don't have many UFOs. She taught me "finish what you start." However, if a project goes unfinished for more than a year, I seriously consider showing it the door, as I'm unlikely to ever finish it, so why let it hang out in my drawers, clogging up my space and assaulting my conscience.

Jan Mast, Lancaster, PA

mid-arm or long-arm machine. You can usually rent one at a nearby shop if you don't own one. *Susan Walters, Newark, DE*

⑰ Before I practice free motion designs on fabric, I practice with a pencil, then practice in the air with a pointed finger. I also finger trace a stitched design until I think "my brain has it." When I first begin to use a new design on a quilt, I use matching thread for the top and backing so any mistakes I make show less. After that, I begin using a contrasting thread that will show the quilting. I often use one thread on top and another color on the bottom. It is easy to know if my thread tension is correct when using two different threads. *Marti Blankenship, Pleasant Valley, MO*

⑱ Relax, relax, relax your shoulders. If you don't, you won't be able to develop a smooth rhythm, and your back will kill you. *Marsha Nelson, Clinton, UT*

⑲ Puddle the fabric around the needle area. Do not roll your quilt up in a roll as this is very difficult to manage. *Audrey Clark, Red Lodge, MT*

⑳ Get to know what works for you and your machine. Traditionally, you are supposed to lower the feed dogs, but what works for me is to keep the feed dogs up and reduce the pressure on the foot to almost nothing. Use the speed control feature if you have that. Reduce it to a point that you can floor the pedal to achieve the right amount of even speed and equal stitch length. And, of course, practice, practice, practice. *Nancee McCann, Wilmington, DE*

㉑ Foliage, especially leaves, is very easy to do. Remember that no two are ever exactly alike in nature. Flowers are also fun, and the echoing disguises errors and adds interest. *Carolyn Vidal, Newport, WA*

㉒ Fit your machine with a darning/free-motion foot, set the stitch length to zero, lower or cover the feed dogs, put in a new needle, and use a slow steady movement. *Rebecca Hoffmann, Plant City, FL*

❷❸ One tip I learned from a friend is to have a glass of wine before starting. Or just relax and have fun. If you are uptight and nervous, it will show in your stitching.   *Karen Martin, Breezy Point, MN*

❷❹ Raise the level of your chair so that you are situated over your work. This will free up your arm to move your project.

Use your finger tips to move the quilt. Don't man-handle it. Don't grip it. Your touch should be like holding a bird. You will have more control over moving the quilt with a lighter touch.

Janice Simmons, Fresno, CA

❷❺ I always put a music CD in when I start quilting, so that once the CD is over, I know it's time to get up and move around to take the strain off my neck and shoulders. Being relaxed is really key when you're quilting. When you feel that starting to slip, you need to take a break and wait a while so that you don't end up making a huge mistake that you will regret later.   *Lisa Hughes, Richland, NY*

F. Quilt-As-You-Go

❶ Quilt-as-you-go can be adapted far more than is commonly thought. I have been making a series of small, mostly appliqué, quilts that depict places we visit. I can use them as wall hangings and later remove the borders and put them together if I want to.

Susan Eaglaton, Maryville, TN

❷ Quilt-as-you-go is very similar in nature to paper piecing, so if you like that, you should like QAYG.   *Sally Eshelman, York, PA*

❸ In quilt-as-you-go, it is necessary and important to cut the batting at least 2" longer than the fabric all around the block. Piece two of your strips right sides together. Place the wrong side down on the batting, then stitch the right-hand side down on the batting through the three layers. Then place a third strip of fabric right side down on the second strip, stitching in along the right-hand edge of the second strip. Make sure to cover the batting each time.

Geraldine Whitley, Washington, DC

❹ My favorite fast quilt to do for charity is a horizontal quilt-as-you-go. I start with 2 strips right side together and stitch them to the middle of the batting/backing layer. I lightly press each seam open after it's sewn on and mark where the raw edge of the next strip should be aligned, in case the previously sewn strip is uneven. I pin the most recently sewn strip in place through batting and backing prior to sewing on the next strip. These steps will keep the back from bunching and the horizontal strips will all be parallel.

If you think about it, many quilts can translate into a degree of quilt-as-you-go. Instead of sewing all my rows one to the other to complete a top, I sew the horizontal rows directly to a prepared batting and backing as described above. Then I sew in the ditch, then sew vertical seams and presto, the quilt is machine basted. I go back in and have fun machine quilting inside the blocks.

Nancee McCann, Wilmington, DE

❺ Make sure the fold-over piece is open all the way, or you will end up with too much bulk and the finished project will be smaller that you wanted.

Karen Benke, Medina, OH

❻ It is recommended that the backing fabric be of a small print for quilt-as-you-go. The joining seams are easy to hide in a busy print. Another plus for printed backing fabric is that when you turn it over, you have another quilt.

Rosemarie Garone, West Islip, NY

It is recommended that the backing fabric be of a small print for quilt-as-you-go.

❼ Cut batting slightly larger than the block and backing a good inch larger than the block. Quilt, leaving the seam allowance free of stitching. Trim back the batting to the seam allowance. This will allow you to join the blocks without covering strips. If you prefer, you can quilt to the edge of the block, join blocks together after trimming to the correct size, and then use covering strips over the joins.   *Marie White, Waiuku, New Zealand*

8 I like to use a piece of 80/20 cotton/poly batting in my squares. I find that the batting is thin enough, yet it adds dimension to the quilt. If I'm making the squares on my machine, then I add a second layer of 80/20 on the back before I stitch in the ditch. I don't like it when I can feel the edges of the quilt blocks.

Mary Jo Millonzi, Mt. Prospect, IL

9 Square up the block and trim the batting to ¼" shorter than the block. I trim the batting only on the side I am joining together. You need to plan ahead a little more when you layer and quilt your blocks to know how much extra batting and backing to have so your quilt blocks can be attached easily. It seems to be easiest to layer your block, having the batting and backing extending beyond the block as you do your quilting and then trim the excess off as you attach the blocks. Quilt-as-you-go quilting designs typically will be contained within the block, not extending across the sashing and/or into a neighboring block. It is possible to add that type of quilting after the project is put together, but typically, the quilting is within the block.   *Rosemarie Garone, West Islip, NY*

> *I blind stitch all the seams on the back of the quilt so the back has a more finished look.*

10 I blind stitch all the seams on the back of the quilt so the back has a more finished look.   *Kathy Kelleher, Kennebunk, ME*

11 I love quilt-as-you-go patterns. I've made quite a few because I could not see paying someone all that money to quilt a quilt for me on a longarm machine, and I had such a hard time forcing a large queen or king quilt into my little sewing machine—and don't get me started on the neck and shoulder pain from handling big quilts at one time!   *Mary Kokoszka, Magnolia, DE*

12 Use all the fancy stitches most machines now have to quilt these quilts. This will make it look like an old time crazy quilt. Remember to use the bobbin thread color to match the backing.

LaVonne Lawrence, Neillsville, WI

13 Don't over-quilt the edges of quilt-as-you-go blocks so that assembly will be easier. You can go back and add a few stitches later, if you want more quilting. *Diane Bachman, Leola, PA*

14 If you are doing a quilt-as-you-go project and there are triangle tips, be careful to leave enough seam allowance so they don't get cut off. *Karen Martin, Breezy Point, MN*

15 Be careful of dense quilting in quilt-as-you-go because it can make it harder to get a good square quilt at the finish.

Joan Oldham, Panama City, FL

G. Long-Arm Quilting

1 I send out quilts to be longarmed quilted. Put everything in writing. Both of you keep a copy. How do you want it quilted? Edge to edge? Highlights? Where do you want the highlights? What color thread? What color bobbin? Is the quilter edging it? How much is it going to cost?

I don't want to spend hours and hours putting my quilt together only to go pick it up and find I don't like what the longarmer has done! *Mary Jo Millonzi, Mt. Prospect, IL*

2 I hired a lady to do long-arm quilting for me who brought 10" squares quilted with samples of her designs. I found that very helpful in picking out a design. *Liz Brown, Annapolis, MD*

3 If you can't afford to have your quilt long-armed, many long-arm artists will baste your quilt for you to do your own quilting. This will save hours on your knees or dollars in spray basting and safety pins.   *Michelle Harrison, Morganton, GA*

4 Prepare your quilt top carefully. Accurate piecing will make the job easier for your long arm quilter. Contrary to what is said, mistakes will not quilt out! Make sure you press and lint roll your quilt top to remove stray threads.   *Mary Dyer, Flagstaff, AZ*

5 Frequently check the underside of the quilt to make sure all is well. It is not fun pulling out stitches if the tension is off. I also like to use purchased pre-wound bobbins because they hold more thread and take less time to deal with.   *Lorraine Vignoli, Commack, NY*

6 I find using an 80/20 blend of batting or 100% cotton batting works best when loading a quilt onto my longarm. I pin my backings and float my battings and tops. The 80/20 or 100% cotton battings "stick" to the backings and make floating the tops easier because those battings have a stickiness or static to them. This holds everything in place until I baste the layers together with the longarm machine.   *Mary Kokoszka, Magnolia, DE*

7 Be sure to ask your long arm quilter how much wiggle room she requires on each side of your project before you purchase batting and prepare your backing.   *Melissa Velik, Kutztown, PA*

8 If possible, rent a longarm machine and take some lessons to see if this is for you. Personally, I love longarm quilting, but I don't have room for a machine.   *Karen Kunte, Rome, PA*

9 The best thing I did was find a web group that exclusively uses the very kind of longarm machine I have. I read all their questions and responses. I've learned more that way than any other. I have a really vibrant, great group.   *Joan Oldham, Panama City, FL*

H. *Learning to Machine Quilt*

❶ I'd say get a very busy print and practice on it, and then your mistakes won't show. Turn it into a tote or something practical, because it's nice to have something useful from those hours of practice. This is what I did when I took a machine quilting class at a local quilt shop. *Patricia Grimm, New Windsor, NY*

❷ One thing I did that helped was to place a small piece of wood under the machine pedal so that I couldn't go too fast and ruin the look of the quilt. The wood just keeps the pedal from going down too far. *Kellie Hewitt, Marion, VA*

❸ I got a wonderful beginner book from Alex Anderson that gave me guidelines for machine quilting. I also joined a block-of-the-month group at my local quilt shop. They were wonderful, and I got to try a lot of different things! *Mary Jo Millonzi, Mt. Prospect, IL*

❹ Make a quilt sandwich with two pieces of muslin and some batting. Mark it off with a large grid and use each grid section for a different stitch. I fill up many of these pieces as I practice machine quilting. Then I serge the edges and donate the pieces to the local animal shelter because they always need bedding for cats and dogs. *Kathleen (Kathi) Miller, Vancouver, WA*

❺ Buy a cheater cloth (pre-printed panel), pin it with backing and batting, and just machine quilt by following the lines on it. Then fill in spaces with free motion quilting. I like to call this method "puzzling" (referring to a jigsaw puzzle). *Roxie Fitzgerald, Cerritos, CA*

Buy a cheater cloth (pre-printed panel), pin it with backing and batting, and just machine quilt by following the lines on it.

❻ Try using the pattern on the fabric as a template for machine quilting designs, especially on borders. I've "connected the dots" of a polka dot fabric to quilt a zigzag design.   *Marsha Hunt, Glenside, PA*

7 Beginners should develop passion for machine quilting by going to quilting shows and talking with the manufacturers of quilting machines. I learned a great deal by observing and watching others at work on their quilting machines. If possible, beginners should go to retreats for quilters and devote concentrated time to machine quilting.   *Geraldine Whitley, Washington, DC*

8 Tape a pencil to your needle and practice moving the quilt sandwich around as if you are quilting. Do this until you are comfortable; then thread the needle and practice your quilting.
Mary Ann Logan, Niles, OH

9 Craftsy online has great classes. If you cannot afford a Craftsy class, look at who teaches them and go to their blogs and websites. They offer so many marvelous tutorials that you can spend a couple of years practicing their tutorials.   *Michelle Harrison, Morganton, GA*

> *I made pot holders and hot pads for practice sandwiches. I practiced, practiced, and practiced and kept reminding myself that machine quilting is a learned skill and I can learn it.*

10 *Done* is better than *perfect*, I think! Use old fabric and batting and just quilt. Animal shelters love these if you cut them up into workable squares and zigzag around the edges. These squares also make great china protectors between dishes in storage or transit.
Carolyn Vidal, Newport, WA

11 I made pot holders and hot pads for practice sandwiches. I practiced, practiced, and practiced and kept reminding myself that machine quilting is a learned skill and I can learn it.
Joyce Ciembronowicz, Lake Zurich, IL

12 In the beginning, use a thread that closely matches the background so mistakes aren't so noticeable. Use a backing that is busy so mistakes blend in. If you make donation quilts for children, practice quilting on them. The children won't notice that your stitches are herky-jerky or inconsistent. You just have to jump in and do it, and before long you will find a rhythm that works with your speed and hand motion.   *Sharon Gregorczyk, Kyle, TX*

13 I took two classes in machine quilting before I purchased a BSR (Bernina Stitch Regulator). What a difference a stitch regulator makes—it's much more fun to machine quilt now! And a tip for beginners: take classes, because different teachers have different helpful hints.   *Sally Berry, Virginia Beach, VA*

14 Don't get caught up in all the high-end machines for machine quilting. They are pricey and not affordable for everyone, and you can quilt on what you have. That's what I do, and my machine is not in any way high end or advertised as a "quilting" machine.   .   *Joyce Ciembronowicz, Lake Zurich, IL*

15 My aunt sat me down with a 36 × 36" quilt sandwich sectioned in four equal squares. I marked one section with dots, one with a flower pattern, one with a feather pattern and one with lines. I quilted the dots with a curve to each, forming a curvey square, echo quilted the flower, used stippling around the feather, and formed squares with the lines. Once I was done, I felt more comfortable with the machine quilting process. Plus, I bound the sample and now use it as a centerpiece on my table.   *Karla Irby, Ft. Lauderdale, FL*

16 I make so many donation quilts that it was a necessity for me to learn to machine quilt. I save hand quilting for that very special top. Long-arm machine quilting was not available forty years ago, so I practiced for many hours on discarded curtains from the second hand stores. The curtains gave me lots of yardage that could be cut into manageable sizes, and they were thicker than cotton, giving me that padded feeling of a quilt sandwich with batting.

        Dianne Deaver, Yuba City, CA

17 All I did was stitch in the ditch for years, as I loved handquilting more. Then a friend told me over the telephone her method. As long as the quilt is pinned properly, do the borders first. I thought it would not work. It did. I quilted 13 tops in a month. I ditched the cotton thread and instead I use Marathon rayon 40 weight embroidery thread in the bobbin and on top of the machine. It quilts beautifully and does not knot or go hard after being washed. It is like machine quilting with silk thread. I use a number 70 needle to do my quilting, changing it after every quilt I quilt.   *Maggie Ziehl, Kanata, Ontario*

18 I started out early by machine quilting ¼″ from seamlines and gridlines. Then I graduated to using stencils to make my designs. Now I have been learning to do free-form feathers and back-fill designs. I have taken Harriet Hargrave's class, and I have a number of books that describe the process.   *Laroletta Petty, Breckenridge, CO*

I. Storing the Machine Quilted Quilt in Process

1 Before I had my current frame, which allows me to roll the width of the quilt on the frame, I always took the quilt off the hoop and gently folded it until I was ready to work on it again. No matter how soon it would be, it always came off the frame, even if just for the night. I didn't want my seams being pulled at any more than necessary.   *Ruth Anglin, Tijeras, NM*

2 I just squish the quilt or just leave it on top of my sewing table. I generally quilt for hours, taking little breaks. I quilt only one project until it is finished, leaving all other projects for another day.   *Maggie Ziehl, Kanata, Ontario*

3 I have a spare bedroom, and I lay my quilt in process on the bed as if it were finished. I place a marker where I left off.   *Mardi Niles, Scotia, NY*

❹ I loosely fold it up and drape it over the back of the couch. I haven't much room, but I do try not to bundle it tightly, which I'm worried would cause creasing and shifting of what has not been quilted.   *Danette Lockler, Denver, CO*

❺ If the quilt is not huge, I will put it on my design wall between quilting sessions. That way, when I walk past it, I can sometimes see other ideas I can do to complement what I've already done.   *Sharon Gregorczyk, Kyle, TX*

If the quilt is not huge, I put it on my design wall between quilting sessions. When I walk past it, I can sometimes see other ideas I can do to complement what I've already done.

❻ I usually leave quilts-in-process right on my sewing table with the needle in the down position. Once I start machine quilting, I usually finish in a day or two.
Kris Newlin, West Chester, PA

❼ I keep the quilt on the machine, if possible. I cover my machine with a cheap, clear plastic painter's tarp between quilting sessions.
Carolyn Vidal, Newport, WA

❽ I try to end at a good stopping point at the end of a row or free motion section. I take the quilt out of the machine, and put it on my quilt rack.   *Peggy Noto, Portland, OR*

❾ I wrap it in a towel and keep it near my machine. That way, when my cats want to nap, I won't be incorporating too much cat hair in the quilt.   *Margaret (Peg) Parsons, New Castle, DE*

❿ When I load a quilt on my quilting machine, I plan to finish it quickly. If I have quilts waiting to be loaded, they are in project bags in a tub under my machine. In the bag is the backing, binding, sometimes the label and a note with the name and dimensions.
Karen Martin, Breezy Point, MN

CHAPTER 13

Embellishments

A. Thread Painting

❶ Use a leather rolling foot for thread painting.

Mary Heidemann, Daykin, NE

❷ Make sure you use a Magic Bobbin Washer in your bobbin. It really helps to avoid those nasty thread "nests." *Pat Deck, Oreland, PA*

❸ For thread painting, I wear disposable rubber gloves to keep a good grip on my fabric. I also set my machine to go at a constant speed so my foot doesn't get over-active. *Pat Hill, Orillia, Ontario*

❹ Use the correct weight stabilizer. A wash-away or iron-away stabilizer is easier on your stitches than a tear-away.

Michelle Massaro, Glenside, PA

❺ Do not be afraid to experiment with different kinds of threads when thread painting. Metallic, glow in the dark, or wool can add dimension to your work. *Marcia Porcelli, Forsyth, GA*

6 When using multiple colors in a satin stitch, use the color last that you wish to stand out. The edge stitches will slightly overlap the previous color/stitch, thus standing out. This is the same idea you use when pressing seams toward one color or another. The piece with the seam allowance will stand out.   *Laura Hilliker, Monterey, CA*

7 I use a strong polyester embroidery thread, preferably Isacord. It is thin but strong to go over areas several times without breaking.   *Nancy McClelland, Girard, PA*

8 Decide which direction the sunlight is coming from in your thread-painted picture. Then the shadows will be on the backsides and undersides of everything. The shadows will need to be darker by at least several shades on the color wheel. You'll start to look for shades in gradient colors next time you shop for thread. You'll want a light, medium and dark shade for many colors you use a lot.   *Rosemarie Garone, West Islip, NY*

9 I have found that with thread painting it's less important to use the best-quality thread, fabric, and batting. You can forgo that to some extent and dwell on the effect you want to achieve—shiny, bulky, rough, etc. You are always working toward that end result pictured in your head. Sometimes you need to go over what you have done with something else. Most of the time there is no ripping out.   *Becky Hahn, Boyceville, WI*

10 A beginner may want to start with a fabric with large prints of an object. My suggestion is a large floral print. Think how awesome these flowers can become with you drawing with thread over the already pretty flowers. You don't have to stay with the same color that is on the fabric, but just play and have fun.

Even if you are no artist, grab a sheet of paper and sketch the flow of lines you think you may want to follow. Do it over and over several times; then go to the sewing machine with this fresh in your mind.

I always use TopStitch Needles for a more even flow of the thread and less breakage. Decide on gloves or the hoop method. I personally like to use quilters' gloves with breathable fabric and rubber fingertips.   *Sharon Beck, Twinsburg, OH*

B. Couching

❶ The use of a couching foot is not necessary but is very helpful and makes the project go much quicker.

Any decorative thread or yarn can be attached to fabric. Use invisible thread for the needle thread and regular sewing thread in the bobbin. Decrease or lower the upper tension so that the bobbin thread pulls the invisible thread below the fabric and the bobbin thread does not poke through to the top of the fabric.

Use a zig-zag stitch. Lengthen the stitch and set the width so that the zig-zag will just go over each side of the decorative thread or yarn you want to attach.   *Carol Young, Wilbraham, MA*

❷ Use a couching foot if possible, and make sure the stitch width isn't too wide. You don't want the yarn to move around under the stitching.   *Patsy Shields, Sellersburg, IN*

❸ If curves are involved, I use a tiny bit of basting glue to set the base thread in place.   *Stephanie Leuthesser, San Ysidro, CA*

❹ Tack and turn your couching. Start with two straight stitches forward and back to tack the end of the yarn in place. Then switch to a zigzag stitch. When you want to change direction, lower your feed dogs, tack (ending with the needle on the side you will be turning toward), turn, tack (again ending with your needle on the side you'll be turning toward), put your feed dogs back up and keep going.   *Rosemarie Garone, West Islip, NY*

Tape a straw to your machine in front of the presser foot and feed the yarn through the straw.

❺ Tape a straw to your machine in front of the presser foot and feed the yarn through the straw.   *Janet Bland, Smyrna, GA*

❻ I learned to do couching on a Christmas stocking. To get a metallic look without using metallic thread and the headaches that sometimes accompany it, I chose a cording that had metallic threads in it. I then did the couching with a shiny poly machine embroidery thread.

Marti Blankenship, Pleasant Valley, MO

❼ I love the three-dimensional effect couching creates for stems on flowers. *Margaret (Peg) Parsons, New Castle, DE*

c. 3-D Objects in Quilts

❶ Quilt your quilt first. You don't want to be going around all of the embellishments. Use embellishments that are compatible with the type of quilt it is and the feeling you want to create. Buttons add a homey quality and sweetness. Jewels and crystals add elegance, light and bling. Shaped buttons can add to a theme.

Marsha Nelson, Clinton, UT

❷ Adding these types of embellishments are really my specialty. I first use a light, nonwoven, fusible interfacing on the reverse of my fabric. When I hand sew beads to fabric, I use beading thread or hand quilting thread; these types of thread hold up to a lot of abuse. I also stitch forward through the bead and then through the fabric, then I stitch back through the fabric and bead again before I put the next bead on and so on. Before I finish a line (like a stem, etc.), I run the thread through all the beads and then back down through the fabric. I then tie off the thread with three double knots, run the thread back through to the other side, and tie it off twice. I then cut my threads and use Thread End glue over all the knots to make sure everything will last many years without damage.

Nanette Meck, Alum Bank, PA

❸ I love doing appliquéd cottages, buildings, etc. I use small buttons for door knobs and sometimes beads and jewels to trim outfits on appliquéd little girls.

I recently made a pink and brown quilt for a great-grand-daughter with all little girls in old-fashioned costumes, some with umbrellas. I enjoyed doing trims on their outfits. I felt like I was playing with paper dolls again as in my childhood! I almost did not want to part with the quilt when it was finished.

Barbara Theriault, Brooksville, FL

I like to "hide" buttons or "made with love charms" on a quilt.

❹ I have used buttons (ladybug on a floral piece) to hide a mistake made when piecing. I like to "hide" buttons or "made with love charms" on a quilt.   *Nancy Chase, Columbus, MT*

❺ Sometimes it may be necessary to cover the items with a fine netting to trap them in place.   *Patsy Shields, Sellersburg, IN*

❻ Putting a small anchor (small plastic disc or button) behind the object on the back of the quilt will help hold a less than very light-weight item and the quilt won't sag.   *Nancy Swanwick, Fort Scott, KS*

❼ When attaching buttons, I use the button sewing foot on my machine, feed dogs down, and the appropriate width zig-zag to quickly attach several buttons to a project. For example, eyes for 20 cats on a quilt, a jar of buttons on a sewing themed quilt, and a paper pieced project.   *Nancy Koyanik, Troy, VA*

❽ Buckram, used for drapery making, is very useful as a stabilizer to make fabric super stiff, so it's great for 3-D objects. Use spray baste or double-sided fusible to adhere.   *Sharon Mominee, Alpine, CA*

❾ Use embellishments with wild abandon. Use up those wonder-ful things you have been saving in your button box, those broken jewelry bits, inspiring found objects. *There will be more.* I often supplement buttons and 3-D objects with perle cotton embroidery or quilting. *Use them* or someone will someday clear out your stash, and it will all go to some thrift store...

Michelle Harrison, Morganton, GA

❿ I created some advent tree wall quilts and sewed 25 little red wooden beads on them. The tiny ornaments are stored in a little pouch at the base of the tree and "hung" on the little wooden beads.

Nancy Swanwick, Fort Scott, KS

⓫ Texture inspires me. I've actually gone outside and picked up sticks and incorporated them in some of my pieces.

Jo Yawn, Jonesboro, AR

⓬ If it is a wall hanging, I glue the embellishments instead of sewing them on.   *Elizabeth Merkle, Levittown, PA*

⓭ I once used O rings as black olives on a pizza quilt. Don't rule out anything!   *Linda Ahn, Mohrsville, PA*

⓮ Three-D objects, like buttons, jewels or beads must be firmly affixed to a quilt. The correct adhesive for the project is of utmost importance. If the quilt will be dry cleaned or washed at a later date, it may be easier to attach buttons and beads with needle and thread. You may want to even remove them before cleaning and reattach again afterward. Never, under any circumstances, put these types of embellishments on a quilt for a baby or a young child.

Marcia Porcelli, Forsyth, GA

⓯ Buttons are a terrific way to embellish a quilt. Place buttons in the center of a block, or in seam joints (this can cover seams that didn't quite match!). Stitch the recipient's initials or full name in nine-hole buttons. Sew them on the quilt to accent a particular area.

Hot fix crystals are a great way to add bling to a quilt. Many colors are available in various sizes. Mix and match them; get carried away, it's all right! And they won't wash off when the quilt is laundered.

Rick rack or other ribbon sewn over seams is one way to cover not-so-perfect construction. Sew the trim on after the quilt sand-wich has been made. This way you will be quilting the quilt and embellishing at the same time! A nice touch to a quilt's edge is to place rick rack in the seam allowance when sewing on binding.

Yo-yo shapes add character to quilts. They can easily be sewn to the quilt after it has been quilted.

Folded fabric, such as prairie points and pinwheels, can be added to a quilt during construction. Prairie points create an edge on a quilt.   *Anna Osborn, Omaha, NE*

D. *Cutter Quilts*

❶ If the quilt has historical significance (like Grandma made it), I proudly display it. If the quilt has enough substance to it and is not "lumpy," I will use it as the batting for a quilt.

Anna Osborn, Omaha, NE

❷ I prefer to make smaller quilts or pillows out of a beloved quilt so it can continue to be loved.   *Pam Angus, Levan, UT*

❸ A friend gave me a prayer bear that was holding a beautiful square from an older quilt that was falling apart. She included a poem with it about the source of the older quilt. It became a treasure for me.   *Kathleen Van Orsdel, Talbott, TN*

❹ I love to use small sections of cutter quilts and glue them to the front of plain cardstock to use as a greeting card. Everyone loves getting these!   *Nancy Henry, Rochester, NH*

❺ A flower or interesting shape can be appliquéd over a worn spot in an otherwise good quilt.   *Netta Pyron, Rolla, MO*

❻ I make bows and flower pendants with pieces of old quilts. They are unique and look so sweet on a denim blazer or in a little girl's hair.   *Annette Crain, Spanish Fork, UT*

❼ I once made a jacket from an old quilt with embroidered areas to cover some holes.   *Carole Brown, Ephrata, PA*

Relationship to Guilds, According to Our Survey

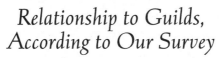

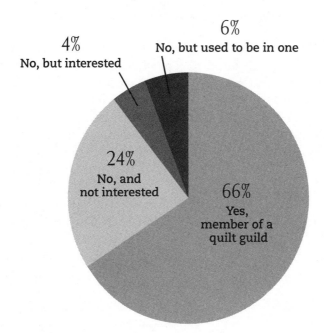

4%
No, but interested

6%
No, but used to be in one

24%
No, and
not interested

66%
Yes,
member of a
quilt guild

❖ Belonging to a guild can add a richness and depth to your quilting life. Yes, you will be asked to contribute to the group via charity projects and holding office, but you will meet wonderful people who share your passion for all things fabric and get the support you need to continue in your glorious addiction!

Annemarie (Nancy) Poorbaugh, Montgomery, AL

❽ One of my favorite projects is to staple a piece of the old quilt to the back of an old window and then hang the window on the wall.   *Carol Young, Wilbraham, MA*

❾ Salvage the good parts of cutter quilts for things like changing pads for babies and potholders.   *Jeanette Searcy, Brunswick, GA*

❿ I like to put pieces of old cutter quilts in a framed shadow box with other relics from past family members, and give them to the girls in the family on their 16th birthdays.   *Barbara Johnson, Dallas, OR*

⓫ I filled a green mason jar with sewing items such as buttons, lace, old spools of thread, etc. I purchased a top for the jar made for an electric bulb. I then purchased a shade that had a detachable paper. I used this paper for the pattern which I cut out from my old quilt that I slept under when I was growing up. The unfinished shade had sticky applied, so I attached the quilt. I then applied trim on the top, bottom and back seam. The grandchildren now have a lamp with my special old quilt.   *Ann Majors, Forest Hill, MD*

> *I cut old quilts in half and rebind them to use on the back of a chair or couch.*

⓬ If possible, I cut old quilts in half and rebind them to use on the back of a chair or couch. Some have small salvageable pieces that make nice pillows.   *Amy Mayo, Havre de Grace, MD*

⓭ I like to use pieces of cutter quilts in framed wall hangings or as doll quilts.   *Mary Heidemann, Daykin, NE*

⓮ I have used old quilt pieces to embellish clothing, such as adding a quilted pocket to a denim shirt or covering a torn area on jeans. I have also used pieces of old quilts along with new fabrics when making purses.   *Nancy Kreisler, Elmira, NY*

⓯ I received a cutter quilt from my grandmother's estate. It was in such bad shape that I fussy-cut around the holes and made a teddy bear out of it. I have him in the room where my grandchildren sleep, and they all know that I made it and what he is made from. I turned a quilt that would have been thrown away into a treasure that will remain in my family for more generations.   *Marcia Porcelli, Forsyth, GA*

16 A quilt my grandmother made frayed around a not-100% cotton block, and I could see that she used a cutter quilt as batting. It made me want to see the rest of the cutter quilt, but I guess I will have to wait a few more hundred years until the rest of the quilt disintegrates.   *Michelle Harrison, Morganton, GA*

17 Sometimes an old quilt is just too hard to cut up. Instead, I will store it in an acid-free box with acid-free tissue and only bring it out to refold or to show it off. I have also finished some old quilts and tried to complete the work of the original quilter in her memory. From other old quilts, I have placed quilted pieces in bags and vests or made teddy bears out of them. I do so lovingly and respectfully. I also thank the spirit of the quilter for sharing their work with me.   *Marianne Udell, Santa Fe, NM*

18 A friend gave me two raggedy quilts, but I cannot bear to cut them. At this time, they serve as a cover on my husband's antique car in our garage. Every time I get in my car, I get to enjoy seeing them. They still have a purpose, even though they are tattered, and I love their patterns.   *Joanne Picicci, Spokane, WA*

19 I have some old quilt tops from a distant relative who died in 1927. I hope to finish them some day. But I will not cut into someone's work to make another object.   *Kris Newlin, West Chester, PA*

E. Repurposing Other Objects and Fabric for Quilts

1 I am making a quilt for my grandson using old shirts from his dad, grandpas, and great-grandpas. I will give this to him for his graduation. I am also saving T-shirts from my granddaughter as she grows up to do the same for her graduation.

Natali Hawley, Montrose, PA

② I have included fabric from some of the dresses my daughters used to wear into doll quilts for their babies to play with.

Jennifer Padden, Austin, TX

③ I have saved many baby and toddler clothes from my grand-daughter. She is now 6, and I am gathering scraps from her clothes to use in an ongoing memory quilt as she gets older. She is helping me with the sewing and enjoying doing the wiggle stitch (zig-zag).

Fran Shaffer, Coatesville, PA

Old flannel sheets can be used when a thin batting is desirable.

④ Denim from old jeans is a great repurposed fabric to use in quilts. Because it is heavier than woven cotton, mix it with flannel from old pajamas and nighties. Used men's shirts, especially plaids, make great fabric for a masculine quilt. Old flannel sheets can be used when a thin batting is desirable, and old comforters make a great puffy batting for quilts. Washable wool blankets are great for a heavier batting. A large cotton tablecloth can make a beautiful backing for a quilt. *Anna Osborn, Omaha, NE*

⑤ Old blue jeans make wonderful quilt throws for watching TV or just lounging. These are great for kids and sleepovers or camping. Pockets can be used as embellishments, as well as the belt loops. Rag quilts using blue jeans are a great, quick project.

Sharon Sutton, Lindsey, OH

⑥ I have repurposed several wedding gowns and veils into ring bearers' pillows and handkerchiefs for many of my friends' grand-children to carry at their weddings. The laces are beautiful and can also be used on crazy quilt corners. *Arlene King, Baldwinsville, NY*

7 When my husband retired, I took a good number of his old dress shirts and ties and made him a memory quilt to commemorate the event. *Barbara Merritt, Brackney, PA*

8 One of my favorite quilts was one I made from old blue and white men's dress shirts. I bought them for 75 cents each at the local Goodwill store. *Stephanie Greenberg, Lawrenceville, NJ*

9 I made a memory quilt honoring my father. I used his old neckties to make blocks that included printed fabric pictures of him. I also glued on military patches and embroidery from his baseball caps. Then I pinned tie clasps and other lapel pins onto the memory quilt. *Nancy Jolley, Tucson, AZ*

10 I love using wool pieces in my quilts. I buy 100% wool skirts and jackets from the thrift store. I cut them apart and wash them to felt them. I store the felted wool in a plastic tote until I need to use in a quilt. Wool is wonderful to use in appliqué because the edges don't ravel. *Annette Crain, Spanish Fork, UT*

11 The only embellishment I've used is felted wool. I like it for tiny pieces, such as birds' eyes. *Amy DeCesare, Delmont, PA*

I like felted wool for tiny pieces, such as birds' eyes.

12 I added ribbons, both ends sewn down into a loop, to a granddaughter's baby quilt. She will love to play with them during tummy time. *Joan Hagan, St. Marys, PA*

13 Sometimes a found object is just the ticket for a hanging. In "Bless this House" I used tiny pieces of a rubber jar-lid gripper as the soles of a child's footed sleeper. In a "green" project, I used plastic mesh to cover the cut-away ground area of the land-fill, behind which were all of the scraps of fabric used in the upper part of the piece. *Sharon Mountford, Canoga Park, CA*

14 I have used snaps for an owl's eyes, small watch hands for animals feet, and hooks and eyes for claws.

Kirsten Schmitt, Baldwin, NY

15 I love putting words on my quilts. I use the foam, sticky-back letters available at the big box quilt shops. Sometimes I spray paint them to change their color. Then I whipstitch them on.

Cheryl Lynch, Broomall, PA

16 I keep the ends of my embroidery threads and sandwich them between either tulle or water soluble stabilizer. Then I free-motion stitch over this, making sure to secure the threads. I have added bits of fabric to the mix and created a lacy type of fabric that can be added in various shapes and stitched to the quilt to accent a block. This works really well on the parts of a block that are a solid, or that act like a solid. Sunbonnet Sue bonnets are great done this way. Any appliqué design can be embellished with this thread lace.

Donna Rowe, Russellville, AR

17 I tie objects onto my quilts or make little see-through organza pockets on the quilt to display things, such as coins.

Cheryl Lynch, Broomall, PA

Antique ladies' hankies can be use for appliqués, cut in half and "draped" over a fabric shelf holding a vase of flowers.

18 Antique ladies' hankies can be use for appliqués, cut in half and "draped" over a fabric shelf holding a vase of flowers. It makes a beautiful center for a quilt. Felted wool roving can be incorporated to give animals soft and fluffy coats.

Colleen Froats, Alanson, MI

19 I made a "Rosie the Riveter" wall hanging honoring my grandmother who helped build airplanes during World War II. I used bolts and rivets to embellish it.

Charlotte Kewish, Gibsonia, PA

⑳ I have used a lot of sea shells, beads of various sizes and upholstery braids and trims. When I use old jewelry, I paint it with clear nail polish so corroding metal is not an issue for the quilt. I have used lots of old cotton lace, and I have dyed some to suit my purpose. I enjoy using sequins, and I have a small stash of square ones. I have no idea why those appeal to me so much—maybe because they are uncommon. I found some flower shaped ones, as well.   *Michelle Harrison, Morganton, GA*

㉑ I have stained chop sticks for fencing on pre-printed panels, and used sequins for fish scales, adding a fishing line and small fish hook.   *Earleen Huebner, Au gres, MI*

㉒ I've used wide ribbons as a frame around blocks, like a matting on a picture. It looks pretty cool.   *Kellie Hewitt, Marion, VA*

㉓ I made a Christmas wall hanging that had a house on it and in the window sat a little cat (an old stud earring that no longer had a match).   *Kathi Levan, Sudlersville, MD*

㉔ As a wedding gift for nieces and nephews, my great-aunt made us each a puff block pillow. Over the years it has flattened, come apart and deteriorated. I took the puff block fabric and ruffle and created yo-yos. I put them together in a diamond setting to make a small wall hanging.   *Eileen D. Wenger, Lancaster, PA*

㉕ My grandmother made lace doilies that I like to put over a quilted piece for the center of a quilt.   *Pam Burress, Mount Washington, KY*

CHAPTER 14

Technology

A. Software Designing

❶ I usually start off designing a quilt by doodling on graph paper. When I have a doodle I like, I move to the free, open-source software Gimp, which is similar to Photoshop. With a little practice, Gimp can do most of what Electric Quilt can do. I use it for every quilt I design or lay out. Gimp has a customizable grid which can be blended in and out and be made magnetic, which makes drawing straight lines kid's play. It's really great—and free!

Amanda Kei Andrews, Vero Beach, FL

❷ I have only used Quilt Wizard, which is a simple program that helps me figure out how much fabric I would need to purchase for a particular kind of quilt. *Susanne Hilton, Laurel, MD*

❸ I frequently add a sketch of a block or a quilt into Photoshop to try different color ways. I also make layers in Photoshop to make patterns for appliqué. *Stephanie Greenberg, Lawrenceville, NJ*

❹ I use Electric Quilt 7 to design new projects. The biggest benefit to me, besides not having to do the math, is I can scan the fabric I intend to use and see if it works. In the past, I have sewn blocks only to find I don't like the way they looked. It saves me a lot of time in the long run. *Patti Goggio, Broadlands, VA*

❺ I use EQ7-Electric Quilt Company. It takes the math challenge out of design. I determine the finished size quilt block I want to use and then can choose layouts and borders to achieve the size and design I want. *Carol Martin, Honey Brook, PA*

❻ I redesign every pattern I purchase. I generally find most pattern designers do a poor job with directions. The only way I can be sure that everything is correct is to draw it myself in EQ7. I also design original quilts and original blocks and create appliqué elements like leaves that can be printed on my printer using freezer paper. Putting a quilt in Electric Quilt also lets me audition fabric in the entire quilt. *Eileen Ellis, Tabernacle, NJ*

❼ I use EQ6. I can start from scratch or use the blocks that are in the block libraries. I also use my Glass Eye, a stained glass program for making quilts or for individual pieces of the quilt. The Eye can print on more than one sheet, and then I tape them together. *Barbara Hill, Huntsville, AL*

❽ Electric Quilt 7 has been a real tool to adjust block size to make sure the quilt is in proportion. It is particularly helpful to design a dogtooth border. If I import scans of the fabric I will use, I can decide if the fabric is appropriate for the design. The ability to print templates and import photographs is an added bonus.

If I import scans of the fabric I will use, I can decide if the fabric is appropriate for the design.

I have used EQ7 to give the customer ideas to choose from, to try different colorways, and to give a customer an idea of what the finished quilt will look like.   *Gail Hurn, Highland Haven, TX*

❾ I have used Excel. Making graph paper allows me to figure out how to lay out squares. The paintbrush feature lets me add colors
Pam Sievers, Powell, OH

❿ I love to "doodle" my possible quilting designs using Photoshop Elements. Placing a number of quilting motifs over a picture of my quilt lets me know what works for the quilt.
Judy Davidson, Palmwoods, Australia

⓫ Since I am a Mac user, the major quilting programs are not usable for me. I do use Illustrator to graph patterns and to figure sizes. I also print out templates from Illustrator.
Sharon Mountford, Canoga Park, CA

⓬ Mywebquilter.com is a nice online site to design quilts or try out color combinations.   *Sally Zimmer, Bark River, MI*

⓭ I use Microsoft Publisher to design my quilts. I photograph the fabrics and import them into my computer so that I can see what the finished quilt will look like before I make the first cut.
Nancy Quade, Newark, DE

⓮ I use the Statler stitcher software to audition quilting designs.
Joan Oldham, Panama City, FL

⓯ I'm a graphic designer, so I use Illustrator to plan out quilts and make my own paper piecing patterns. I'm really lucky to know the program so well because of my profession. It might be a little overkill for the average quilter, and I have to be savvy enough to do my own math to calculate how to cut my pieces and how much yardage I will need. I still sketch on graph paper when I just want to get some ideas out, though.   *Kari Vojtechovsky, Centennial, CO*

16 I do not use computers for quilt design, although I am very computer savvy. There is something about paper, pen, and design together that just feels right. I buy spiral notebooks on sale during back-to-school sales for $.10. I have filled many with ideas and graphs and calculations. *Kris Newlin, West Chester, PA*

B. Photo Transfer

1 I have only used regular cotton fabric ironed onto freezer paper and printed on my Stylus R1800 printer. I haven't used this for pictures of people, but it has worked well for buildings, details, scenes and clouds. *Sharon Mountford, Canoga Park, CA*

2 I have also used my scanner and printer when repairing old quilts. I carefully cut out a piece of the torn fabric, place it on the bed of my printer/scanner and create an image of the fabric. Then I print it out again on paper-backed fabric with my inkjet printer. I found this to be a great way to repair antique or aging, much-loved quilts.

Barbara Merritt, Brackney, PA

I have used my scanner and printer when repairing old quilts.

3 I just finished a T-shirt quilt for my daughter. I photo transferred not only her team and individual pictures from her childhood, but some of her certificates. They are interspersed in the quilt with her uniforms and T-shirt blocks. *Susanne Hilton, Laurel, MD*

4 I used the photo transfer technique to make a special pillow showing a picture of our family to send to our daughter who was going through chemo and radiation treatments for cancer. She kept it with her to remind her that we were all with her despite the miles between us. *Mary Phinney, Lancaster, PA*

5 I made a quilt with houses on it for a grandson. Every window had a family member in it. *Joan Hagan, St. Marys, PA*

6 I included a photo of my newborn granddaughter in her first quilt to make it very personal. *Janis King, Huntly, Australia*

7 I made a quilt for my 87 year old father. When I told him I made a quilt for him, he wasn't very excited. When he unfolded the quilt, he noticed that I had taken all his World War II pictures that he had saved to a CD. I printed them on special photo fabric and sewed them into a quilt. Needless to say, he was speechless. *Lucy Esposito, Granbury, TX*

8 My husband went to Kilimanjaro a few years ago. I had him pick 16 pictures from his trip, transferred them to fabric and made a wall hanging out of them. *Sue Hurley, Princeton, NJ*

I made a Broken Dishes quilt for a missionary's child, using photos on the plain squares. The photos were of her sophomore year in the States.

9 I made a Broken Dishes quilt for a missionary's child, using photos on the plain squares. The photos were of her sophomore year in the States.
Helen Elliott, Hendersonville, NC

10 My sister and I used this method to make a 50th wedding anniversary quilt for my parents. It was our first attempt, but the results were wonderful, especially the looks on my parents' faces when they opened the gift. I am going to attempt this in the future for my children and my grandson. I think the gift is priceless. *Mary Calkins, Brooklyn, WI*

11 I have made a number of quilts in which I use photo transfer. I have made them for special birthdays and anniversaries. They become a photo album on a wall. Recently, I realized that three of my quilts were displayed in the nursing home rooms of friends. I had made them for the ladies' 80th and 90th birthdays and for a 50th wedding anniversary. The quilts were a conversation starter for staff and visitors and helped connect the ladies with their lives before entering the nursing home. The one made for the 90 year old was displayed at her funeral, which was one month before her 101st birthday.   *Beth Bigler, Lancaster, PA*

12 I've used photo transfers for labels. In fact, I couldn't find a good picture of my son and myself together, so I used two of our photos and put them side by side on the printer to label his Confirmation quilt. He loved it! I'm also planning to make a memory quilt using photos, and I'll be transferring some of his artwork from elementary school to put in his memory quilt.

Patricia Grimm, New Windsor, NY

13 I was able to find pictures of my husband's old Air Force base, various jets, and logos for his unit, which I printed on transfer fabric, to use in a military-themed quilt and wall hanging for him. He was thrilled with the results!   *Pam Barman, Magnolia, TX*

14 I use photo transfer to commemorate an anniversary or birthday or special happening. When my grandson was born, I made a set of quilted bumpers for his crib with large trucks, cars, and trains going all around all four sides and a photo of every family member in one of the vehicle windows. I even put a photo of my sister's dogs on one of the flat bed cars of the train! My idea is that he would get familiar with all the names and faces in the family, even some that are no longer with us.   *Pamela Capen, Suffern, NY*

15 I have a project planned using my grandparents' wedding photo surrounded by crazy quilt patches made up of their old clothing.

Kim Patterson, Yacolt, WA

16 I wash the fabric to remove sizing, pretreat it with Bubble Jet Set, iron the fabric to freezer paper, print on my computer, let it dry a day or two, ironing occasionally to really set the ink, peel off the freezer paper, rinse with Bubble Jet Rinse, immediately pat it dry, and maybe even use a blow dryer to ensure no ink bleeding occurs. Follow the manufacturer's instructions and don't take any shortcuts!   *Marcia Guza, Brick, NJ*

17 I find photo transfer doesn't tend to look nice after a few washings. I do some in wall hangings or things I don't wash.

Susan Walters, Newark, DE

C. Other Computer Applications

1 The internet is my best friend. I can gather ideas for hours at a time. I can take classes, visit blogs, and find free tutorials. I can buy that one missing piece from a fabric line that my local quilt store has "almost all" of. I can join groups of like-minded quilters and find wonderful new friends for whom I do not have to clean my house because they like me just the way I am, sometimes in my pajamas, and sometimes with a glass of wine in my hand!

Michelle Harrison, Morganton, GA

> *To make personal labels for each quilt, I print onto fabric using Word.*

2 Excel is wonderful for recordkeeping—contacts and addresses and costs of each quilt.

I also keep photos of the quilts I make in folders on my hard drive. I plan to put all the photos in a hard bound book.

To make personal labels for each quilt, I print onto fabric using Word.   *Gail Hurn, Highland Haven, TX*

3 I use Excel to keep a list of the quilting books I own so I don't buy things I already have. It's a long list. Also, I use the internet to read inspiring quilting blogs and to shop for fabric, books and patterns.

Lisa England, Ashland, KY

4 Mostly my digital camera and Photoshop have helped me enormously. I photograph every quilt that takes my interest at local shows. Often I might only take a photo of a border or a block. Sometimes it's the quilting I'm really trying to capture. I load all these photos on my computer and sort them in styles or color or quilting. Then I have my own personal resource.

Jann Dodds, Kenthurst, Australia

❺ I have saved photos of my quilts on Picasa in order to review them when I need inspiration.   *Doris Carbone, Dracut, MA*

❻ Quilter's Cache has an abundance of quilt and quilt block patterns which can be sorted by size. I enjoy using them for my guild's monthly Lucky Buck. I buy a 10" square of fabric and using a pattern of my choice to turn it into a 12½" quilt block.

Sally Berry, Virginia Beach, VA

❼ I use my cell phone and/or camera to take pictures of work in process or for auditioning borders. I take a picture and send it to my computer. When I view it on my computer screen, I can see if blocks need to be rearranged or if the colors (borders) are pleasing together.   *Janet Bland, Smyrna, GA*

❽ I love Pinterest and Google images. If I know what block I want to make, or even when I don't, they offer a wealth of inspiration.

Other computer programs apps I have include: Dear Jane, Block Base, EQ 3, 4, 5, 6 & 7 and add on programs to EQ such as Baltimore, New York Beauty and Sue Spargo.

IPhone apps I've used include lock Fabb, Convert Units, Robert Kauffman Quilt Calc and Quilting Daily.

I use them to help me design quilts, calculate fabric yardage and convert metric and imperial measurements.

Louise Lott, Healesville, Australia

❾ I love Google Images. I download the images, enlarge or reduce the image, make a pattern and create the image out of fabric. Our youngest grandson requested an airplane border for his transportation quilt. I'm currently making the border with 20 different images of airplanes.   *Pat Smith, Sidney, NY*

10 I have taken classes over the internet and have used quilting ebooks. This is particularly useful in longarm quilting because I can have the demonstration playing right next to my machine.

Diane Linker, Scarsdale, NY

11 Triangulations is a great computer application. I use this for all half square triangles and quarter square triangles. You get all 56 sizes on the disk, you don't load it on your computer, so you only print what you need.   *Karen Benke, Medina, OH*

12 I love the instructional DVD's for quilting because you can stop and start, replay until you understand what you need to know. It is so helpful to hear another quilter talk you through a new technique at any time of the day or night.

Olivia Kuebler, Kansas City, MO

> *YouTube is always a help to learn a new technique or a ruler when you just can't grasp what the written instructions mean.*

13 YouTube is always a help to learn a new technique or a ruler when you just can't grasp what the written instructions mean.

Patty Smith, Urbana, IL

14 I use Print Master to make custom labels for my quilts. Lots of fun.

Peggy Tummarello, Central Valley, NY

15 I use a Microsoft product called Visio which is a drawing tool. You can customize the scale, there are lots of built-in shapes, stretching capabilities, set precise sizes to a thousandth of an inch, import fabric swatches and countless other bells and whistles. One of the features I use the most is being able to label each section with both the finished size of the piece as well as the size to cut; this saves lots of mistakes in cutting.

Stephanie Leuthesser, San Ysidro, CA

16 Having access to the best quilting technology out there is no substitute for an artistic vision of what you want to create. Any technology out there is only a tool to be used, like an artist uses a paintbrush. It might make some things easier or faster, but their effectiveness is limited by the creativity with which they are used.

Kari Vojtechovsky, Centennial, CO

⑰ I do not use computer applications other than downloading patterns from sites, free or purchased. Being able to use a pattern that is downloaded rather than wait until the mail carrier brings it is awesome!   *Susan Kirk, Edgewood, MD*

D. Dream Sewing Machines

❶ My dream sewing machine would have to be a new Husqvarna. I sew with a Quilt Designer now and have had her quite a long time, but she is wearing out because I've used her so much. I might enjoy a new machine that has embroidery capabilities, but would first and foremost, give me all the quilting options I have now. Ever since I discovered how wonderful the sensor foot is, I can't imagine ever sewing without it, so my dream machine would have to be another Husqvarna.   *Francis Stanley, Slidell, LA*

❷ The Husqvarna Diamond Deluxe would be my dream machine. The designer diamond sewing machine has a large extended sewing surface, making it really easy to sew. There are various hoop sizes, which would help me to add variety to my designs. There is an automatic sensor system which senses thickness of fabric and adjusts automatically, making sewing a breeze. With the touch of a button, the adviser sets the stitch parameters per the fabric and the sewing technique you feed in. There is an adjustable light system which helps reduce the strain on your eyes. But the added feature is that the machine comes with 380 embroidery designs and 4 embroidery alphabets in 3 different sizes with both upper and lower case letters.   *Rosemarie Garone, West Islip, NY*

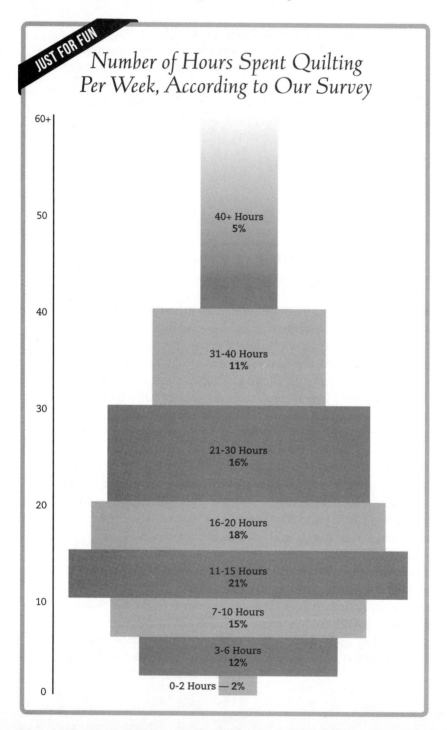

JUST FOR FUN

Number of Hours Spent Quilting
Per Week, According to Our Survey

40+ Hours
5%

31-40 Hours
11%

21-30 Hours
16%

16-20 Hours
18%

11-15 Hours
21%

7-10 Hours
15%

3-6 Hours
12%

0-2 Hours — 2%

❸ My dream machine is an Avante longarm. I have a Pfaff 2.0
Expression and am satisfied with what it will do. It meets my
needs for piecing and small quilting projects. The Avante 18" is big
enough for my own personal use but not so big that it would take
over the house, since I do not plan on making a business out of my
hobby, and not so expensive that I feel it has to pay for itself.

Debra Shirey, Kittanning, PA

❹ If I could make the throat and embroidery area bigger on the
Pfaff 2170 I now have, it would be my dream machine.

Sally Eshelman, York, PA

❺ I really do not like the fancy machines. My dream sewing
machine is no longer made. It was a Singer sewing machine with
the built-in bobbin winder. I hate having to take the bobbin out
and wind it on top of the machine. I have a Project Runway Brother
machine, and the only thing I would change is the width of the
neck to make it easier to quilt.   *Amy Kentera, Highland Mills, NY*

❻ Gratefully, I have my dream sewing machine. I have a Janome
10000 that I purchased when I retired in 2002. I love the machine
and have never wanted to trade it for another.

My second dream machine is soon to be delivered: an Innova
longarm quilting machine. After having had another brand of longarm machine, I am more knowledgeable about getting a machine
serviced. I rate servicing right up there with brand purchase.

Marti Blankenship, Pleasant Valley, MO

❼ I currently have a Janome Horizon 7700. It is very close to a
dream machine. It has a large throat area to allow decent sized
quilts to be quilted at home. The "accufeed" system works very
well—much, much better than a walking foot on my previous
sewing machine. Little things, like needle down when you stop; a
choice of using the foot pedal or a start-stop button to make the
machine "sew"; being able to move the needle left or right to get
the perfect stitching line; good lighting; and a variety of presser
feet to accomplish many sewing tasks all add to the ease of sewing

with this machine. About the only feature it does not have is a low-bobbin warning. That would be a great addition.

Nancy Koyanik, Troy, VA

If my house was on fire, I would try to save my 1897 Davis Reliance treadle machine above all my other possessions!

8 I actually just got my dream sewing machine: a Janome Horizon. It is one of the new ones with 11" between the needle and the machine. It has 5 LED lights and a thread cutter. All the feet, etc. store in the top of the machine. It is the most well-thought-out machine I have ever seen.

But I must admit I equally love my 1897 Davis Reliance treadle machine. She still sews as smoothly as when she was new. She has so many attachments I don't think I will ever use them all. She was the Lexus of her day, and I still love her and love to sew on her. If my house was on fire, I would try to save this sewing machine above all my other possessions!

Diane Bachman, Leola, PA

9 I have my dream sewing machine. I use the Brother Quattro. I am able to do a lot of editing on screen without going into the software all the time.

Patsy Shields, Sellersburg, IN

10 I love my Brother 6000D. It has a deep throat, and because it is a sewing and embroidery machine, it does many things. I can also sew when the embroidery unit is connected, so for those times when I have been embroidering and have a little sewing to do, I can just change to sewing and take care of it without having to take apart the machine.

Patti Goggio, Broadlands, VA

11 My dream machine is a domestic machine with a wide enough area for large quilts to fit in. I love my Bernina 440 QE, but do wish I could manage larger quilts. I think I'd especially love a mid-arm that I could use while seated.

Paula Loges, Sims, NC

⑫ I would love a Bernina 710. I think it would be nice to have a wider throat area for machine quilting. The Bernina 700 series has 10" of space.   *Beverly Landis, Quarryville, PA*

⑬ I have been sewing with Berninas for 30 years. I am really looking at a new 750. I like the BSR (stitch regulator for quilting), the larger bobbin, the larger arm opening and the LED lights under the sewing machine arm. It feels like a good fit for my sewing/quilting needs.   *Penny Ford, Sundre, Alberta*

⑭ I've loved all my Berninas, but my 820 just takes the cake! Of all its features, it's the extra-long free arm, that wonderful space, that makes it so fantastic. I don't use the stitch regulator because I'm a darning foot and feed dogs down girl, nor do I use the computer memory thing, but that extra maneuver room is tops.   *Penny D'Aloia, Coburg, Australia*

⑮ My dream machine is a Bernina 820 QE because of its extra large work area. I also love the jumbo bobbin because it's less likely to run out of bobbin thread in the middle of a project. The 820 QE also has a stitch regulator for machine quilting. Ah, a little bit of heaven!   *Joan Paul, Stuttgart, Germany*

⑯ I just bought the Bernina 759QE, so I think the dream machine is in my house. I love the lighting (which I think could bring in an airplane), the size of the harp, the variable needle positions, scissors, and variable widths and lengths of stitches. It has 837 stitches which should see me through to the next millennium! Also, when I'm using decorative stitches, it shows me on the touch screen exactly where I am in the pattern. Too many features to cover them all, but it's a beauty.

Marie White, Waiuku, New Zealand

The Bernina 759QE has 837 stitches which should see me through to the next millennium!

⑰ I would love to have my maternal grandmother's treadle singer machine because I learned to sew on it with her when I was very young.   *Pamela Olson, South Windsor, CT*

18 My dream sewing machine would tell me when my bobbin thread is running low. I always run out at the wrong time.

Marilyn Pearlman, Fuquay-Varina, NC

19 My dream machine is one that you can put a spool of thread on the top and on the bottom for your bobbin thread. They would run out at the same time and you wouldn't have to change the bobbin all the time!   *Linda Ahn, Mohrsville, PA*

20 I'd love an old hand crank machine so I could sit outdoors and quilt.   *Debbie Paige, West Springfield, MA*

21 I want a pre-World War II Singer Featherweight. I do *not* need fancy stitching. I need portability with a dependable straight stitch because I have back issues. I am no longer able to lift my machine from the car and haul it into class. I have audited several classes and gone home to sew, but I would love to be able to sew in class with a Featherweight.   *Michelle Harrison, Morganton, GA*

22 I'd want the biggest throat possible to allow for larger quilts and to be able to do free motion quilting. I would want it to have the embroidery feature as I make labels for every quilt. There would be a separate blanket stitch for appliqué, and a large enough post or area to hold larger spools of thread. I currently have a Viking, and I like the automatic sensor for fabric thickness and auto tension. No messing with tension controls. I make clothes for my little granddaughter, and the decorative stitches are nice.

Pam Sievers, Powell, OH

23 I would love a machine that has a really wide throat space, a few types of stitches but not hundreds, great speed control (going fast when I want and slower when I want), a thread cutter, a bobbin alarm, needle up/down, 1-step button hole feature, built-in extension platform, lots of great feet and a built-in walking foot. That would get all my favorite features of my two machines in one. That would be a dream!   *Kari Vojtechovsky, Centennial, CO*

E. Social Media

❶ Someone is always ready to share a new tip or design on social media. Quilters are some of the most generous people I know.

Leslie Emma, Raleigh, NC

❷ I have often found the answers to problems I was having with a particular sewing method or pattern on a sewing website. The very first year I was a quilter, I could not figure out how to do a binding to save my life. In the wee hours of the morning, a fellow quilter was online and talked me through the process. I have never forgotten that lesson and have talked many others through the process and taught it over and over again. *Susan Chandler, Solon Springs, WI*

❸ I find social media extremely important in keeping me up to date with the latest and greatest quilting trends.

I have used YouTube so much when I am stuck on a technique and need a little review.

Seeing my favorite quilting bloggers just gives me a shot of adrenaline and makes me want to run downstairs and create something in my sewing room. *Annette Crain, Spanish Fork, UT*

❹ I belong to the Sylvia's Bridal Quilt Yahoo group. Each week the moderator posts the block for the week. Each quilter uploads a photo of her completed block to that block's file and also to her own file. I enjoy seeing other interpretations and color choices, and quilters' comments, and interacting with other quilters through messaging. *MaryJean Bower, Bloomsburg, PA*

❺ Blogging has expanded my quilting beyond my wildest expectations. Because of it I've tried new techniques and methods I would have never tried without it. I've gone way out of the box in quilting since I began blogging. *Candace Pekich, Walla Walla, WA*

Blogging has expanded my quilting beyond my wildest expectations.

❻ Blogging is a two-edged sword. It keeps me working on a project so I can show it off to all of my family and friends as I work. I live away from almost all of my family and friends, so they can see what I do on a daily/weekly basis.

Blogging and reading blogs also causes me to have many UFOs when I see so many beautiful projects being worked on by other bloggers. I want to stop what I'm doing and try that new pattern, especially if I have hit a rough spot on my current project, or if I'm at a point that I don't love, such as basting.　　*Diane Meddley, Parrish, FL*

❼ I don't blog myself, but when I'm in the mood for some eye candy I enjoy surfing other bloggers and Pinterest.

Melynda Cash, Forest, VA

❽ I am addicted to quilting blogs! They are my main source of inspiration when I can't sleep at night. There is something for everyone out there, no matter your quilting style. I can be part of a quilting community even if I don't live around other quilters.

Peggy Quinlan-Gee, Salt Lake City, UT

❾ Reading blogs and entries in social media can offer inspiration for new ideas, as well as encouragement from a variety of quilters, from novice to expert. It is also a "virtual" quilt guild and is available 24/7 for busy quilt lovers.　　*Signa Ferguson, Pelham, AL*

❿ I have learned so much from my Yahoo groups and quilt forums. They're great places to ask questions and get answers. There are some things I can't learn from a book.

Emily Galea, Boca Raton, FL

⓫ Most of the quilts I make are called Chemo Comforters and are given to cancer patients undergoing chemotherapy. I post them on my Facebook page for Chemo Comforters to help get out the word that these quilts are available.　　*Susan O'Keefe, Rochester, NY*

CHAPTER 15

Binding

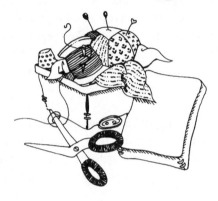

A. Choosing a Binding Style

❶ Sometimes I want the binding to disappear and sometimes I want it to stand out, like a miniature frame. I usually can't pick what will make that happen until the quilt is completed, with backing and whatever quilting design is chosen.

Terri Overton, San Tan Valley, AZ

❷ Think of the binding as a design element. I rarely make the binding the same color as the final border. Consider using decorative stitches on the binding or inserting a ruffle, piping, or flange.

Rachele Howard, Van Buren Point, NY

❸ I like a darker binding, generally speaking, since a quilt reminds me of a picture in a frame.

Olivia Kuebler, Kansas City, MO

❹ Binding is an opportunity to add another design element to your quilt. I love using a scrappy binding, or adding a flange, piping or rickrack. Stripes are always fun and can be cut straight or on the bias.   *Karen Martin, Breezy Point, MN*

❺ For binding a quilt, I always choose the binding fabric after the quilt top is done. I audition several fabrics that I think may look good and a few "wild card" fabrics. I do this until I find the one that I think makes the quilt sing. Your eye should not be drawn to the binding, but instead, the binding should balance the quilt and complete the message you are trying to communicate.

Karen Price, Blackfoot, ID

❻ Some quilts look really good with a fairly wide binding, and some are much nicer with a really narrow one. Fold your binding fabric over and audition it before cutting strips to see which you prefer. It may be different with each quilt you make.

Colleen Froats, Alanson, MI

❼ For a striped binding, I love bias binding. Also, on small quilts where a bulky, double straight binding would look out of place, I use a single fold bias binding.   *Karen Martin, Breezy Point, MN*

❽ I like to audition the binding when my quilting is completed. Sometimes, what I thought would be the perfect binding, just does not work. I gather several fabrics that might work and tuck them under the quilt with just enough of the folded edge showing to mimic binding. I stand back or take a digital photo to see what looks good, and usually the "perfect" frame to my quilt is easy to spot.

Ann Liebner, Pine Grove, PA

❾ For several years, I used a black and white country-style fabric for binding most all of my quilts. It was my signature. But the truth be told, it was easy to cut and fold, using the checks as guides.

Kathy Perry, Sugar Land, TX

❿ I love the look of plaid fabric used in bias binding, especially for manly quilts.   *Janice Simmons, Fresno, CA*

⑪ Match the thread to your binding, not the quilt color.

Bernadette Bird, Oregon, IL

⑫ I love to use rickrack in my binding. To keep it in place while stitching, I use a basting glue. Pins distort the seam too much.

Karen Martin, Breezy Point, MN

⑬ I like for my binding to be a statement, so I rarely bind with a fabric that will be lost among the piecing of the top.

Pam Barman, Magnolia, TX

⑭ I like to take one of the bolder, but less prominently used, colored fabrics in my quilt for binding fabric.

Amanda Kei Andrews, Vero Beach, FL

> *I like for my binding to be a statement, so I rarely bind with a fabric that will be lost among the piecing of the top.*

⑮ I like to use a couple of different fabrics on the binding, either making two sides the same or making all four different. This helps to bring all the colors and fabrics together.   *Grace Lively, Wolf Lake, IL*

⑯ I like to have a little extra batting on the edge of the quilt so the binding is filled up and not floppy.   *Patti Prince, Lake Isabella, CA*

⑰ I machine stitch the binding front and back. The awesome machines we have now have many decorative stitches that can add to the beauty of a quilt when used on a binding.

Janet Jaeger, Silver Springs, FL

⑱ I have done facings on more modern style quilts where I don't want the stripe that binding adds to a quilt.

Stephanie Greenberg, Lawrenceville, NJ

⑲ I think wider binding (at least 3" wide) is easier to work with, makes beautifully mitered corners, and I don't have to cut off extra batting. It can be worked into the "look" of any quilt.

Roberta Whitcomb, Emmaus, PA

20 I do not like ¼" bindings because I feel they are generally out of scale with most of my projects. I prefer a ½" finished binding.

Sharon Mountford, Canoga Park, CA

B. Measuring for Binding

1 I measure the quilt and use the Robert Kaufman iPhone app to determine the number of strips I need to cut. I sew my binding on to the front of the quilt and hand sew it down to the back.

Peggy Quinlan-Gee, Salt Lake City, UT

2 Fold the quilt in half side to side and measure the width, then double that number. Fold the quilt in half top to bottom, measure that length, and double that number, too. Add those two numbers together for quilt perimeter and add another 10–12".

Elizabeth Flavin, Wilmington, NC

3 To figure out the length of binding I need for my quilt, I measure both sides and both tops, add those totals and then add an additional 12" for the mitered corners.

Rita Goff, Asbury, WV

C. Applying Binding

1 Make sure when you sew the binding to the back of the quilt that you cover the seam from attaching the binding to the front of the quilt. You don't want it to show on the back of the quilt.

Kathy Kelleher, Kennebunk, ME

② Before sewing the binding on, I like to square up the quilt and make sure all my edges are clean and even.

Janet Jaeger, Silver Springs, FL

③ I always machine sew the binding on to the front of the quilt and hand sew it to the back. I don't like to see the machine stitches on either side. My hand stitches are very small to make those invisible also. It is a cleaner look.   *Sharon Stoddard, Bridgeport, CA*

④ I use straight grain binding, cut 2½" wide. I fold the binding in half, line up the cut edge with the raw edge of the quilt, and stitch with a ¼" seam. I then line up a rotary cutter ruler, placing the ½" mark on the ruler on the seam I've just sewn. Then I cut off the rest of the batting and backing (this means there's ¼" of batting and backing beyond the raw edge of the quilt and binding). I sew each side of the quilt to within ¼" of the end of the edge. When all four sides are sewn on, I sew the corners of the binding to create the miter, trim the corner, wrap the binding over to the back side, then slip-stitch it down by hand.   *Nancy Swanwick, Fort Scott, KS*

⑤ I prefer to sew the binding to the front of the quilt by machine and finish the back with a hand sewn blind stitch. I think it looks neater that way, and I can hand stitch while I watch TV.

Mary Caldwell, Howell, MI

⑥ I finish the back by hand because it is my calm, final, personal touch.

Carol Bordwell, Chewelah, WA

⑦ I like to hand stitch the binding. It's a nice opportunity to visit with my quilt before I give it away.

Ellen Mueller, Acton, MA

I like to hand stitch the binding. It's a nice opportunity to visit with my quilt before I give it away.

⑧ When I'm handstitching down the binding on the back, I usually knot along the way, so that if the binding should catch and begin to tear out, it reaches a stopping point quickly, making less binding to repair.   *Karen Asman, Martin, OH*

9 Just recently, I have started making my own binding for quilts. I make 1" double-fold binding which I sew to the back side of the quilt with the machine, then fold over and hand stitch to the top. Before this, I left about 4" of the backing all around the outside edge of my quilt top and turned it over and hemmed it with mitered corners. The double fold binding looks neater, but the fold-over hemming is faster.   *Jenn Martin, Prattville, AL*

10 My attempts at full machine binding have not always resulted in seams being covered. Often my seams were as wavy as the ocean. I prefer sewing on the raw edges of the binding by machine and then hand stitching the edge in place. I like this because I'm certain that the seam line of the binding and quilt is covered by the binding and that my corners miter smoothly.

Debbie Daugherty-Ball, Salisbury, MD

11 I choose a spot about two-thirds of the way down the right hand side of the quilt and pin the beginning of the binding. Then I take the binding around the quilt without pinning to check that no binding joins will be at the corners. If they will be, I adjust the starting point of the binding and recheck it. When I'm happy, I sew it on by machine, using my walking foot.

Janice Goodburn, Foxton Beach, New Zealand

12 Sew a binding with a faux piping/flange by cutting 1½" width of binding fabric and 1¾" of piping fabric, the length needed to go around quilt, plus 10". Press the seam allowance towards the binding fabric. Fold in half as a normal binding and a ⅛" piping/flange will appear. Machine sew onto the quilt back and bring to front. Use the Sewline or Fons & Porter glue stick to secure the binding down. Machine stitch in the ditch of the piping.

Shari Nyles, Fleetwood, PA

13 To bind a quilt, I use a 2¼" wide strip cut straight of grain or bias. Stitch it on the front, with the right sides together, using a ¼" seam width. I add a strip of batting cut ¾" and sew with long stitches to the quilt top inside the ¼" seam line. Then I fold the binding to the back, grab my Bernina high/low foot and stitch in

JUST FOR FUN

There's too much _____ in my stash and never enough _____.

❖ There are too many <u>odd-shaped scraps</u> in my stash and never enough <u>continuous yardage</u>. *Jan Mast, Lancaster, PA*

❖ There's too much <u>batik fabric</u> in my stash and never enough <u>1880 reproductions</u>. *Karen Martin, Breezy Point, MN*

❖ There's too much <u>"going to save for something special"</u> in my stash and never enough <u>"need for the current project."</u>
Georgia Ricci, Midway, GA

❖ There's too much <u>fabric</u> in my stash and never enough <u>time to use it</u>. But just looking at and stroking it does the soul good!
Marie White, Waiuku, New Zealand

❖ There are too many <u>overly bold (but beautiful) florals</u> in my stash and never enough <u>blenders</u>. *Laroletta Petty, Breckenridge, CO*

❖ There's too much <u>cat hair</u> in my stash and never enough <u>time to launder</u>. *Kay Hinkelma, Florissant, MO*

❖ There's too much <u>blue</u> in my stash and never enough <u>yellow</u>. And yet when I buy new fabric, I invariably come home with more blue... sigh... *Nancy Henry, Rochester, NH*

❖ There's too much <u>of everything</u> in my stash and never enough <u>of anything</u>! *Susan Louis, Briarwood, NY*

❖ There's too much <u>happiness</u> in my stash and never enough <u>to make me stop collecting</u>. *Barbara Papp, Kings Park, NY*

the ditch from the front (I have also handstitched the binding to the back). This creates a perfect machine sewn binding that's a bit poofy—a lovely look!   *Diane Johansen, Naperville, IL*

> *I run a small basting stitch by hand all around the quilt ⅛" from the edge so it will be covered by the binding. This stitching eases in the edge so it is never rippled.*

14 I always use double-folded, continuous bias binding. But first, I run a small basting stitch by hand all around the quilt ⅛" from the edge so it will be covered by the binding. This stitching eases in the edge so it is never rippled.   *Sharon Nungester, Berwyn, PA*

15 I prefer hand binding quilts for myself because it produces a nice clean look. Charity quilts will get a lot of use and many more washings, so I machine stitch these for extra durability. I use a zigzag stitch which, to me, looks much nicer than a straight stitch.

Nancee McCann, Wilmington, DE

16 If I'm sewing the binding all by machine, then I sew it to the back and bring it around to the front and topstitch it, usually with a blanket stitch. I find if I stretch the binding just the least little bit, it helps it to lie flatter than if I'm trying to ease it in to fit.   *Sally Eshelman, York, PA*

17 I use 2½" doubled bias binding with a ⅜" seam allowance, so when I wrap it to the back, it is a full binding.

Jennifer Padden, Austin, TX

18 Attach the binding with a ¼" seam all the way around, then when you get ready to sew the ends together, overlap the binding the same width as the binding. If your binding is 2½" wide, overlap it by that much and cut it off. Turn one end 45° and sew it like you did the other strips. When you straighten it out to sew down the last bit, it will be exactly right, and you can't tell where you started or stopped.

Shirley Valk, Ellerbe, NC

⑲ To join the ends of the binding after I sew it on the quilt, I again use the mitered seam. Seams in the binding are not obvious, and the diagonal seams spread the bulk. Then I fold the binding to the back and whipstitch it into place.   *Debbie Daugherty-Ball, Salisbury, MD*

⑳ Always use a double binding and always have it separately attached to the quilt. The very first place a quilt wears is the binding. Having a double thickness will slow down the wear process, and if it is separately attached (as opposed to turning excess backing to the front for a binding), you can always take it off if it does fade or wear and attach a new binding without having to cut the quilt.   *Nancy Henry, Rochester, NH*

㉑ I don't do one continuous bind. I bind the sides of the quilt first, then the top and bottom.   *Yolande Smith, Titusville, FL*

㉒ I *always* bind before I quilt. I got into this habit because it seemed like I was always rushing to meet a deadline. You can always cut back on the quilting if you are short of time, but you can never submit a quilt with a partial binding! Then I found I liked not having raveling and stretched edges and block seams popping open as I wrestled the quilt under the needle for machine quilting. It was so much neater, and the quilt didn't get stretched and distorted.
          Valerie Turer, Brooklyn, NY

D. *Binding Tools*

❶ I use a walking foot to apply all bindings. Careful pinning and slow, but accurate, sewing with gentle stretch-to-fit techniques gets the binding applied.   *LynDee Lombardo, Olympia, WA*

❷ Even though I pin ahead of my stitching, I still use a stiletto tool to hold the binding firmly in place in front of the needle.

Joyce Finch, Golden, MO

❸ I use a binding tool for joining the binding on the bias. The tool tells you where to cut the binding for a perfect bias fit.

Frances Courson, Maryville, TN

❹ When I'm binding a quilt, I use a piece of wrapping paper tube and neatly wrap my prepared binding around it. When I'm ready to put the binding on the quilt, I put a string or ribbon through the tube, put it around my neck and apply the binding to the quilt. This is much easier than having the long strip on the floor, table, etc.

Nancy Peet, Fairport, NY

❺ I like to use glue sticks (Fons & Porter or Sewline) to secure the binding instead of pins. This allows me to sew the entire binding by machine without the distortion involved with pins.

Shari Nyles, Fleetwood, PA

❻ Using my quilt gloves as I machine sew the binding strip to the right side of the quilt is a great help in keeping the binding from slipping. I can keep my left hand on the quilt while guiding the binding with my right hand.   *Patricia Grimm, New Windsor, NY*

❼ When I need to quickly apply a binding, I apply binding initially to the back, fold it to the front, and top stitch on the front, using a #38 Bernina foot. This foot keeps the top stitching straight, and it looks more professional.

Nannette Konstant, Flourtown, PA

> *I use hair clips, the snapping kind, to hold down the binding before I hand-stitch it to the back of the quilt.*

❽ I use hair clips, the snapping kind, to hold down the binding before I hand-stitch it to the back of the quilt. It is more effective than pins, and I don't stab myself.   *Joan Trautwein, Belle Mead, NJ*

❾ Instead of using the very expensive binding clips meant for quilting, I buy binder clips from an office supply. They are less expensive and hold very well. *Susan Dyer, Ashland, MA*

E. *Straight Grain Bindings*

❶ Unless there are curved quilt edges involved, bias binding, which allows stretch, is unnecessary and overall more challenging to work with. Stick with straight binding unless you're working with scalloped or curved edges. *Jan Mast, Lancaster, PA*

❷ Bias binding is nice for curves, but most of the time, straight binding will work, especially if it is cut length of grain instead of across. *Beth Cates, Carroll, IA*

❸ Straight-grain binding is easier to calculate and has fewer seams. *Kris Newlin, West Chester, PA*

❹ Some people think bias binding wears better/longer, but my first quilt was on my bed for 15 years, and the straight-grain binding still looks fine after all that time and many washings. *Mary Caldwell, Howell, MI*

❺ Straight binding creates fewer "bubbles" or less warping when folded to the back side. Bias binding is best if used on a curved or scalloped quilt edge. *Georgia Ricci, Midway, GA*

❻ Straight cut binding is very easy to cut, and usually the grain is not completely straight, so you don't have to worry about one thread on the end wearing out. *Shirley Valk, Ellerbe, NC*

F. *Bias Bindings*

❶ If you have any curves, or maybe your measurements are slightly off, a bias binding is much more forgiving than a straight one.

Sandy Glass, Cibolo, TX

❷ I was taught that bias binding would hold up longer. If a thread breaks, there are thousands more on the bias. If a thread breaks in straight binding, one thread runs all the way down.

Sandy Cornelius, Camarillo, CA

❸ I love a scalloped binding, and they just cannot be done with straight binding. I usually use straight binding for straight edge quilts, though. Bias binding on a straight edge quilt just wastes fabric. To attempt a scallop or other undulating edge with a straight of the grain binding is just foolish. You will find that you can waste fabric that way, too.

Michelle Harrison, Morganton, GA

> *Bias binding seems to sort of "hug" the quilt edge into straightness.*

❹ My favorite binding is a double-fold bias binding because I believe it to be more durable than a straight-of-grain binding. It also seems to sort of "hug" the quilt edge into straightness. I create the binding by cutting a square, and then cutting it in half diagonally. I sew the top and bottom edges into a seam, which is then pressed open. I now have a parallelogram which I take to my cutting board and, folding it in half, cut into 2" strips. I then sew the ends of the strips into seams until I have one long bias strip. I do this instead of creating a continuous bias because I seem to have a better strip of bias when I'm finished.

Ruthie Hoover, Westerville, OH

❺ Bias binding absolutely lays so much nicer with no puckers or wrinkles. And it takes no more fabric to cut on the bias. Should a thread in the fabric break, with bias it crosses on the diagonal, just like seaming on the bias distributes the fullness. It doesn't leave a straight line that is easily followed. Bias edges don't unravel either, making it easier to bind with bias.   *Karen Asman, Martin, OH*

6 I continue to use a walking foot to apply bias binding, sewing carefully around the curves. If there are inner points, such as the points in the binding of a Double Wedding Ring quilt, I stop my machine at the point and backstitch. Again, adjusting the binding into a miter, I start the machine at the ¼" point, backstitch for a few stitches and then continue on around the curve.
                                              Ruthie Hoover, Westerville, OH

7 I only use bias when the print is a check or crossgrain stripe, because those look really cool on the bias. Otherwise, crossgrain cut strips work just fine, and I am not left with weird triangle-shaped scraps.   *Annemarie (Nancy) Poorbaugh, Montgomery, AL*

8 I do not use bias binding because it's a waste of fabrics and has too many seams. I have not yet had a binding that has worn out.
                                              Kris Newlin, West Chester, PA

G. Mitered Corners

1 To miter a corner: stop ¼" from the corner with your stitching and back stitch. Then fold the binding at a 90° angle away from the quilt corner. You will have a triangle at the corner. Then fold the binding down over the triangle and start sewing from the corner down the next side. This little extra piece of fabric gives you a nice mitered corner when you fold it over to the other side to stitch down. When I come to the end of my stitching, I fold back the binding so that it matches the other binding and press. I then align the two pressed pieces right sides together and sew them closed before finishing the edge.   *Sandy Howell, Highland, UT*

❷ I mark a little dot ¼" from each corner, and I stop stitching at that mark. I then miter the corner by folding straight up away from me. I finger crease and pin, then bring the binding down, lining up to the raw edge of the quilt. I proceed to stitch, being careful of the pin, and then stitch to the next corner

Teresa Caldwell, Long Valley, NJ

❸ I use a Frixion marker and mark ⅜" from the end of each corner. I also mark the end of the corner. I sew to the first mark, back stitch 3 stitches, sew back to the line, then sew on the diagonal off the edge of the quilt at the second mark. I raise the presser foot, turn the quilt, insert the needle at the first mark (⅜" from the end) and repeat at each corner. When I take the quilt from the machine, I use a seam ripper and take out the stitches that I made on the diagonal. This method ensures a perfect miter each time.

Frances Courson, Maryville, TN

❹ I use the high five method to miter corners: sew to ¼" from the corner, remove quilt from machine, pull the binding up as in a high five movement, line the top up to the edge, lay the binding down, and continue sewing.   *Roberta Whitcomb, Emmaus, PA*

❺ I use Eleanor Burns' method. Her books are great, and I always advise new quilters to use them. They are clearly written, with lots of pictures and simple to follow descriptions.

Vickie VanDyken, Everson, WA

When you use binding tape, the corners are so easy to miter and look very neat.

❻ When you use binding tape, the corners are so easy to miter and look very neat. I have just folded over the backing and hemmed with square edges if it complimented the quilt top.

Jenn Martin, Prattville, AL

❼ When I am hand-tacking the binding to the back of the quilt, I remember to close each corner angle on both front and back with a ladder stitch.

Michelle Harrison, Morganton, GA

8 Be sure to stitch miters closed if the quilt will be judged!

Cathie Shelton, Montgomery Village, MD

9 Negotiating corners makes me smile—now! I used to avoid it because I never understood written directions. Way too confusing. And then I made friends with the oldest quilter I could locate. She lived on a farm in Kinsman, Ohio. I called her and asked if I could bring cookies and talk quilting. I treasure that day. I learned so much that perfected my quilting skills, including negotiating corners. She handed me a sample that looked like a pot holder and said "Practice." So I wish I could write perfect directions, but I can't. But now *I'm* older and if you bring cookies, we can talk quilting, and I'll give you a sample to learn from and practice.

Kathy Perry, Sugar Land, TX

10 If you want to avoid mitering, use a round ruler or even a plate to round off the corners before binding. If the radius of your curve is small, you should use bias binding for a rounded corner, but with a larger radius, straight binding works fine.   *Marcia Guza, Brick, NJ*

CHAPTER 16

Records

A. Types of Records

❶ In addition to always putting a label on my quilts with my name, my home town and state, date, and the quilter's name if applicable, I photograph everything I complete. I used to keep them in a small scrapbook with all the pertinent information regarding the piece. Now I've started taking a picture with my iPad and creating a folder for each year. Whenever I think I'm not being very productive, I can look back and see just how busy I've been.

Sharon Gregorczyk, Kyle, TX

❷ I take photos of the quilts I make. With the photos attached in a diary, I write about the quilt: who it was made for and the reason I made it. If it is a particularly difficult quilt or has many pieces, I add things like how long it took, how many pieces, how many fabrics, etc. I also add if I learned a new technique in the process or used a special ruler or tool. This diary also serves as a reference tool.

Diane Meddley, Parrish, FL

❸ I take a picture of the front of the quilt as well as the label, backing, and close ups of any special quilting patterns. I also snip small pieces of the fabrics I used and paste them into a type of collage that I keep with the pictures in a journal. I also write down the name of the quilt, who it was for, the date and where I made it. If I get a thank you note, I will also include that. If I had any epiphanies during the creation of the quilt, I journal that as well.

Linda Pace, McDonough, GA

❹ I take photos of each project and keep them in a folder on my computer. I also have them backed up on a sky drive in case my computer ever crashes.   *Candace Pekich, Walla Walla, WA*

❺ I take photos of each step of the process and, of course, the finished product. The labels contain information for future generations to know the history of my quilts   *Laura Gilmartin, Stafford, VA*

❻ I like the computer program Quilt Album for record keeping. I also print out the pages so that I have a physical copy that I can flick through.   *Anne Couzens, Diggers Rest, Australia*

❼ Each quilt I make for a specific person has a mini journal to go with it. Contained in the journal are the details of how the quilt came to be: the inspiration I used for the quilt, brainstorming diagrams, patterns, fabric swatches, layouts, quilting patterns, and label details.

If any of the fabrics have a history, I'll include that, too.

Sharon Siacci, Khandallah, New Zealand

❽ I have saved the selvage edge from nearly every fabric I have ever used. I save the portion with the manufacturer, fabric line and the color dots. I have written the month and year of purchase with permanent marker on the more recent ones. I am putting these into a quilt that is entirely made of selvage edges. This will be another type of record, in addition to the photos I take of each quilt

Susan Chandler, Solon Springs, WI

9 Depending on the quilt, I sometimes keep tiny swatches, the original pattern, sketches, and notes. I don't do this for most of my quilts, just ones with very special purposes. I do keep a daily journal, so many times there are bits of information about the quilts in progress in there as well.   *Nancy Swanwick, Fort Scott, KS*

10 When I'm handquilting, I measure each piece of thread as I cut it and keep a running tab and tally it up when I'm finished. Of course it helps when I use a whole spool of thread because that's already measured.   *Carol Forestell, Robersonville, NC*

11 I keep a log of fabric and notion purchases (with receipts), plus a photograph of each completed quilt with small swatches of fabrics used, along with the fabric manufacturer and collection name (if applicable). I also include notes about measurements and variations from the printed pattern.   *Signa Ferguson, Pelham, AL*

12 I have a longarm machine. Just recently I started keeping track of the quilts I quilt on it—the size, the panto (or design), the thread type and color, the bobbin thread (if different than what I used on the top), and the number of bobbins used. I wish I had started keeping these statistics sooner. It's interesting to see what threads or pantos I use most often and also how often I use the machine.
Sue Hurley, Princeton, NJ

> *I take notes while I'm making the quilt. If I find something I'd like to try another time, or wish I'd done, I can go back and make notes about that as well.*

13 I have a sewing journal that I've recently started. I take notes while I'm making the quilt. If I find something I'd like to try another time, or wish I'd done, I can go back and make notes about that as well.

Amy DeCesare, Delmont, PA

14 I like to note the date I started and finished a quilt. I like to document the fabrics I used in the quilt, along with swatches of the fabrics used. If

I purchased the fabrics on a special outing with friends, I like to document that as well. *Melynda Cash, Forest, VA*

⓯ I have an Excel Spreadsheet with tabs
* Quilts to be Started
* Quilts in Process
* Quilts Finished *Patricia Boyle, Bedford, TX*

⓰ I use an Excel spreadsheet with columns for name, designer, type (pieced, etc.), date started and ended, who the quilt was given to, who did the long arm quilting, an embedded picture, and any comments. *Stephanie Leuthesser, San Ysidro, CA*

⓱ I keep an Excel spreadsheet with the following columns: date completed, title, height in inches, width in inches, area (computed), calculated price (based on size and current average costs of materials), actual price for which I would sell the quilt or value if donated to charity (takes into account complexity of construction and quilting), basic description of pattern and quilting, final destination (who owns the quilt or to whom it was donated).

In addition I keep a photo record in iPhoto and post quilts currently available on our family website.

Sharon Mountford, Canoga Park, CA

⓲ For quilts that are gifts, I like to include a card that explains how I chose the fabrics or design for the quilt. I try to choose those to reflect the recipient's style or personality. Sometimes these elements are subtle, so a card gives me the chance to point out the connections or the hidden meanings. If it's special, many people save cards as a remembrance. *Amy DeCesare, Delmont, PA*

⓳ If you are doing a sampler, keep a record of the name of each block, along with a picture of the block. I made a quilt with 140 6" blocks, with each block being a different pattern. I wrote the story behind the quilt and included this information in a photo album just about that one quilt. I later learned that this is important if you are having your quilt appraised—the more documentation you have, the better. *Linda Long, Bloomfield, IN*

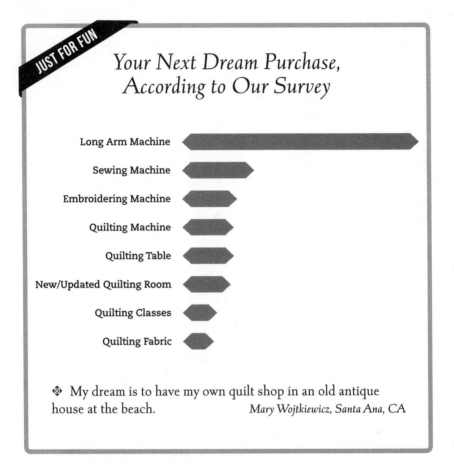

JUST FOR FUN

Your Next Dream Purchase, According to Our Survey

Long Arm Machine

Sewing Machine

Embroidering Machine

Quilting Machine

Quilting Table

New/Updated Quilting Room

Quilting Classes

Quilting Fabric

❖ My dream is to have my own quilt shop in an old antique house at the beach.   *Mary Wojtkiewicz, Santa Ana, CA*

⑳ My husband and I publish an annual "Dahk and Jan Scrapbook" that we give to family and friends, and it includes the quilts I have made that year, along with who they were for. We also include any ribbons I may have gotten at our County Fair.

Jan Knox, Mosheim, TN

㉑ I put my finished quilts out on Facebook for my long distance friends and family to see my latest projects.

Barbara Theriault, Brooksville, FL

㉒ I have a blog and post about all the quilts I make and have made.   *Janet Olmstead, Calgary, Alberta*

㉓ I start with a graph paper drawing of the pattern, in color. If the quilt has different blocks, I draw a larger scale drawing of each block and attach a swatch of the different fabrics to the drawing where that fabric will be used. After the quilt is finished, I take a picture of the quilt and attach it to the graph paper. I date the drawings and log where we are living, since we have lived in 12 states. I have a notebook with dividers with pockets where I keep the pattern and fabric swatches and pictures. On the back of the quilt I make an embroidered label, saying who the quilt is for, my name as the quilt maker and the date. If the quilt is for a special occasion, I add that to the label.   *Sheryl Waddington, Ellenwood, GA*

㉔ Until recently, I've written a quilt journal. I put info in regarding giftee name, pattern, size, fabrics, and pictures. Since that is full, I recently purchased QuiltAlbum2 so I can keep the information on my computer. I'm gradually transferring all the older quilts from the journal to this program.   *Joanne Scott, Peotone, IL*

㉕ I have several methods of keeping records. I have a book I purchased in an art department of a craft store that has lines on one side and blank pages on the other. I write information about when I started/finished, who it was for, where the idea came from, etc., on the lined side. On the blank side there's room for a 4 × 6″ photo and small swatches of the actual fabrics used.

I keep photo records. I blog, but I also have a folder where I keep my finished projects (I also cross-stitch). At the beginning of a new year, I turn those photos into a small hard-bound book, like a yearbook, to keep on my shelves.   *Terri Overton, San Tan Valley, AZ*

B. *Photo Poses and Uses*

❶ I take photos in natural settings on the porch or in the yard. I store them on my computer. I also record them on a form which is submitted to my quilt guild for incentive awards.

Janet Bland, Smyrna, GA

❷ My favorite way to pose a finished quilt is to roll it up and get a binding shot.

Amy DeCesare, Delmont, PA

❸ When I have very special or expensive quilts, or quilts I plan to enter in shows, I take them to my local university where they will photograph them professionally at a fairly reasonable price.

Nancy Henry, Rochester, NH

❹ I take many photos of a finished quilt: full shots of it hanging, lying on a bed if it is intended for the bed, close up shots of the blocks and fabrics, and close up shots of the quilting. If the recipient lives near me, I take a picture with them and the quilt, but if not, I request a photo from them. The photos are put in my quilt diary, along with the information on making the quilt.

Diane Meddley, Parrish, FL

❺ I hang my quilt on the clothesline and take my shots in the morning sun. The photos get downloaded to the computer and stored there, with copies going into a display book

Barbara Falkner, Wellard, WA

❻ I take close ups and "art" shots. Mostly I try to get them hanging straight and get the color just right. Color means a lot to me, and I want people to have the same color experience looking at my photos that I have looking at my work in person.

Michelle Harrison, Morganton, GA

❼ I try to take a full front and full back photo, close-ups of the block detail and the quilting detail, and a photo of the label. A copy gets put into the journal of those quilts that have one, and I keep a copy in my brag-book/photo album.

Sharon Siacci, Khandallah, New Zealand

❽ I try to get a shot with the quilt hanging on a wall when possible; otherwise I put it on the driveway with a clean drop cloth under it and climb a tall ladder for as flat a shot as possible. I also take close-ups of the quilting. Then I store the photos in my quilt diary (a.k.a., Excel spreadsheet).   *Stephanie Leuthesser, San Ysidro, CA*

> *I put it on the driveway with a clean drop cloth under it and climb a tall ladder for as flat a shot as possible.*

❾ I take typical digital snapshots and sometime close ups if the quilting is especially grand. I upload them to my computer and then to a web based photo company that stores them. I order prints and keep them in an album (I am on album #4). The website for my photos offers a free share site. I have a share site for family photos and one for my quilts so my family and friends can be members and view my photos.   *Annemarie (Nancy) Poorbaugh, Montgomery, AL*

❿ I usually take photos with my SLR (digital camera) and upload them to Flickr to share with my friends and family.

Amanda Kei Andrews, Vero Beach, FL

⓫ I once took a picture of a friend's sampler quilt on display, and had note cards made with no borders, just the quilt, on the front. When I presented the notecards to her, she glanced at them and thanked me. When I suggested she take a closer look, she exclaimed, "That's *my* quilt!"   *Nancy Chase, Columbus, MT*

⓬ My sister-in-law once took a photo of a stack of my quilts without my noticing and had the photo made into a mouse pad for my computer at work. What a great gift!

Lorraine Vignoli, Commack, NY

13 I have taken pictures of quilts I have inherited from my grandmother, with details of who made them, how to fold and store them, and washing instructions. My kids will know who made them and how to care for them.   *Nancy Chase, Columbus, MT*

14 I take digital photos and process them myself with a Canon Selphy photo printer. I love this little machine. I put my photos in special albums designated just for my quilt pics and write the info about each quilt off to the side.   *Francis Stanley, Slidell, LA*

15 If I win a ribbon for a quilt in a quilt show, I will attach a photo of the quilt to the ribbon.   *Sharon Gregorczyk, Kyle, TX*

16 I photograph every finished quilt I make and write a short story, journaling the inspiration behind the quilt and any challenges or joys I had in making the quilt. I also record finished size, and finished block size as well as the date started and the date completed.   *Carol Martin, Honey Brook, PA*

Since we have members of different skill levels in our group, pictures of quilts or techniques used to make a specific kind of quilt are a useful teaching tool.

17 My quilting club takes detailed photographs of all completed quilts brought to "show and tell." These include close-up detailed shots and whole quilt shots. We share them online through Shutterfly and periodically print a book of work produced by our members, which is kept by our club historian. I store hard copies of the photographs of my quilts in my journal. We also have a blog that members use to share photographs. Since we have members of different skill levels in our group, pictures of quilts or techniques used to make a specific kind of quilt are a useful teaching tool.   *Betsy Scott, Richmond, VA*

18 I take 4 × 6 digital photos of many of my quilts and keep them in a photo album on my coffee table.   *Shari Haines, Batavia, IL*

⑲ Some special photos of my quilts are printed and framed for my sewing rooms.   *Marcia Dionne, Laconia, NH*

⑳ I have a digital photo frame that changes photos from my computer sitting in my living room. You see my family and my quilts!   *Kristi Wilson, Irving, TX*

C. Signing and Dating Quilts

❶ I like to quilt my initials and the year into the quilts I quilt by hand.   *Janet Olmstead, Calgary, Alberta*

❷ On my grandchildren's quilts, I write "grandma" somewhere on the front of the quilt for them to find. I also sign and date my quilts on a label on the back.   *Toni Heckler, Martinsburg, WV*

❸ I like to hand embroider my labels. I include my name and date, who and what occasion the quilt was made for, and usually an appropriate Bible verse.   *Diane Bachman, Leola, PA*

❹ I use the lettering on my regular sewing machine and stitch important info onto a label for the quilt. The stitching does not wash out as some pen ink is likely to do.   *Jennifer Padden, Austin, TX*

❺ I machine-make a label for a completed quilt. My sewing machine is able to do letters and numbers, so I make a label with date, name, and for whom the quilt is made. I put my name and address, phone number, and usually a little figure of some sort that goes with the theme of the quilt.   *Patricia A. Ensey, Duluth, MN*

6 Generally, I use a Frixion pen, embroider over it, then iron out the ink. I put my initials and the month and year, although if it is a significant presentation, I may put the recipient's name, also.

Michelle Harrison, Morganton, GA

7 I use an Encre Pigment Textile Marker with purple ink, my favorite color, and sign my name and date somewhere near the edge of a quilt or runner. On a purse, I sign on a pocket.

Sherrie Mazzocchi, Annandale, NJ

8 I do a secret message and signature hidden in the quilt in permanent fabric pens. You have to hunt for them.

Sharon Beck, Twinsburg, OH

9 I create a fabric label with a Micron pen. I attach it to the lower right hand corner by a running stitch. My quilts are not finished until the label is on!   *Eileen D. Wenger, Lancaster, PA*

10 I use a piece of muslin as a label that I slipstitch to the back of a quilt. I use a thin line permanent marker and write in calligraphy the story of the quilt. This always includes my full name (including my maiden name—I'm adamant about this), my town, and the date. If the quilt has a special purpose, as most of them do, I include this in the label.   *Nancy Swanwick, Fort Scott, KS*

⓫ I make a label, usually with fabrics from the quilt, and then sign and date it with a Pigma Ink pen. I usually put my label in the back corner of my quilt before I bind the quilt so I can catch two sides of the label with the binding.   *Twila Sikkink, Clear Lake, WI*

⓬ I used to stress over the fact that I could never come up with clever titles for my works of art; hence no label on my finished quilts. However, I have since come to accept that naming a quilt is not nearly as important as signing and dating it. To that end, I keep it simple: my name, city/state and date. That much is easily achieved. I write it with Pigma pen on appropriate fabric and stitch it into the binding or incorporate it into the quilting design so it cannot be easily removed. Because in my old age I have become increasingly neurotic about getting credit for my workmanship, I will also write said information under the label directly on the quilt back. This keeps the dishonest people honest.

Nancee McCann, Wilmington, DE

⓭ My quilts have labels with the name, pattern, date, and, if made for another, their name and reason for the quilt. Several of my quilts have a pocket for the label with a special private note tucked inside.   *Tamara Gross, Wichita, KS*

⓮ I type several labels on Microsoft Word and print them out using the InkJet Printable Fabric. By putting two or three labels on one sheet and cutting them apart, I can justify buying the printable fabric.   *Nora Manley, Athens, AL*

⓯ I make labels on PrintShop and print them out onto fabric. Often I will use a photo of the person or an object in the quilt. I print the title, information about the pattern if it's not original, and my name and the date, and print it on the fabric. Then I fuse it on and hand stitch around it.   *Nancy Robertson, Scituate, MA*

⓰ I purchase ready-made labels with my name on them. I add the year I finished the quilt to the label.   *Anna Osborn, Omaha, NE*

17 I like to use the Printmaster software and Printed Treasures fabric sheets to create my quilt labels. I like to individualize every label according to what kind of quilt it is or who it's going to. This lets me do all sorts of creative things.   *Francis Stanley, Slidell, LA*

Occasionally, I make a fabric envelope that closes with a button and opens up to embroidered details.

18 Sometimes I just sign my quilts with a fabric pen, but mostly I cross-stitch "The best kind of sleep beneath Heaven above, is under a quilt handmade with love." Occasionally, I make a fabric envelope that closes with a button and opens up to embroidered details.

Nancy Chase, Columbus, MT

19 I fuse and sew a label on every quilt I make. Occasionally I will use a Pigma pen and write on the back of the quilt. Every label I make for my quilts tells a story about the journey of the quilt and who and why someone got a quilt. There have been some labels that have answered questions about circumstances surrounding the quilt. It's my way of preserving the quilt history of each quilt I make.

LaNan Eldridge, Paullina, IA

20 I always include my name, including my maiden name, and city. The date is always an interesting question. Did I start and finish in the same year? Do I put the start date, or the finish date if they are different? I recently finished my first quilt which had a 25-year span.   *Olivia Kuebler, Kansas City, MO*

21 I like to make the label to match the theme of the quilt; for example, if the quilt is an ocean scene, the label might be in the shape of a fish.   *Sharon Gallegos, Midlothian, VA*

22 I never sign or date my quilts. God knows what I have made and done for others.   *Karen Benke, Medina, OH*

23 I have quilts my grandmother made for me, and she never labeled them, which was typical of the era. I have decided to label her quilts with the quilt-maker information and any additional information I feel is important to my family or the future caretaker of these quilts.   *Maryjo Kaszubinski, Celebration, FL*

24 The women in the past made quilts for very practical reasons. Some recorded their work but most did not. Which are more "valuable"? In the present generation, we look for labeling of the past as being very important for historical reasons. But when I look at a tattered old quilt, my eyes see the woman sitting by a dim light, contemplating what had occurred that day, just quietly stitching away, just so happy to have a minute to herself or expressing the love she has for the recipient of this personal endeavor. Record the quilt with whatever is important to you at the time you make the quilt.   *Stephanie Maslak, Syracuse, NY*

25 I don't sign and date my quilts. The quilt is not about me but about the recipient. I do, however, try to embroider on the back of each quilt "cancer sucks."   *Susan O'Keefe, Rochester, NY*

CHAPTER 17

Competing, Selling, or Giving

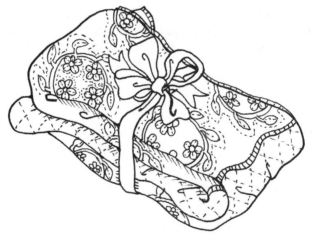

A. *Contests*

❶ I like the challenge of complying with the rules and time constraints of most contests. Even if I don't complete the quilt by the due date of the contest, I usually have a backup idea of what I will do with each quilt I take on. Maybe a wedding present or a birthday gift. I generally really like the fabrics, so entering a contest for the goal of winning recognition or a prize is a secondary motivation for me.　　　　　　　　　　*Deborah Vivrette, Hidden Valley Lake, CA*

② I have only entered one quilt in a contest at a local quilt show. I just made sure that it was cleaned, pressed, had no loose threads and a secure label. Guidance from our quilt guild was provided to those making quilts specifically for the show which included:

+ Bury all knots
+ Ensure bindings are full
+ Sew all mitered corners on bindings front and back
+ Ensure all points are precise and seams are secure
+ Quilting should enhance the design of the quilt
+ Tension on quilting must be even
　　　　　　　　　　　　　　Barbara Merritt, Brackney, PA

③ The only contest I entered was a complete fluke. I was more than halfway finished with my quilt when I read about the contest and realized that my project fit the criteria. When I was able to finish my quilt by the deadline, I entered just for fun and was surprised to be chosen as a finalist. I was very flattered when I realized that some of the other entrants were professional designers. I didn't win a top prize, but it was an exciting experience.　　　　*Karen Martin, Breezy Point, MN*

④ I like challenge quilts and try to enter challenges often. I like the idea of a theme or fabric to get me started. I have entered the Hoffman challenge for years and twice was in New Quilts from an Old Favorite, but haven't won anything nationally.　　　*Margo Ellis, Key West, FL*

⑤ Generally I look for contests after my quilt is done. It usually takes me one year to think about the quilt and up to two years to construct it. Usually there is not sufficient lead time to know the particulars of a contest before construction. Certainly some types of quilts do better in some shows than others. I look at past winners of shows to get a sense of what is receiving ribbons and then select shows accordingly. Sometimes I send a quilt to a show so family members in that area have a chance to see the quilt in person.
　　　　　　　　　　　　　　Georgia Pierce, Seattle, WA

6 Talk with quilters who regularly enter quilts for competition. Find out how to start entering. If a quilt wins big in one guild, chances are good that it will earn top awards again. Keep entering the same quilt in future contests. There are some contests that pay big rewards to winning quilters.   *Marti Blankenship, Pleasant Valley, MO*

7 Judged quilts are subjectively judged, and you should always look at the judges' comment sheets to see what constructive criticism is there. Let the rest roll off your back. It is only one person's opinion.   *Jennifer Padden, Austin, TX*

8 I am currently quilting for shows. I compete in shows to get feedback from judges in areas where I need most improvement. I strive to make a better quilt than the last one. I get satisfaction from having a quilt selected for a show, and when a prize is awarded, I have a great sense of satisfaction.   *Georgia Pierce, Seattle, WA*

9 Figure out *why* you want to enter competitions. Is it for the positive reinforcement? If so, you may be disappointed. If it is for prizes, you will have to make your quilts with perfection as a goal. There are so many ultra-talented quiltmakers out there, and the competition is stiff at big shows. Start with smaller shows: your guild show, county fairs, state shows. You will have a lot more positive feedback from a show like that than at a national show.   *Nancy Henry, Rochester, NH*

In the end, you're bringing your quilt home, so make it to please yourself, not the judges.

10 In the end, you're bringing your quilt home, so make it to please yourself, not the judges. And don't think your quilt isn't nice just because it doesn't win a prize or ribbon.   *Amy DeCesare, Delmont, PA*

11 Choose a pattern and fabrics that make you feel good. Because if you have a smile and take your time and enjoy the process, you've already won.   *Susan Kieritz, Braunschweig, Germany*

12 I wish shows would distinguish between computer-aided precision and hand-guided precision. Two totally different animals, in my opinion.   *Mary Beth Schrader, Cameron, MO*

13 You'd better be awfully good to compete in quilt shows. I've been to a few quilt exhibits where I feel bad for the people who think they're better than their work proves to be.
        Kay Hinkelma, Florissant, MO

14 You must have a great deal of confidence to enter quilts in contests and not get upset if you hear or see any comments that are critical. You cannot please everyone, so don't try.
        Susan Taylor, San Ramon, CA

15 Understand that judges are very critical, which can be good and bad. They identify your weaknesses, which should encourage you to do better. The criticism can also damage your self-esteem in something that you are very proud of. I would be very selective in the category in which I would enter a quilt, as there is an enormous amount of competition out there. Years of experience and technique certainly do reap the rewards in competitions.
        Sharon Sutton, Lindsey, OH

16 Look at and study the quilts that win at the shows you attend. Look at the categories, the quality of design, the density and quality of the quilting stitches and compare to the ones that did not win. Pretty soon, you will be able to pick out the details to know why one won and the other did not. Check out books about quilting and communicate with judges regarding what they look for in a competition quilt.   *Jennifer Padden, Austin, TX*

17 Before a quilt goes to a contest, I block it (soak in cool water, spin in washer, block on 2" thick, styrofoam insulation batts). Pin and square and allow to dry. I remove any lint, animal hair, etc. Check for loose threads. Pack and ship. I insure all my quilts as a rider to my homeowner's insurance policy.   *Georgia Pierce, Seattle, WA*

18 Be sure the binding is done well for contests. The judges always look closely at the binding technique.　*Sue Glasnapp, Delray Beach, FL*

> *With the many, many machine quilters out there, it is hard to win a competition by just hand quilting.*

19 With the many, many machine quilters out there, it is hard to win a competition by just hand quilting. Machine quilters have a definite advantage.

Fran Shaffer, Coatesville, PA

20 Print out a calendar for each month and plan your year towards the competition by filling in each day you want to work on your quilt. Stick to it as much as possible. This will help eliminate a lot of stress by pacing yourself throughout the year. Make sure family and friends understand that you are working on your allocated days to sew and don't want interruptions.　*Susan Borgas, Booleroo Centre, Australia*

21 I do not compete with my quilts. I have always been skeptical about competitions in the art world. How do you compare things that may be beautiful in different ways?　*Stephanie Wagner, Bear, DE*

22 I have realized my goal is not to get a blue ribbon, but to make quilts that assist people where their personal need is. Most award-winning quilts will never be on a bed or be useful, so that is not where I want to spend my time. Also, most award-winning quilts travel quilt shows, and they are from a different part of the world or country. That is not motivation to me.　*Marlys Wiens, Edina, MN*

23 I find that when I try to make a quilt for the purpose of exhibiting it, I lose my creative energy, along with the joy of making the quilt. It seems that I get too involved with making it just right, losing the spontaneity of just creating. I get too worried about how the judges will view it, when I know that an element of judging is very subjective. My art quilts have to come from my own core, from my inner creative urge, and must be part of my process. Otherwise, I have lost my own individual expression.

Susan Louis, Briarwood, NY

B. Venues to Sell Quilts

❶ The ones I make to sell, though, I make for *me*. I feel that if no one wants to purchase it, if I love it, I will love to have it in my house.   *Nancy Henry, Rochester, NH*

❷ When I was younger, I used to make quilts on consignment to earn money to take classes at the university.   *Karen Nick, Lutz, FL*

❸ Consigning any art work really only works if the artist works at the store on a part-time basis. You must be able to tell people about your work.   *Kevin Kern, Paradise Valley, NV*

❹ I have done craft shows for about 18 years and have built up quite a following.   *Mary Jones, Manchester, MI*

❺ I have sold quilts by word of mouth. In my experience, quilts made for boutique tables and craft shows do not sell.
Susan Riley, Hingham, MA

❻ I've only sold one quilt, which was commissioned. I was asked if I could make a quilt for a baby boy soon to be born. His grandfather had died before the baby was born, and Grandpa used to wear a lot of Polo dress shirts in soft blues and lavenders, beautiful pastel colors. The family gave me a bag of his shirts, and I cut squares, rectangles, and sashings, using the Polo logo when I could. I fused them to a light fusing material (MistyFuse), which worked great. I then pieced them together and found a perfect, baby blue fabric with wispy clouds on it for the backing and binding. I stippled it on the machine. The parents and grandmother absolutely loved the quilt; they cried when they saw it. I was very glad I agreed to make this quilt, a real keepsake for that family.
Patricia Grimm, New Windsor, NY

❼ I have never actively tried to sell my quilts, but on occasion someone will stop and ask about a quilt I've made that they've seen on a social networking site or when I'm shipping them at the post office. Then they'll ask me to make one for sale, and we set up the transaction then.   *Lisa Hughes, Richland, NY*

8 I have a wide network of friends, some who also quilt and many who do not, but do enjoy the art. From this network, I have been able to schedule home quilt parties about every other month. Completed quilts are displayed with the opportunity for party attendees to purchase and/or order similar items in their desired colors. This "Tupperware party" approach is very personal and fun as we play games with quilt items as prize gifts.   *Kathie Arbuckle, Colchester, CT*

9 I display my quilts at non-profit organizations to get my quilts out there.   *Audrey Clark, Red Lodge, MT*

10 The local live theater likes me to exhibit in their large lobby in conjunction with a town-wide arts fair each year. The fair is advertised as Third Thursdays and takes place May through September. If the play that is running is something appropriate, I sometimes leave the display for the run of the show.

Sharon Mountford, Canoga Park, CA

11 I sell quilts at our guild QuiltFest. The guild takes a percentage of the sales. I volunteer to work the boutique, and I get to help set up and keep the tables and shelves looking pretty. It is so much fun!   *Michelle Harrison, Morganton, GA*

12 Some quilt guild shows will allow you to sell the quilts you enter/display during the event, or maybe sell them through an associated "country store" at the quilt show. Local crafts boutique/ fairs are good, but you generally can't get a decent return for your cost of materials and labor. My best success in selling quilts is through word of mouth, or if someone sees my work at a local museum event, arts show, or maybe charity/donation baby quilts at the local hospital, or with a new mother or grandparent.

Deborah Vivrette, Hidden Valley Lake, CA

JUST FOR FUN

Top 10 Designs on Your
Bucket List, According to Our Survey

#1
Double Wedding Ring

#2
Baltimore Album

#3
Dear Jane

#4
Mariner's Compass

#5
Log Cabin

#6
Storm at Sea

#7
Drunkard's Path

#8
A quilt that I design

#9
Irish Chain

#10
Cathedral Windows

❖ I'd like to design and make a quilt using free-form designs. I've never done this before and would like to step out of my box and make something entirely different than the traditional pieced quilts that I love to make.

Sue Glasnapp, Delray Beach, FL

⓭ I have sold a few quilts on eBay, as well as at garage sales.

Terry Green, Attica, NY

I've seen new sellers open a shop, only to have their product priced way too low, which sends the wrong signal. If you don't believe in your product, you can't expect anyone else to!

⓮ I used to make quilts just for family members and myself. Then I discovered Etsy, and I can't say enough good things about it! Etsy is an online market place for handmade goods. There are a lot of tips and hints for being successful on Etsy— there are over a million sellers now I recently learned!—but first, do your homework. Study other shops that sell what you want to sell. Become familiar with pricepoints. I've seen new sellers open a shop, only to have their product priced way too low, which sends the wrong signal. If you don't believe in your product, you can't expect anyone else to! Selling my quilts on Etsy allows me to generate a little extra income and continue to be a stay at home mom.

Celeste Collier, Guntersville, AL

⓯ I joined an online community specifically for selling quilts (QuiltsforSale.ca) and post new quilts if they haven't sold before I can get them there.

I post pictures on my Facebook site where quite often, friends will see them and call me to ask if they can buy it, or I show them off at group gatherings, birthday parties, my sewing group, wherever I'm going where a few people I know will be there. When I've finished a quilt, 9 times out of 10 someone wants it right then! I also take special orders and commissions, so it is normal for me to be working on 3–4 customer quilts at all times.

Colleen Froats, Alanson, MI

⓰ I sell quilts at a large quilt store about an hour from my house. It displays them online and in the shop. I also have a shop on Etsy. It was easy to open, and the commissions they take are miniscule.

I have sold quilts to people all over the world, and I love thinking about my "babies" in their new homes!   *Nancy Henry, Rochester, NH*

⑰ If you are going to take the leap and start selling quilts online, it is critical that you have (or have access to) a good camera. Since the customer can't touch and feel your quilt, your pictures have to convey the beauty of your quilt. Consider the setting you put your quilts into for photographing, and always opt for natural lighting.
Celeste Collier, Guntersville, AL

⑱ I do not use sites such as Etsy and Ebay. I've browsed there a few times and do not understand how anyone can sell a quilt for the prices they let them go for. I have had very good luck with the QuiltsforSale site, which is a consignment venue. They are receiving more and more traffic, the consignment fees are very fair, and the quilts are presented in a very good way.
Colleen Froats, Alanson, MI

C. Fair Pricing to Sell Quilts

❶ I was told that a quilt should be priced at three times the value of the materials, then add the cost of the quilting.
Susan Walters, Newark, DE

❷ Coming from an art background, if I were to sell my quilts, the price would be calculated on the following: fabric cost, original design by me, demand on my quilts, time put into making the quilt, and, also, how generous I feel at the time.
Susan Borgas, Booleroo Centre, Australia

❸ I might ask how much the person is willing to pay for a quilt that I make, and then I will tailor the finished quilt to that amount if it is within reason. I take into consideration the cost of the overall materials I will use, the complexity of the pattern, and the hours needed to make the quilt. If the person cannot afford much, then I would suggest something extremely simple, or if I have donated fabric and can use that, the configuration of what I would do for them would change. I might even suggest a smaller item.

Susan Louis, Briarwood, NY

4 I "guesstimate" the amount of fabric I have used, the batting, thread, and so on. I try to pay myself $10 an hour for my time, but one can never really charge for all the time spent making a quilt. For machine quilting, I charge the local standard rate which is 1½ cents per square inch for basic quilting. Thread changes and more complex quilting are 2½ cents per square inch.

Audrey Clark, Red Lodge, MT

5 I have figured the cost of materials and adjusted the price over the years. I also take into account the time required for construction. Currently I use $.10/square inch as the base price. That is increased for complicated piecing and/or hand quilting. I only try to make $10/hour for my time, and frequently I will sell to someone for less than my listed price if they really love a piece.

Sharon Mountford, Canoga Park, CA

6 Once I established a name for myself, knowing the quality of my work, I charged a specific price per square inch, depending on the difficulty level of the pattern. I had set prices for easy, medium and hard. I included a specific number of hours for hand quilting in the price. For every so many hours above that, I added an additional rate. I added to that the cost of all materials involved. If I use a machine quilter, that cost is added to the cost of the quilt, and not the hand quilting cost. 　　*Sharon Rehrig, Nazareth, PA*

7 I charge the cost of fabric plus minimum wage for the estimated time spent making the quilt. 　　*Sally Berry, Virginia Beach, VA*

8 I have heard just recently that someone has come up with a guideline of $.20 per square inch for selling quilts. I don't know whether this would be a good number or not— 100×100 would run $2000. That might be fair, but would someone pay that much?

Joan Oldham, Panama City, FL

❾ A good basis for pricing a quilt is twice the cost of the materials, plus $100 on average, depending on the difficulty of the pattern. I think most quilts should be at or under the $400 to $500 range, unless they are really something special. People can always buy a quilt in a department store for less.   *Carle Kouri, Santa Clarita, CA*

> *A good basis for pricing a quilt is twice the cost of the materials, plus $100 on average.*

❿ Generally I start with the cost of materials times 3–4, then I take into account complexity, time involved, size, occasion, who is buying it. I may sell a quilt for $350 to a family member or friend, but price it much higher online. If it is a very special, complex quilt, I pay for an appraisal, and then base the price on the appraisal.

Colleen Froats, Alanson, MI

⓫ These are my formulas: crib quilt is $6/sq. ft. + cost of fabric; a simple quilt is $25/sq. ft. + fabric; a complicated quilt is $30/sq. ft. + fabric; and a complex quilt is $40/sq. ft. + fabric.

Myrna Paluba, Wayne, PA

⓬ I would have an official certified quilt appraiser determine a value for sale, as well as for insurance purposes.

Jennifer Padden, Austin, TX

⓭ Check out copyright laws dealing with quilts. You may need the pattern designer's permission to sell a quilt made from a purchased pattern or book or magazine.   *Sue Hurley, Princeton, NJ*

⓮ I start with what I've paid for fabric and round it up. If I make back my costs and make some space in my stash, I'm happy. My prices are way too low, I'm sure. I only sell a quilt once a year as a fun thing.   *Verna Fitzgerald, West New York, NJ*

⓯ As I am retired from 30-plus years in healthcare in a high stress job, I only price my quilts to recover cost of the fabric and thread. I love to quilt and enjoy the non-stress environment, so I do not charge for my time.   *Kathie Arbuckle, Colchester, CT*

⓰ Two of the four quilts I've sold were for the cost of the fabric and notions. The other two, much larger and more difficult, were for fabric and notions, plus that same amount for labor. For me, happiness comes from making them, not selling them.

Jeanne Bartleson, North Augusta, SC

> *Quilters, stand strong and never give it away for a song!*

⓱ In 99% of the cases, someone wanting to purchase a quilt you make for them is clueless about the cost of materials and the required skill or time involved. When you give them a price, they will be in sticker shock. These are the people who should be told to head to Walmart or a department store. Quilters, stand strong and never give it away for a song!   *Nancee McCann, Wilmington, DE*

⓲ When I was in grad school, I didn't have a lot of time to quilt, but I made a queen-size Baltimore Album quilt 10 minutes at a time whenever I had the time. It took me 9 months. It was labor-intensive and it was very expensive to have custom quilted. If it does not sell at the price I have put on it, I am happy to own it myself. Works of love are like that—someone has to love it as much as I do for me to part with it!   *Nancy Henry, Rochester, NH*

D. *Insuring Quilts*

❶ I have taken digital photos of special quilts and have told my insurance agent of award-winning quilts. The value was determined by the cost of professional quilting, estimated fabric cost and an assumed $30 per hour for time spent piecing. If there are many quilts to insure, my agent said a separate rider would be needed.

Marcy Leland, Afton, MN

❷ The best thing is to have a quilt appraised by a certified quilt appraiser. One of my last quilts was appraised for $2250 . But since I made it for my handicapped daughter, I would never sell it.

Karen Nick, Lutz, FL

❸ To have a quilt insured, you need to have it appraised, and the high fee for that is not worth it to me. None of my quilts are heirloom quality. I make them for the fun of it.

Annemarie (Nancy) Poorbaugh, Montgomery, AL

❹ I lost several quilts in a tornado, and I priced them for what it would take to buy them. For instance, I had a tiny Flower Garden that took me two years to hand-piece. I priced it at $1500 because I wouldn't take less than that for it.   *Judy Williams, Stockton, MO*

❺ I understand that even when a quilt is lost in the mail, the USPS will only reimburse you for the value of fabric unless it was appraised by a licensed appraiser.   *Cheryl Marion, Grahamsville, NY*

E. *Charities*

❶ For the past five years, I have made patriotic quilts for Quilts of Valor because I believe the veterans returning from Iraq and Afghanistan, as well as veterans from previous wars, need to know they are appreciated and their service and sacrifice are acknowledged. I feel this is a fitting way for me to share my time, talent, and treasure to express my gratitude to those who serve.

I also make charity quilts for children in trauma situations, as well as for disadvantaged children, homeless families, and mothers and children in domestic abuse environments. These quilts give comfort and warmth to those who especially need them.

Sue Glasnapp, Delray Beach, FL

2 My bee ladies and I are currently making quilts for Brooklyn, NY, families who were left homeless after Hurricane Sandy. Our community needs us now more than ever, and we feel that there is no greater comfort than to be wrapped in a handmade quilt.

Kirsten Schmitt, Baldwin, NY

3 I have made quilts for The Road Home, a facility that helps the homeless, because a quilt can make the place feel a little more homey, especially for someone who is new to this unfortunate situation.

Ann Johnson, Salt Lake City, UT

4 I quilt about 200 quilts a year for Children's Mercy Hospital of Kansas City, MO, the North Kansas City Hospital Hospice Care, and Hillcrest Ministries. Hillcrest Ministries is a restart program for families that bottom out for reasons of mismanagement, unemployment, drugs, etc. A bed-size quilt is given to a family unit who completes the restart program. If they do not graduate, they do not receive a quilt. We hear this is a valid incentive that some families work toward.

Marti Blankenship, Pleasant Valley, MO

5 I have donated quilts to my place of employment, and then we sell raffle tickets, and the money goes to the arthritis foundation.

Loreen Wise, Egg Harbor, NJ

6 I have made quilts for my church. They sell at auction, bringing in from $300–$1900 each, which totally depends on who's bidding.

Kris Newlin, West Chester, PA

7 I am a teacher and adore books/reading, so I've donated fun quilts to the local library for them to have drawings to raise money.

But the charity I've donated to most is a horse rescue place. I have horses who are near and dear to my heart, so this is a big one for me. I've made them pillows, wall hangings, and a quilt, and they sell them in various ways to raise money.   *Karla Santoro, Stanley, NY*

8 I have made quilts for my granddaughters' annual school auction. They go to a private school that is not federally funded. They have these auctions to raise funds for school equipment, computers, phys. ed equipment, art supplies, etc.

Ann Ouellette, Meriden, CT

9 I make quilts for Project Linus. I was a pediatric nurse and saw firsthand how much these quilts meant to those who received them.

Denece Turner, Evans, GA

10 I have made upwards of 75 baby quilts for neonatal units for area hospitals. Those little guys and their parents need to know some extra love at a critical stage in their lives.   *Barbara Johnson, Dallas, OR*

11 Through my local quilt guild (Ladies of the Lake), I make five or six baby quilts each year. These quilts are given to every baby born at St. Helena Hospital at Clearlake, CA. I make these quilts partly because our county is relatively poor, and many families who have their babies at this hospital don't have many or any new items for their babies. This charity also helps our quilt guild keep our tax-exempt status. I have also made quilts for donation when I was with the Napa Valley Quilters group. These quilts were carried in fire trucks and police cars for distribution and use, and distributed in emergency situations.   *Deborah Vivrette, Hidden Valley Lake, CA*

> *I make these quilts partly because our county is relatively poor, and many families who have their babies at this hospital don't have many or any new items for their babies.*

12 When Mennonite Central Committee came to me to assist in fundraising through quilting, they caught my interest. Quilting used to be what you did with your scraps. Because of the North America Relief Sale Meetings in Ontario, Canada, Bev Patkau and I looked at each other and said, we should share "love" and use a heart as a symbol. My job was to send out some emails and let people around the world know that we were collecting heart blocks.

To our surprise, my emails to a few friends had a life of their own. By the time we were done collecting, we had probably 4,000 blocks! I made a quilt from patches from a 90 year old lady, Mrs. Harder, from Mountain Lake, MN, who sent me 50 striped hearts. Together with Blue Meadow Design Love, Joy, Peace fabric, I made a quilt, and Bev made hers in Canada. Our two traveling quilts made between $150,000 to $200,000 for MCC to assist in their global work.

That also leads to my connection with Good Books and the book, *Passing on the Comfort*. The US author originated in Mountain Lake, Minnesota area and Mrs. Harder is the only person I have found that remembered making quilts that were used in the story of *Passing on the Comfort*!   *Marlys Wiens, Edina, MN*

⓭ Going through the cancer journey inspired me to make quilts for cancer patients. Words of encouragement and Bible verses that are written on the quilts send out hope and comfort to all who receive them.   *Sandy Testerman, Conowingo, MD*

I know that I get more from making these quilts than those who receive them. It is so nice to know that something you can do is received and appreciated by someone in pain.

⓮ A group of women got together over 10 years ago to make Blankies for Grown-Ups, lap quilts for people who have been diagnosed with breast cancer. We give them a "blankie" to take to chemo and other treatments so they have something to keep them warm and to know they are not forgotten. These "blankies" go to anyone who needs or wants one. There are no stipulations put on anyone to receive a blankie, other than they have been diagnosed with a life-threatening disease. As you will hear from almost anyone who does this kind of quilting, I know that I get more from making these quilts than those who receive them. It is so nice to know that something you can do is received and appreciated by someone in pain.

Susan Taylor, San Ramon, CA

15 A few years ago I donated a special Angel Quilt that I made to the Bassett Cancer Center in Cooperstown, NY, that cured my husband's cancer. Ironically, this year I was diagnosed with breast cancer, and for four months, I walked by that Angel Quilt on the wall and reflected on those angels. The nurses at the clinic told me that their patients also appreciated the quilt and were very pleased to meet its maker. I am presently working on another quilt that will be donated to our newly renovated clinic to mark my remission and cure.   *Barbara J. Flynn, Ilion, NY*

16 Most of my quilts are charity quilts because I am a cancer survivor! While on that journey I discovered many people with no support system. It was heartbreaking to think so many had to go on this journey alone, so I started the Sew and Reap Community quilt project. We make quilts for cancer patients and Soldiers Angels who distribute them to our Wounded Warriors.

Sandy Testerman, Conowingo, MD

17 I've donated quilts to my local public radio station fundraiser. I love both quilts and public radio, so using one to benefit the other seems very fitting.   *Mary Coudray, Belleville, WI*

18 There is a local women's club that I've supported with quilts. They have a Holiday Craft Auction every November, and all proceeds go to local scholarships and a local charity. I prefer to see the community I live in benefit directly from my donations.

Mary O'Donnell, Las Vegas, NV

19 I participate in a monthly charity online quilt bee called the Happiness Circle at Do Good Stitches. It gives me a wonderful feeling to know I am helping put together a quilt that will brighten someone's day who is in need.   *Stephanie Zito, Sudbury, Ontario*

F. Quilts for Life's Milestones

1 I make runners, placemats, table toppers, pillowcases, purses, baskets, etc. and keep them on a gift shelf. When a shower or wedding pops up on the calendar, I go to my stash and see what might fit that person and occasion. I like giving a gift that I made because it is personal!   *Sharon Stoddard, Bridgeport, CA*

2 When you've been a quilter for a long time, it is amazing how many occasions your family members want you to commemorate with a quilt: weddings, births, entering college, graduating from college, moving to a new home, the list goes on. Mostly I am happy to cater to them because they are my family and I love them, as long as they don't tell me exactly what colors they want in the quilt.

Betsy Scott, Richmond, VA

3 I have the hope of making at least one quilt a year, with special love and care paid to the special milestone events in our family life like graduations, weddings, baby showers, etc.

Jan Mast, Lancaster, PA

4 I have made small "get well" art pieces and baby quilts. I have made Mother's Day quilts and Father's Day quilts. I have made Going to College quilts.   *Michelle Harrison, Morganton, GA*

5 My Moma just passed away and I am making three quilts from the dresses she made to share with my two sisters. We can still get a hug from Moma in a way as we snuggle under the quilt.

Diane Meddley, Parrish, FL

6 I have given many quilts as shower gifts. I truly believe that I am invited to baby showers because they know that they will receive a baby quilt. I made the most recent one in 25 days.

Elaine Zeitler, Akron, NY

7 Our family tradition for at least four generations is to make a quilt for new babies.   *Signa Ferguson, Pelham, AL*

8 I make quilts for births, get well, weddings, holidays, graduations, birthdays, and memorials because that is how I show that I care. Some people cook and bake—I quilt.

Annemarie (Nancy) Poorbaugh, Montgomery, AL

> *Some people cook and bake—I quilt.*

9 Births usually get a person motivated to make quilts. Right now I am making twin and full size scrap quilts as my seven grandchildren are in full-length beds now and their little crib quilts are too short. Grandchildren can be real ego builders for a grandma because they love it if "Grandma made it."   *Sharel Etheridge, Lennon, MI*

10 I have a friend who has a closet full of fun lap-sized quilts and larger ones that she has enjoyed making. She allows each grandchild to choose a quilt whenever they hit a milestone: confirmation, graduation, marriage etc. She actually had one granddaughter rush to enroll in confirmation classes to beat out a cousin who also had her eye on one specific quilt in Grandma's closet and was going to graduate earlier.   *Carolyn Vidal, Newport, WA*

11 I make a quilt for each of my grandchildren on their 16th birthdays. I have 25 grands—made 17 quilts so far, 8 more to go.

Esther S Martin, Ephrata, PA

12 It seems every time I am ready to make a quilt for myself, a wedding is planned or a grandchild is on the way (and I am not complaining). None of my grandchildren can own just one quilt. They have them to cuddle with and drag around, some with pockets and toys hidden in them, as well as bed and crib quilts.

Nancy Chase, Columbus, MT

13 Right now I have four quilts in my closet waiting for my granddaughters' special occasions to happen: graduation, wedding, babies, housewarming gift, etc. I want the quilts to signify an important milestone in their lives.   *Jeanne Bartleson, North Augusta, SC*

14 In my PA German culture, quilts are a traditional wedding gift. The more quilts a bride gets, the longer her marriage will be!

Diane Bachman, Leola, PA

15 I made a very special quilt for my sister-in-law to keep her warm during her chemotherapy appointments. I stitched words of encouragement and love and designs that represented the strong women in our family. I added the date I finished the quilt, and when I gave it to her, she teared up. I hadn't realized that the date was her mom's birthday. We lost her mom earlier that year. I told her it was her mom's way of reassuring her that she will be all right, and yes, she is one year cancer-free.

Laura Gilmartin, Stafford, VA

16 Instead of taking a lot of pictures of traveling that someone will eventually have to throw away, I have made quilts to remember my trips. When we visited cousins in Northern Ireland, we saw an antique quilt in the Ulster/American Folk Park that I recreated when I came home. When we were in Sedona, AZ, I found the perfect quilt kit that will always make us remember the colors and our time in the southwest. In Italy, I took pictures of floor tiles and have now completed my Italian Tiles quilt.

Nancy Swanwick, Fort Scott, KS

G. Giving Quilts Away

1 I always can't wait to see what people are going to think of their gift when I make them quilts. Most of the time, I keep the quilt a secret until it is done. I am dying to tell, but it is a pleasant surprise for them.

Tamara Jones, Lindsay, Ontario

2 The making of my quilts comes from the deepest part of me, during periods of sadness, distress, happiness and joy. It is my way of sharing myself with the world around me. When I give a quilt, it is the most heartfelt present that I can think of giving.

Susan Louis, Briarwood, NY

3 It is nice to make and give for no reason other than to make someone happy. I went to a doctor appointment and the technician was not ready for the holidays due to a hurricane hitting our area. I felt so bad that she lost so much and had a young daughter that I made her a quilt for the holiday. She sent me a thank you note saying that I put her back in the holiday spirit. That made me feel good. *Robin Levine, Wantagh, NY*

4 I made a quilt for a lady I worked with who lost everything she owned in a fire. *Tami Pfeiffer, Janesville, WI*

5 I enjoy letting a recipient select their own quilt from my finished pile. *Barbara Augustine, Woodbridge, VA*

6 The very first quilt I ever made went to my mom. She was the one who inspired a love of crafts and creating in me in the first place. I have made quilts for my nieces and nephews when they got married, had babies, etc. My goal is to make a quilt for each and every member of my family. This past Christmas, we were up to approximately 40 immediate members, so I pretty much have my work cut out for me. If possible, I'd like to make a couple to keep for myself as well. *Marsha Brasky, Algonquin, IL*

7 I pray for the person I am making the quilt for while sewing on it.

Joan Hagan, St. Marys, PA

8 When I make a quilt for adults, I like to make a storage bag of the same fabrics. When I make a child's quilt, I make a pillow case of the same fabrics and put the quilt inside. *Susan Kieritz, Braunschweig, Germany*

When I make a child's quilt, I make a pillow case of the same fabrics and put the quilt inside.

9 I have bartered a quilt. I made him a quilt, and he made me a beautiful wooden wood box for my firewood.

Elizabeth Stine, McDonough, GA

10 When I give a high school graduation memory quilt, I package it in a plastic bin lined with wrapping paper. This way the bin can be used to pack for college.   *Annette Starr, Cottage Grove, MN*

11 I send quilts to new homes to make way for me to make even more. My daughter and daughter-in-law "go shopping" through my quilts. The rule is that I can say "no," but they usually leave with whatever pops for them.   *Joyce Finch, Golden, MO*

12 I let my quilts hang around my home and studio. Then when someone comes for a visit and they make an "I like that" comment, they receive it as a gift.   *Brenda Card, Larsen, WI*

13 I am currently making quilts for my son, niece, and seven nephews. When I grew up, my grandmother crocheted afghans for us grandchildren. I love my afghan and think about it often. I want my son's generation to have something from a previous generation as well. Also, due to my husband's military service, I have always lived very far away from my extended family, and I want them to have something from me.   *Terri Overton, San Tan Valley, AZ*

I like to wrap mine with a bow and let the quilt be the wrapping paper.

14 I like to wrap mine with a bow and let the quilt be the wrapping paper.

Paula Clark, Ethridge, TN

15 I think it is important to tell the recipient about the care required for a hand made quilt. I once gave a quilt to someone whom I thought would enjoy it and perhaps launder it once or twice a year. To my surprise, she washed the quilt several times a week, and it wore out. She asked me to fix it and there was no fixing that could be done. It was a rag.

Michelle Harrison, Morganton, GA

⓰ When I'm making a baby or toddler quilt, I keep extra binding fabric and border fabric if I have some. That way if there is a tear, or the binding doesn't last, I have fabric for repairs. I fold it and label it and put it away in a storage container with other repair fabrics for other quilts. *Diane Meddley, Parrish, FL*

⓱ Our sons and their wives each received 1–2 pages of typed information concerning all aspects of their individual quilts: who helped to quilt, whom I consulted concerning any part of the process, which stores I bought fabric from, any number of books, patterns or magazines used, the title of the pattern, how many yards of quilting thread used, even when we even started the process, how they decided on the pattern they wanted, was it with children in tow or on a road trip, the process of marking the quilt and tools used, their wedding date, who made the quilt and where, the year—and more! Also, I pass on information about how to care for and clean or wash the quilt. *Eileen D. Wenger, Lancaster, PA*

⓲ Include a couple pieces of leftover fabric from the quilt in the pocket that is made to be the label on the back of the quilt. If the recipient keeps those scraps in the pocket when the quilt is washed, the fabric will match if the quilt needs to be patched. *Debbe Meade, Houston, TX*

⓳ Remember, once you give the quilt away, it is no longer yours, and you have no control over what happens to it. Some people treat quilts like heirlooms, and others treat them like blankets. Not everyone sees a quilt in the same way as the person who created it! *Debra Shirey, Kittanning, PA*

H. And Keeping Them

❶ If a quilt isn't for a gift, I will try to display it somewhere in my home by hanging it or folding it over a rack or ladder or on a table or piece of furniture. I love to decorate with quilts because of the warmth they add to a room.   *Karen Martin, Breezy Point, MN*

❷ I hang quilts in my house or place them on beds or over sofas and chairs. My son jokes that our house has padded walls!
          Deborah Gross, Willow Grove, PA

❸ I display my quilts in the living room until they next one is finished. Then they go into a special quilt closet my husband built. Some are brought out for special occasions such as Christmas and Valentine's Day.   *Barbara Augustine, Woodbridge, VA*

> *I use the quilts on a rotational basis in my home. I like having the color and patterns change throughout the year.*

❹ I fold and store each one that I am keeping. Then I use them on a rotational basis in my home. The smaller ones I hang on the wall as an art display. Some quilts are seasonal. I like having the color and patterns change throughout the year.
          Carle Kouri, Santa Clarita, CA

❺ Most I keep because I love them and can't bear to give them away. Some I do make for family or friends. I made a quilt for a family member's new baby, and I couldn't part with it, so I made them another one just a bit different!
          Vicki DiFrancesco, Conowingo, MD

❻ Most of my quilts stay at home because I get so attached to them while making them that I can't stand to part with them, so they get well used and loved by my family.
          Stephanie Zito, Sudbury, Ontario

❼ I have a quilt cabinet that I put some completed quilts in. This way when special people come to stay at my house for an overnight, they can wrap themselves up with love.   *Terry Miller, Alexandria, VA*

❽ I have a quilt whose top was made by my paternal grandmother and it was quilted by my maternal grandmother. It is carefully folded and stored on the top shelf of my bedroom closet. When I don't feel well, it comes down, and I cuddle up in it. I am sure when they made this quilt, it was meant to be utilitarian, but it has been much more to me. Quilts are made with love and should be used with love.   *Nancy Chase, Columbus, MT*

CHAPTER 18

Caring for Quilts

A. Long-Term Storage

❶ Flat is absolutely the best if room is available. Especially for old quilts, being stored flat eliminates stress on the fabrics and the stitching and, of course, avoids fold lines. Rolling is probably second best since it avoids fold lines and doesn't cause too much stress. Folding is okay if precautions are taken, such as padding the folds with acid-free paper and re-folding the quilt on a regular basis.   *Carol Nussbaumer, Estes Park, CO*

❷ Using the core from a roll of batting is a great way to store large quilts. Wrap the core with archive quality tissue before wrapping your quilt around it. Sew up a tube and slip the entire rolled quilt into the fabric tube to protect it. Never store your quilts touching wood (like in a wooden chest). It will stain them and leave brown marks.   *Janice Simmons, Fresno, CA*

❸ I'm not lucky enough to have an extra bedroom where I can lay quilts flat on the bed, but I do have an unused bathroom where I hang a lot of quilts over the shower rod!

Karen Martin, Breezy Point, MN

❹ Flat storage eliminates creasing. I have two large portfolios made of heavy fabric with a full zipper closure and handles which I purchased on clearance. My miniatures and smaller wall hangings fit in them nicely. I layer them with acid-free paper, put a tag listing the contents on the handle, and store the portfolios horizontally. They are breathable and keep the contents clean and crease-free. Wall hangings that are too large for this method are stored in a rolled manner. I have swimming pool noodles that are stiffened with a length of 1 × 1 wood down the center hole. The noodles are wrapped in plastic and then the quilts are rolled around the noodle in layers. The whole thing is slipped into a storage bag I made of ripstop nylon with a draw-string closure. It also has a tag that lists the contents. For the largest quilts that do not conform to either method, I fold them using acid-free paper between layers and store each in a pillowcase or self made bag of muslin. On the outside is a tag with the name of the quilt *and* the last date it was refolded. Refolding is necessary, especially if it is being stored for a long time, to decrease the potential for permanent creasing.

Nancee McCann, Wilmington, DE

❺ Flat is best if you have the room. I stack quilts on my guest bed for storage, turning the one on the top of the pile right side down. They lie flat, and only the back of the top one is exposed to light. When guests come, I fold the extra quilts and stack them on a nearby shelf. They add such a homey feel to the room.

Susan Dippon, Alexandria, VA

6 I usually fold the corners up diagonally, then fold the quilt into a rectangle and then roll the rectangle. I do not have room to leave quilts flat or to keep them rolled because I make many large quilts.

Joan Oldham, Panama City, FL

7 I was always told to fold a queen size quilt in thirds, then roll it like a sleeping bag to cause minimum fold lines/creases.

Leanne Skoloda, New Holland, PA

> *I fan fold my quilts. My theory is that each time I fold the quilt, it is along a slightly different line so a permanent fold doesn't develop.*

8 I fan fold my quilts. My theory is that each time I fold the quilt, it is along a slightly different line so a permanent fold doesn't develop.

Anna Osborn, Omaha, NE

9 I read somewhere that a quilt artist ships her quilts in a box and just stuffs them into a box with instructions that they send them back the same way— no creases.   *Linda Ahn, Mohrsville, PA*

10 I roll my quilts, put them in a cotton pillowcase, and then store them in my cedar chest.   *Karel Umble, New Holland, PA*

11 Because I have cats, I use a lint roller on all my quilts before storing them to get the majority of hair off them.

Kathleen Van Orsdel, Talbott, TN

B. *Laundering Quilts*

1 I launder quilts with organic detergent in the washing machine. Unless a quilt has gotten really dirty, I use the delicate cycle. I always line dry quilts with their backs to the sun.

Wendy Akin, Terrell, TX

② An old quilter told me once that she launders her quilts with just a squeeze of dish soap to remove oils. She doesn't use any detergents unless absolutely necessary for dirt removal. For stains, she uses Grandma's Spot Removal. I took her advice to heart and have used all of her methods since I started quilting and have never had any problems. *Lisa Hughes, Richland, NY*

③ Our state quilters' organization toured the restoration area of the Kansas Historical Museum several years ago. They had a special display up for us; one part I will never forget. They had several identical quilt blocks displayed. One had never been washed, one washed once, and so on until the last had been washed 10 times. That last one was just a rag; it was shocking. At that minute, I decided to limit the times my quilts would be laundered. They also told us that they didn't try to get antique quilts "clean," but rather just tried to stop any further deterioration. They put a screen over the top and vacuumed the quilt through the screen. I was convinced to try to gently use my quilts, but not to launder them to death. *Nancy Swanwick, Fort Scott, KS*

④ If a quilt absolutely needs laundering, I put it in the washing machine with warm water and gentle, quilt-friendly soap. I use Ivory. I let it agitate for 3 seconds, turn it off and let it soak overnight. I spin the water out, fill the washer again with warm water for a rinse session, let it soak overnight, then spin it out again. I then remove the quilt and spread it on a clean sheet where I can leave it undisturbed to dry flat. This technique is friendly to the fabric and batting fibers. *Lauren Devantier, Amherst, NY*

⑤ For laundering a quilt, I use my daughter's front-loading washer because it is more gentle than my agitator type.
Joanne Picicci, Spokane, WA

⑥ My quilts are all made to be used and loved, so regular washing is expected. I usually make the quilt the only item in the load and wash it with cold water on the gentle cycle with a gentle permanent

press cycle in the dryer. The quilt comes out damp, so I spread it
on the bed and keep the ceiling fan on until it is completely dry.

Jennifer Padden, Austin, TX

7 The quilts I own I launder with mild laundry soap and a cup of
white vinegar. I have never had colors bleed into each other or into
the background fabric. The white vinegar helps set the colors. I do
not dry them in the dryer, but wait for a nice day and then hang
them on my wash lines with a thin sheet over them to protect them
from birds.   *Barb Carper, Lancaster, PA*

8 I put the quilt in the machine for a regular wash. I put the
quilt in the dryer and partially dry it. Then I take it out, put it on
the floor in my sewing room and square the quilt by sticking pins
through the quilt into the carpet. I let the quilt finish drying.

Marti Blankenship, Pleasant Valley, MO

9 I fill the bathtub with lukewarm water and mild soap, put the
quilt in, and knead it gently. I drain the water, refill with cool water,
and knead to rinse. I repeat this until the soap is gone. The best
way to dry a wet, heavy quilt is to put a sheet out on the lawn away
from birds and lay the quilt out on it.   *Kathy Kelleher, Kennebunk, ME*

10 Art quilts and many small decorative wall quilts may not ever
need laundering, but they may need vacuuming using a protective
material, such as netting, over the vacuum suction.

Patricia Dews, Gainesville, VA

11 I learned you should use soap on quilts, but not detergent. I
use Orvus paste which I buy at Farm & Fleet for about $8–$10/
gallon, which lasts several years. I think its intended use is for
washing animals.   *Mary Coudray, Belleville, WI*

c. Removing Spots from Quilts

❶ I spot clean quilts with LOC from Amway, and then hang them in the sun so the sun can bleach it.   *Wendy Oyler, Canandaigua, NY*

❷ I use a product called Vintage Textile Soak in the washing machine with warm water when I have a stained quilt.
Lauren Devantier, Amherst, NY

❸ I have found that dabbing rubbing alcohol on stubborn stains, rinsing with clear water, and then rubbing in dishwashing detergent and rinsing again works best.   *Barbara Merritt, Brackney, PA*

❹ I use the old-fashioned Fels Naptha soap to pre-treat any stains before washing the quilt.   *Donna Hill, Brimley, MI*

❺ Cat throw-up is the type of stain I get most often. For that, I remove the throw-up with either a paper towel or soft towel, and wipe with water, followed by Nature's Miracle, which is specifically formulated for pet accidents.   *Patricia Dews, Gainesville, VA*

❻ I have used baking soda and vinegar soaks on just the spots. Then I lay the quilts in the grass and let the sun and the chlorophyll in the grass do their work.
Ann Roadarmel, Elysburg, PA

I lay the quilts in the grass and let the sun and the chlorophyll in the grass do their work.

❼ Recently a friend spilled water on red fabric and it bled to the white background of the quilt. My suggestion was to use Spray N Wash with a Q-tip. I placed a towel behind the spot so the liquid would not spread. It took several tries, but it did work. I was careful to rinse out as much Spray N Wash as possible.
Mary Andra Holmes, Prescott, AZ

8 I put some club soda on a Q-tip and lightly dab the spot.

Yolanda Hernandez, San Antonio, TX

9 For unknown stains on newer quilting, I have had great luck with Vivid bleach. It's my go-to stain remover.   *Kim Loar, Lancaster, PA*

10 One of the hardest stains to remove, and one that really upsets me, is if a quilt has been pulled off the bed and is lying on the floor and someone comes in and steps on the quilt, particularly with black rubber soled shoes. That really ticks me off. Removing that black rubber mark is nearly impossible, and it always occurs on a light-colored quilt! Resolve Carpet Cleaner is the best thing I have found to use. I would not use that product on a vintage quilt, but I do risk it on a quilt that I can replace.

Marti Blankenship, Pleasant Valley, MO

11 I've used Grandma's Secret Spot Remover, Oxyclean and peroxide. They all work well. I soak the spot, rub as little as possible, and soak some more if needed. Usually one of these three products will work.   *Vicki DiFrancesco, Conowingo, MD*

12 First I try a gum eraser to remove a spot. Then, I use an old handkerchief dipped in water and Dial liquid dish detergent.

Donna Oertel, Midland, MI

13 I use Tide Stain Release. This does not affect colors and is excellent at removing anything.   *Sally Zimmer, Bark River, MI*

14 Recently, I was ripping apart a vintage, badly hand sewn, incomplete top which had some stained squares. I put them in a salad spinner and gave them a good soaking in water and a product called Retro Clean. I rinsed and spun them several times, and the squares came out clean.   *Nancee McCann, Wilmington, DE*

15 I use Dawn dish detergent for grease spots and Carbona stain removers for others.   *Leslie Emma, Raleigh, NC*

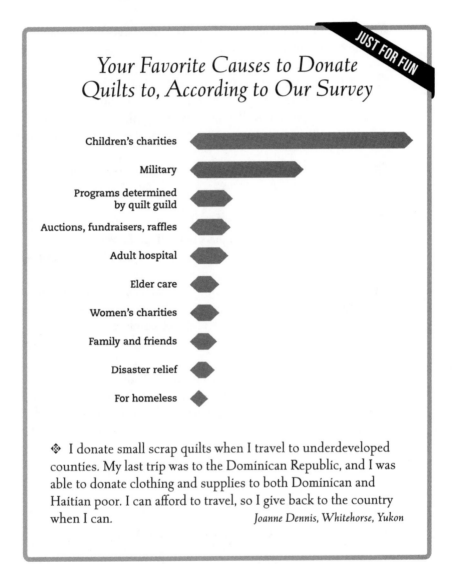

Your Favorite Causes to Donate Quilts to, According to Our Survey

JUST FOR FUN

Children's charities

Military

Programs determined by quilt guild

Auctions, fundraisers, raffles

Adult hospital

Elder care

Women's charities

Family and friends

Disaster relief

For homeless

❖ I donate small scrap quilts when I travel to underdeveloped counties. My last trip was to the Dominican Republic, and I was able to donate clothing and supplies to both Dominican and Haitian poor. I can afford to travel, so I give back to the country when I can.   *Joanne Dennis, Whitehorse, Yukon*

16 I have a quilt soap bar (Quilter's Soap by Sallye Anders) that I bought in Lancaster, PA. It has never failed to remove stains in quilts or other clothing. It isn't pretty and doesn't smell good, but it is a wonderful product.   *Carol Baruschke, Dunedin, FL*

17 I mix a little rubbing alcohol and Dawn detergent and gently rub the stain with a toothbrush.   *Wilma Scholl, Kaufman, TX*

18 The best trick I know is to coat the stain with a thick layer of natural yogurt before machine washing. I recently did this with a blood- and coffee-stained Baltimore Album quilt, and the results were astounding.   *Sue Sacchero, Safety Bay, Australia*

19 Obviously, do not dry a stained quilt in the dryer because the stain will set.   *Liz Brown, Annapolis, MD*

20 I have had some success with a Tide stick or other detergent cleaners. If all else fails, appliqué a butterfly or flower over the stain.   *Myra Tallman, Mindemoya, Ontario*

21 As a last resort, I've used hair spray and a quick rub between my hands, dunking in warm water immediately. If that doesn't work, I love the stain/spot, just as I do my wrinkles on my face.   *Nancy Fairchild, Crossville, TN*

22 If there was still a spot on an antique quilt after a normal washing, I would probably just leave it. To me, the spot would just add character to the quilt. I might even make up a story to explain how it got there!   *Susanne Hilton, Laurel, MD*

D. Other Tips for Caring for Quilts

1 For "the favorite" quilt that's on the couch and used regularly, I always try to fold it differently when straightening up the room. That way, folds aren't in the same place, putting stress on the same threads. I also fold the quilt with the outside bound edges tucked inside rather than sticking out on the edge, as they get a lot of wear with use as it is. Bound edges don't need to be exposed to more wear, like someone's back leaning and rubbing against them.

Anne Zinni, Hertford, NC

❷ I use canned air to do quick air bursts on wall hangings to clean off dust and dirt.   *Colleen Potts, Pottsville, PA*

❸ I hang quilts up outside in the shade to get that fresh air scent back in them. Nothing smells as fresh as a quilt hung outside!

Liz Herrara, Mays Landing, NJ

I hang quilts up outside in the shade to get that fresh air scent back in them. Nothing smells as fresh as a quilt hung outside!

❹ If quilts need a quick freshening up, I run them through the dryer with a damp cloth that has a tiny drop of lavender essential oil.

Marsha Woodruff, Greeley, CO

❺ Keep quilts out of direct sunlight. Air them monthly on a slightly windy day.   *Fran Shaffer, Coatesville, PA*

❻ I store quilts out of sunlight in a metal shelving unit. The rods which form the shelves allow air circulation. The unit is covered by a canvas cover made for it. I tie lavender sachets inside the unit on the posts, not touching the quilts, to repel moths and other bugs.

Katherine Schaffer, Lima, NY

❼ To iron a large finished quilt, I lay it on my bed and iron it there.   *Carol Baruschke, Dunedin, FL*

❽ I *never* store quilts in plastic bags of any kind. I either use acid-free tissue paper or a cloth covering.   *Kim Loar, Lancaster, PA*

9 I always make at least one matching pillowcase to use for storing the quilt when it's not in use. A matching pillowcase also makes it quick and easy to find the quilt I'm looking for.

Trudy McKinnon, Redcliff, Alberta

10 I hang some of my antique quilts on rods around the house. They are rotated as the year moves along. One extremely fragile quilt, dated 1840, I store in an acid-free box. A couple of times a year, I re-fold it and put it in new acid-free paper.

Carol Nussbaumer, Estes Park, CO

11 I constantly rotate the use of my quilts. Every week when I change the beds, on all three beds I change quilts as well. If it was on the quilt rack, it goes to the bed. If it was on the bed, it gets rolled on pool noodles and goes back to the closet. There is always a new look to every room.

Denise Monday, Jacksboro, TN

12 We go away for the winter so, before we leave, I take every quilt, table runner, and wall hanging and lay them all out on the bed in the guest room to relax over the winter.

Betty Gray, Denver, IA

Index

Just for Fun Index

About The Old Country Store

A Historic Destination

Since 1978, The Old Country Store, located in the heart of the village of Intercourse, Lancaster County, PA, has provided its customers with a wide assortment of fine wares. Today, The Old Country Store, with its selection of more than 6,000 bolts of fabric, gorgeous locally-made quilts and crafts, array of books and notions, and irresistible collection of locally preserved foods, remains a destination for visitors and locals alike.

Today, locals, including many Amish and Mennonite craftspersons, and visitors choose their fabric from the extensive selection in the fabric rooms.

The grand three-story brick building was built by the Eaby family in 1833 to provide local customers with clothing, housewares, appliances, and fabric. Today, locals, including many Amish and Mennonite craftspersons, and visitors choose their fabric from the extensive selection in the fabric rooms.

The staff at The Old Country Store are highly experienced at sewing and quilting. They offer help and advice to customers—and they quilt and sew for pleasure themselves.

Locally Handcrafted Items

The Old Country Store's old-fashioned shelves are filled with thousands of locally handcrafted items—from potholders, to redware pottery, to Amish dolls. The Store remains committed to supporting local craftspersons, most of them Amish and Mennonites, by featuring their handmade crafts, rather than items from nationally manufactured gift lines.

Quilting Supplies

The Store also provides everything one needs to make a quilt, including an impressive selection of quilting notions and supplies, quilt books, and color-coordinated fabric packs, as well as a wide variety of patterns kits, carefully assembled by the Store's experienced staff.

Locally Made Quilts

"*One of the 10 best quilt shops in the United States.*"

— Better Homes and Gardens' Quilt Sampler

Named "One of the 10 best quilt shops in the United States" by *Better Homes and Gardens' Quilt Sampler* magazine, The Old Country Store carries high quality, locally-made quilts of all sizes, each individually selected by the Store's experienced staff.

The Quilt Museum at The Old Country Store

The Quilt Museum at The Old Country Store fills the second floor of the historic building. The Museum features a permanent exhibit of quilts commissioned by the Store and made by selected quilt artists. In addition, the Museum hangs a changing exhibit each year, showing work by nationally known quilt designers and makers. For information on the current exhibit, go to **www.ocsquiltmuseum.com**.

Classes at The Old Country Store

Expert quiltmakers and seamstresses teach Classes at The Old Country Store. The hands-on Classes cover a wide variety of sewing and quilting subjects, and each is geared to a particular skill level. A Bernina sewing machine is available for each person who registers. For information about upcoming classes, go to **www.theoldcountrystore.com/sewing-classes**.